Falling Back

CRITICAL ISSUES IN CRIME AND SOCIETY

Raymond J. Michalowski, Series Editor

Critical Issues in Crime and Society is oriented toward critical analysis of contemporary problems in crime and justice. The series is open to a broad range of topics including specific types of crime, wrongful behavior by economically or politically powerful actors, controversies over justice system practices, and issues related to the intersection of identity, crime, and justice. It is committed to offering thoughtful works that will be accessible to scholars and professional criminologists, general readers, and students.

For a list of titles in the series, see the last page of the book.

Falling Back

Incarceration and Transitions to Adulthood among Urban Youth

Jamie J. Fader

Rutgers University Press

New Brunswick, New Jersey, and London

Library of Congress Cataloging-in-Publication Data

Fader, Jamie J.
Falling back : incarceration and transitions to adulthood among urban youth /
Jamie J. Fader.
    p.   cm.—(Critical issues in crime and society)
Includes bibliographical references and index.
ISBN 978–0–8135–6074–8 (hardcover : alk. paper)-ISBN 978–0–8135–6073–1
(pbk. : alk. paper)-ISBN 978-0-8135-6075-5 (e-book)
    1. Juvenile delinquents—Pennsylvania—Philadelphia. 2. Juvenile delinquents—
Rehabilitation—Pennsylvania—Philadelphia. 3. Juvenile corrections—
Pennsylvania—Philadelphia. 4. Juvenile justice, Administration of—
Pennsylvania—Philadelphia. 5. Mountain Ridge Academy. I. Title.
    HV9106.P5F33 2013
    365.'420974811—dc23   2012033333

A British Cataloging-in-Publication record for this book is available
from the British Library.

Visit our website: http://rutgerspress.rutgers.edu

Manufactured in the United States of America

To my dad, James Frederick Fader

"This is a terrible hardened one," they says to prison wisitors, picking out me. "May be said to live in jails, this boy." Then they looked at me, and I looked at them, and they measured my head, some on 'em,—they had better a measured my stomach—and others on 'em giv me tracts what I couldn't read, and made me speeches what I couldn't understand. They always went on agen me about the Devil. But what the Devil was I to do? I must put something in my stomach mustn't I? Tramping, begging, thieving, working sometimes when I could—a bit of a poacher, a bit of a labourer, a bit of a wagoner, a bit of a haymaker, a bit of a hawker, a bit of most things that don't pay and lead to trouble, I got to be a man.

—Magwitch, in Charles Dickens's
Great Expectations (1861)

Contents

Preface   *xi*

Acknowledgments   *xiii*

Introduction   I

1   *No Love for the Brothers: Youth
Incarceration and Reentry in Philadelphia*   19

2   *"Because That Is the Way You Are":
Predictions of Failure and Cultural
Assaults Inside Mountain Ridge Academy*   43

3   *"You Can Take Me Outta the 'Hood, But You
Can't Take the 'Hood Outta Me": The Experience
of "Reform" at Mountain Ridge Academy*   56

4   *"Nothing's Changed but Me":
Reintegration Plans Meet the Inner City*   77

5   *"I'm Not a Mama's Boy, I'm My Own Boy":
Employment, Hustling, and Adulthood*   102

6   *"I Just Wanna See a Part of Me That's Never Been Bad":
Family, Fatherhood, and Further Offending*   127

7   *"I'm Finally Becoming the Person I
Always Wanted to Be": Masculine
Identity, Social Support, and Falling Back*   163

8   *"I Got Some Unfinished Business": Fictions of Success*
     at Mountain Ridge Academy's Graduation Ceremony   190

     Conclusion   208

     Notes   233
     Index   249

PREFACE

Above all, we do not have enough studies in which the person doing the research has achieved close contact with those he studies, so that he can become aware of the complex and manifold character of the deviant activity.

—Howard Becker, *The Outsiders*

WHEN I STARTED A Ph.D. program at the University of Pennsylvania, I had no reason to suspect that I would become an inner-city godmother, drive a getaway car after my companion provoked a high school basketball team to form an angry lynch mob, deliver a group of pallbearers to an eighteen-year-old's funeral, or take an overnight road trip with several former and active drug dealers. I could never have predicted that my SUV would be used as an ambulance for a young woman who believed she was losing her baby, or that I would be asked to hang out while my companion provided a urine sample for his probation officer. I could not imagine hearing that a young man had been shot to death on the very street corner where I had stood with him only five days earlier.

I did know that, after six years of crunching numbers to evaluate delinquency programs, I wanted to understand the experience of juvenile justice from the perspectives of the young people inside the system. Researchers so rarely ask youth to share their insights, perhaps because we dismiss them as inarticulate or immature or because we worry that they might hesitate to make themselves vulnerable to strangers, particularly white, middle-class ones. Scholars have not always kept such distance from their subjects. In the early twentieth century, sociology students were regularly encouraged to leave the college campus to conduct in-depth community studies and collect life histories of gang members and other delinquent youth. Robert E. Park, a former journalist and founder of the Chicago School of Sociology, famously exhorted, "Go and sit in the lounges of luxury hotels and on the doorsteps of the flophouses; sit on the Gold Coast settees and on the slum shakedowns; sit in the Orchestra Hall and in the Star and Garter Burlesque. In short, gentlemen, go and get the seat of your pants dirty in real research."[1] Park inspired several classic ethnographies, including Clifford Shaw's *The Jack-Roller*, Harvey Zorbaugh's *The Gold Coast and the Slum*, and Paul Cressey's *Taxi-Dance Hall*, as well as more recent depictions of crime and deviance such as Elijah Anderson's *Code of the Street* and Mitchell Duneier's *Sidewalk*.[2] These gems convinced me that, by talking to young people, I could gain valuable knowledge about the ebb and flow of criminal careers among adolescents at the cusp of young adulthood.

ACKNOWLEDGMENTS

I OWE SPECIAL DEBTS to several mentors who had a hand in crafting this book. I am grateful for the mentorship and guidance provided by Elijah Anderson, Kathryn Edin, Lawrence Sherman, David Bayley, Hans Toch, and Michael B. Katz. Without institutional support from the University of Pennsylvania Graduate School of Arts and Sciences, the Otto and Gertrude K. Pollak Summer Research Fellowship, and the Ford Foundation Diversity Fellowship, this work could never have been completed. My research would have been impossible without the permission of and encouragement from Joyce Burrell at Philadelphia's Department of Human Services, Judge Myrna Field at Philadelphia's Family Court, and the administrators and staff at the institution I call Mountain Ridge Academy.

Several other scholars have provided me with ideas, support, and feedback along the way, including Patrick Carr, Randall Collins, Jeff Ferrell, Frank Furstenberg, David Grazian, Paul Hirschfield, John Laub, Robin Leidner, Shadd Maruna, Mary Poulin, Stephen Richards, Eric Schneider, and Tukufu Zuberi. Thanks also to Peter Mickulaus at Rutgers University Press; Grey Osterud, who provided much-needed editorial guidance during the revision of this manuscript; Kate Babbitt and Joseph Dahm, who assisted with copyediting; and Jeaneé Miller, who developed maps for the section on racial segregation in Philadelphia.

My colleagues in graduate school and beyond generously offered moral support at times of stress and doubt: Faye Allard, Rene Luis Alvarez, Bob Apel, Janel Benson, Keith Brown, Rachelle Brunn, Gniesha Dinwiddie, Marie Garcia, Alice Goffman, Jaime Henderson, Megan Kurlychek, Ke Liang, Catherine Mayer, Dana Peterson, Allison Redlich, Meredith Rossner, Janet Stamatel, Lindsay Taggart-Rutherford, and Wendy Thompson.

I owe a great debt to my real and extended families, including my "Philadelphia dad," Phil Harris, and his wife, Ellen. Thanks, too, to the Fountain, Kelly, and Park clans, who have offered constant encouragement and important diversions from writing. Paul Gordon, my former husband, supported both my research and my return to graduate school. Thank you to my lifelong friends, Rachael Bennett, Greg Diltz, Shannon Hurley, the late Michael "Kupe" Kuperman, and Susan Rochard, for being a constant presence in my life no matter how far away I move. My parents, James Fader and the late Nancy Allen Fader, pushed me to excel and refused to accept any limits on what I could become. I thank my dad for his support, even though I know he doesn't understand why I want to hang out with people who break the law. I am grateful to my mother for passing on her spontaneity and fire. My husband, Chris "Kit" Kelly, came into my life unexpectedly and changed it forever. He is my spiritual and intellectual partner and my most supportive critic.

Finally, and most importantly, thanks to the young men who allowed me to write about them, Akeem, Eddie, Gabe, Hassan, Isaiah, James, Keandre, Leo, Luis, Malik, Raymond, Sharif, Sincere, Tony, and Warren, as well as their family members and friends who shared their insights. You had little reason to trust a "newsy" (nosy) white lady who wanted to write a book about your lives, but you did anyway. You made me laugh hysterically, broke my heart, and inspired me with hope for the future, all at the same time. I hope I have done your stories justice and represented you with depth and humanity. A special thanks to Sincere for giving me some of my best ideas, for offering excellent chapter titles, and for serving as a superb guest speaker in my courses.

Falling Back

Introduction

A FIVE-HOUR DRIVE FROM Philadelphia, nestled deep within a dense forest in western Pennsylvania, is Mountain Ridge Academy, a reform school for delinquent youth. The facility's sprawling ninety-acre campus contains eight dormitories, each of which houses thirty-two young men between the ages of fourteen and eighteen. The dorms, school, gym, and administration buildings are all clad in brown clapboard, giving them a rustic feel that is at home in its rural surroundings. The well-manicured grounds extend to the forest's edge, inviting deer and other wildlife to pass through. Although the facility has no fences, razor wire, bars on windows, or locks on doors, counselors play up the dangers of the forest to discourage escape attempts. Sidewalks crisscross the grounds, and groups of residents travel together between dorms, the cafeteria, and the school in single-file lines, hands behind their backs. The first in the line opens the door, and as each of his dorm mates files through, they exchange thirty-one "thank yous" and "you're welcomes." Staff members watch carefully as the young men troop by, pointing out pants that need to be pulled up or shoelaces that are tied improperly. The recipient of such feedback thanks the counselor for his comment.

Constant feedback about behavior is part of Mountain Ridge's regime of change, which is based on the notion that offenders think in fundamentally different ways from their law-abiding counterparts. The "criminal thinking errors" approach aims to help young people identify patterns of thinking that lead them to delinquency and supplant them with prosocial, corrective thoughts. According to this philosophy, when thinking changes, behavior will follow. Behavioral change, such as following the facility's rules, is thus indicative of improved thinking patterns. Only when rule-abiding behavior is sustained for a period of many months can a young person be considered for release back into his community.

The latest one-day count of juveniles in residential placement found over 48,000 young people living in facilities like Mountain Ridge Academy (with an additional 20,500 housed in preadjudicatory detention).[1] At an average cost of $240.99 a day per youth, stays at these institutions cost taxpayers $5.7 billion annually.[2] Despite such high costs, little is known about what happens inside such facilities. Media accounts generally alert us only when young people are injured or killed, such as when Darryl Thompson died inside Tryon Facility in 2006 in upstate New York. Thompson was physically restrained by staff after repeatedly asking when he was going to get his "rec" (recreation) during his morning routine, when kids are required to be silent.[3] Few researchers have gained access to juvenile institutions to better understand the strategies they use to promote healthy development among troubled teens.[4] Even rarer are scholarly accounts of the experience of incarceration from the viewpoints of youths who spent time in confinement.

I first visited Mountain Ridge and about thirty other juvenile institutions in 1999 as part of a team of program evaluators for the city of Philadelphia. I was immediately fascinated by the stark contrast between verdant, pastoral settings of these facilities and the gritty urban landscapes of Philadelphia. At reform schools, kids learned horseback riding and ropes courses, with daily routines that were highly structured—down to the three minutes they were permitted to use the shower or toilet. Meanwhile, their urban counterparts hung out on corners, with days characterized by long periods of boredom or, for those engaged in the social service system, waiting, punctuated by spontaneous periods of excitement generated by conflict between residents or with the police. While incarcerated, youth were under constant scrutiny by staff for signs of commitment to criminal lifestyles, while on the outside, this surveillance was conducted by video cameras, police cruisers, and helicopters.

When I met these young men, all were residents of what social theorist Erving Goffman termed a "forcing house for change,"[5] a mandatory institutional program for juvenile drug sellers and users, which I call Mountain Ridge Academy to protect the identities of its staff and clients.[6] Each had been arrested and identified by the juvenile court as requiring reform and rehabilitation to curb his criminality. While at Mountain Ridge Academy, these young men were informed that their delinquent behavior stemmed from their regular practice of "criminal thinking errors" and that they would not be released until they had learned to identify and correct those errors. I started my research here because I wanted to learn how they understood the staff members' attempts to promote personal transformation and the challenges they faced in demonstrating internal, cognitive change through external, behavioral change. At a more fundamental level, I was curious to find out what happens when change is required of individuals by an external, coercive force.

After these young men demonstrated sufficient change to earn their release or, more typically, staff members determined that they had changed as much as they were ever likely to, they faced a new transition as they returned to their homes and communities in Philadelphia. Criminologists generally refer to this period of becoming a free person again as "reentry" and/or "reintegration" and point out that this process entails multiple and serious challenges.[7] The youth in my study had been removed from the poorest and most violent neighborhoods in Philadelphia and been incarcerated in a lush, bucolic setting in the middle of a forest. They returned to the city to find the same problems they had faced at the time of their arrest: neighborhoods plagued by violence and open-air drug markets, conflict with the police, and a lack of legitimate employment opportunities.

Although these conditions remained the same, many things had changed while these young men were away: children they had fathered before their arrest had already achieved such milestones as birthdays and first steps, romantic relationships had been strained during the long separation, bedrooms had been taken over by their younger siblings, and the trust of parents and guardians had been destroyed by the inevitable lying associated with selling drugs. Many young men who had long been dreaming of the day they would be freed suddenly realized the difficulty of renegotiating their place within families, households, peer networks, and neighborhoods. Moreover, the transition from institution to community brings with it the involvement of professionals such as probation officers and reintegration workers. Former offenders must meet the conditions of probation, including weekly drug screens, and stay out of trouble while under harsh scrutiny.

This book's title, "Falling Back," has two meanings in stark contrast to one another. The young men I studied used the term "falling back" as synonymous with "going straight" or relaxing one's efforts in the drug game.[8] I explore this as a central concept because Mountain Ridge Academy was ostensibly designed to promote falling back and because most of the young men sincerely wanted to fall back and stay out of trouble when they returned to Philadelphia. However, as I demonstrate in detail, most were unable to fall back as consistently as they had planned. In fact, most found themselves "falling back" into their old patterns of criminal activity or falling backward, losing progress toward becoming what they called "productive adults." I document the ways in which they tried to fall back in the positive sense, as well as the structural, cultural, and developmental barriers that led many to fall back in the negative sense.

At the time I met them and began to document their lives, these young men were facing yet another transition—from youth to adulthood. Aged between seventeen and nineteen, many were already fathers who intended to develop active relationships with their children after release, most had completed high school or a GED while incarcerated, some intended to move in with their girlfriends or "baby mamas," and four had plans for college or technical school. In many measurable ways, these young men were in the process of becoming men.

This book tells the stories of fifteen young men who belong to the most vulnerable group in the United States: young men of color from inner-city neighborhoods who have been incarcerated before turning eighteen. These youth are unlikely to have grown up in a two-parent home, to have attended school regularly, and to have lived with parents or guardians who brought in a steady income sufficient to meet the family's needs. They are extremely likely to have witnessed violence, to suffer from mental health problems, to have had family members in and out of prisons and jails, to be fathers themselves, and to be behind their peers academically. While many have had adult responsibilities such as taking care of younger siblings from an early age, they are unlikely to accomplish the transitions that generally lead to law-abiding adulthood. They are less likely than their suburban, white, or even female counterparts to finish high school, enroll in postsecondary education or vocational training, find jobs, and establish stable work histories. They are significantly less likely than white men to marry, perhaps the most powerful gateway out of criminal activity. As adults, they are more likely to be incarcerated than to finish college or be enlisted in the military, and they are markedly more likely to die in their twenties as the result of homicide than members of other racial-ethnic groups.

In this work, I explore how precariously situated young men achieve manhood and the sources of change in their lives. I focus on the intersection between the formal, institutional attempts to reform youth within the juvenile justice system and their own conscious attempts to attain adult milestones and stop offending. My questions are the following:

1. How do these young men experience and interpret the experience of incarceration?
2. What role (if any) did incarceration play in helping the young men "fall back" and become healthy adults?
3. How did the young men navigate the dual transition from facility to community and from adolescence into young adulthood?
4. What social factors promoted healthy adult development and "falling back" from criminal activity?

The next section outlines the steps I took to answer these questions.

"WHATCHU KNOW 'BOUT THAT?" RESEARCH DESIGN AND CONSIDERATIONS

I used ethnographic methods to explore the transition to adulthood for young men of color returning home from reform school. Between 2004 and 2007, I carried out intensive participant observation and interviews with fifteen young black and Latino men who were adjudicated and found delinquent by the juvenile justice system in Philadelphia and ordered to Mountain Ridge Academy, a reform school targeted toward youthful drug sellers and users.[9] I began my research inside the facility in November 2004, conducting limited observations of the program's operations, including a day spent in training with new staff members, and pre-release interviews with young men of color who were preparing to return to Philadelphia.

Between December 2004 and July 2005, these men trickled back into their communities in Philadelphia. I documented their experiences

for the next three years as they struggled to fall back and become productive citizens.[10] I spent time in courtrooms, in living rooms, on street
corners, on front stoops, in corner stores, and on basketball courts. I
accompanied these young men on weekly visits to their probation officers, to complete job applications, to their first day of technical school
and on their last day before going away to college, to care for younger
siblings, to appointments with doctors, and to family members' funer-
als. I visited some in detention and treatment facilities and had ongoing
correspondence with others during their incarceration in adult jails and
prisons. As part of this ethnographic fieldwork, I got to know parents and
other family members, friends, girlfriends, and children of the young men
in the study. I conducted regular record checks of both juvenile and adult
records and spoke with probation officers and reintegration workers in
order to verify some of the young men's claims about events such as drug
tests and new charges.

Thanks to my years as an evaluator for Philadelphia juvenile justice
programs (1997-2002), I had a thorough understanding of the system
and of the specific institutions and stakeholders that compose it. More
important, perhaps, I had a level of access to programs, courtrooms, and
records that would be unlikely without the groundwork of years of relationship building. Before developing the longitudinal research design,
I conducted eighteen months of preliminary field research examining
various stages of the reentry process. Between March 2003 and August
2004, I immersed myself at "Powelton Aftercare," a community-based
program that provided transitional services to young people returning
to Philadelphia from a number of reform schools. I was assigned a desk
and shared an office with caseworkers, who generously allowed me to
accompany them on home visits with parents, recreational outings, and
courtroom appearances. I helped in the GED class, attended staff train-
ings and retreats, and worked with administrators to help make sense of
the city's call to "reinvent aftercare."

As part of a research team at the Fels Institute of Government at the
University of Pennsylvania, I worked in spring 2004 with court administrators to identify gaps in their planning and recording of aftercare
services for probationers. I observed hundreds of review and discharge
hearings in "J-Court," the courtroom specially designated for this type

of proceeding, and reviewed hundreds of court files to document the presence and contents of aftercare plans developed by probation officers. I worked with young people and their guardians to improve attendance at the Re-entry Transition Initiative—Welcome Return Assessment Process, an assessment program designed to transition returning youth back into the public school system, typically into alternative disciplinary schools,[11] and I spent two full days observing classes at the program.

This preliminary research allowed me to establish relationships with reintegration workers and probation officers that proved useful later when I was following several of the young men on their caseloads.[12] Finally, it provided me the opportunity to interact with young people themselves, giving me confidence that I would be able to build rapport with them as I moved onto the next phase of research.

Getting In and Developing Rapport

Many excellent ethnographers have documented the challenging process involved in "getting in" to a social setting, which really means "getting in" with the people who inhabit it.[13] Given the fact that I am a blond-haired, blue-eyed, highly educated, middle-class woman—nearly opposite in every way from those I hoped to engage in my study—I am frequently asked how it was possible for me to establish rapport with young people so different from myself. My answer is always that it is deceptively simple, that people of all backgrounds are eager to share their stories—including inner-city African American males who have suffered the stigma of justice system involvement and confinement. Stories and interpretations by socially marginalized groups are rarely elicited and typically take a backseat to the privileged accounts of more powerful groups.

The young men in my study were eager to meet with me at Mountain Ridge to tell their stories. Although I offered a small financial incentive for the pre-release interview, I believe that was secondary to other motivations. Meeting with me alleviated the boredom and monotony of an institutional schedule. Even more important, behind the closed door of the interview room, the young men had complete freedom to speak their minds—to criticize the program or their counselors and to use slang and curse words. Because such language is prohibited inside the facility's walls and their communications are carefully controlled and monitored by the staff at all times, speaking freely was a rare privilege. Venting about the real or perceived injustices they experienced allevi-ated some of the stresses of confinement. Many of the young men used our time together to hear news of the goings-on in Philadelphia; being from their city when they were so far away proved an invaluable tool for establishing commonality. I updated them on how the Sixers were playing, local gossip (e.g., rapper Eve was imprisoned in a federal facility in Center City during this time), and the rising rate of gun violence in Philadelphia.

I explicitly employed several other strategies to gain these young men's trust. Being a straightforward person led naturally to sharing infor-mation about myself, not just asking probing questions about them. While making sure that the topic of conversation was firmly focused on them, I was open to answering questions about my personal back-ground and professional life, reducing the vulnerability associated with a unidirectional flow of information. A meaningful difference between interviewers and ethnographers is that we seek to establish an ongoing relationship with those we study. I set out to be as honest as possible with them and to allow them to see me as human and therefore imperfect. This was easier when I was going through my divorce in 2006 and sub-sequently experienced substantial downward mobility in my standard of living. I am also naturally somewhat self-deprecating, which helped the young men realize that I did not view myself as morally or intellectu-ally "better than" them. Living on the border of the North Philadelphia ghetto throughout my twelve years in the city also helped reduce the social distance between us.

Instead of allowing race to be unspoken, I purposely and openly acknowledged our differences. I pointed out how their neighbors reacted to me as one of the only white persons who regularly entered their com-munities. I asked questions about their perceptions of the differences and similarities among people of different races or ethnicities, with the intent of letting them know that I was open to discussing race. Moreover, as I got to know them better, they realized that race and racism was a profes-sional interest of mine as a sociologist and that their status as black males was a central concern in my writing about them. I listened with interest as they discussed racial profiling by the police and their experiences traversing territory they considered "white." Over time, as I tested new theories with them, a common refrain became "whatchu know 'bout that?," a title of a hip-hop song performed by TI that was popular at the time. When they asked me what I knew about that, they teasingly challenged my depth of and rights to knowledge about their lives. They wanted to know how their world would be represented in a book. Sometimes it was said with admiration, as a form of encouragement when I was indeed able to tell them what I knew and it was consistent with what they knew.

I anticipated correctly that their initial responses to me, particularly during their period of confinement, would be sexualized in nature. They were, after all, pubescent boys who had been deprived of contact with young women for an extended period of time. When I thought they were making subtle advances or expressing romantic crushes during these early encounters, I discouraged this by dressing as nonprovocatively as possible and emphasizing my status as a married person and our age difference. Over time, most realized that our relationship was going to be more enduring and more important than the typical sexual fling. Being "just" friends was easier after they returned to Philadelphia and I built ties with their girlfriends and babies' moms. My then husband occasionally accompanied me, and they liked and respected Paul. There are a limited number of roles that women occupy in this setting: romantic or sexual partner, which would violate fieldwork ethics; social worker, which would create complications with their official caseworkers; and mother, sister, or friend. I believe I most commonly fell into the last category for most of these young men. Many dubbed me "a member of the family," "one of us"; some said I was "from the 'hood"; one even called me "Mommy."[14]

People often wonder whether I was fearful for my safety when I spent time with these young men, some of whom had admittedly done violent things in the past. I ventured into inner-city neighborhoods during a period of escalating gun violence in Philadelphia. It would certainly have been foolish to think that bullets hit only the people for whom they were intended or that my race, gender, and education offered me any protection. However, I felt comfortable because inner-city neighborhoods are pretty ordinary most of the time. The vast majority of the citizens are just trying to meet the demands of the day: getting to and from work, picking up their kids from school, or preparing meals. Certainly, living in North Philadelphia on the border of one ghetto and working in West Philadelphia on the perimeter of another made contact with young black men a fairly common occurrence in my daily life. Because of my preliminary field research with young people returning from reform schools, little they said surprised me.

The young men themselves never made me feel fearful; they quickly recognized that I was one of those rare people who never demanded that they earned my respect. I just gave it, which, over time, made them very protective of me. I also gave lots of hugs and after a while came to believe that, in contrast to sex and fighting, those hugs were a sadly uncommon form of physical contact for them.

I would have felt less safe had I chosen to do field research at night instead of during days and evenings. I knew from driving through these neighborhoods that they underwent a fundamental shift after dark. Grandmothers who spent the day on the front porch supervising small children pack up and go inside. The energy of the street increases dramatically as males take over public space, congregating in larger numbers on corners and front stoops. I missed some things by avoiding those times, particularly the opportunity to learn more about peer relationships among men. I got a glimpse into that society whenever Paul tagged along with me. He had excellent rapport with the young men in my study and served to define my relationship with them as nonsexual early in my research. What I did not expect, and found profoundly interesting, was how drawn they were to him. They were mesmerized by everything he said, recounting his jokes over and over again in stories they shared with their friends. They asked about him nearly every time I saw them and often begged him to make plans to spend social time with them at the gym, strip club, or massage parlor, activities they perceived as masculine. Their interest in and attachment to him suggested a deep desire to relate to other men in ways that they saw on television and in movies, and provided a telling commentary on the consequences of growing up without male role models.

People often ask me how much I influenced the young men I followed. I offered them some material forms of assistance, such as a small payment for each of their audio journals, occasional meals, and frequent transportation. I helped them fill out job applications and gave my phone number as a reference, though I never received a phone call from a prospective employer as a result. When young men got locked up, sometimes I visited or put money "on their books" to be used for the commissary, where they could buy socks, deodorant, food, envelopes, and stamps. Given their extremely precarious finances, these contributions were appreciated but insignificant.

The contribution that likely had a greater impact was the social support I offered in the form of hugs, listening, and dispensing advice—though only when asked. Teaching me about their world made them feel that they had something to offer the world. The knowledge that an adult who was not a social service or corrections professional cared about what happened to them was very powerful. For example, James phoned me when he was stabbed. Over the yelling in the background, I shouted for him to leave the house where his roommate was wielding a knife. After he was taken to the emergency room, I met him there and rode in the ambulance that took him to another hospital that had not yet reached its limit of indigent patients. I also demanded to know why the police had shackled the arm that was bleeding. Without me, he would have done that alone. As the narratives in this book show, social support by adults and connections to the mainstream can make an important difference between those who were able to leave the drug game behind and those who continued to be involved in some small or large way with this illegal enterprise.

The strength of ethnographic methods comes from the close, personal relationships formed with the people being studied. This approach is a self-conscious departure from the positivist premise that scholars should remain detached and distanced from their subjects in order to reduce the potential for bias.[15] While ethnographers must indeed pay close attention to how their associations with those they study shape what they see and do not see and what they write or fail to write, the strategy of systematic and repeated observations over months and years allows the researcher to understand and represent people's choices within a larger structural and cultural context. The trust stemming from these relationships provides access to information—especially sensitive information—that is simply unavailable to researchers using other methods. If carried out with care, ethnography provides a rich representation of people as complex and contradictory individuals, neither all good nor all evil.

The bleak picture of these young men's existence after release reveals that if my goal had been to change the course of their lives, I did a poor job. Indeed, if caring and consistency were enough to alter someone's life trajectory, the state could have alleviated its budget shortfall by employing me as the least expensive program in history. But the causal forces behind the precarious position of young men of color are structural and cannot be disassembled by one person's good intentions. As urban ethnographer Tim Black says, these young men need a social movement, not a social worker.[16]

Protection of Research Participants

During the initial interview, potential participants were presented with an informed consent form approved in advance by University of Pennsylvania's Institutional Review Board, which we read out loud together to ensure their full understanding and allow them to ask questions. Two of the youths were under eighteen, so in addition to their consent, I secured the consent of their parent or guardian. Participants were told that if they chose to be part of the study, they could change their minds at any point in the future. During tape-recorded interviews, I advised them to skip any question that made them uneasy or they believed they could not answer truthfully. The young men I recruited for the study were eager to participate. All who were eligible, who were from Philadelphia and presumably returning home soon, agreed to participate.

The names of the study's participants and the agencies with which they were affiliated have been changed to protect their identities. The young men were given the option of choosing their own pseudonym, which Sincere and Leo elected to do. Transcripts and field notes were maintained on a secure computer that remained in my possession and was password protected. Signed consent forms and interview and journal tapes were stored in a locked, fireproof safe. A confidentiality agreement from the National Institute of Drug Abuse provided an additional layer of protection. With it, neither my field notes nor I could be subpoenaed for use in a legal case against the study's participants in the future. All were advised that sensitive information would be kept confidential, with two important exceptions: as a mandatory reporter, I was obligated to report any incidences of child abuse that I witnessed and any instance in which a young man in my study planned to do imminent harm to himself or others. Thankfully, this never arose.

THE MAKING OF MEN IN PHILADELPHIA:
THE STREET AND THE SYSTEM

The first chapter, "No Love for the Brothers," introduces the young men whose stories unfold in the book and sketches their lives before their incarceration and as they returned to the city after release. Their stories intersect with a social and cultural description of Philadelphia that belies its moniker as the city of brotherly love. The "hidden Philadelphia" that inner-city residents inhabit is marked by rising property taxes, limited public services under threat by budget crises, a staggering murder rate, aggressive attempts by the police to curb drug sales, and vanishing job opportunities. The "two Philadelphias" are characterized by an astonishing degree of racial residential segregation, competition between ethnic groups for jobs, loosely organized drug markets, recent waves of immigration, urban renewal efforts, and close geographic proximity of rich and poor.

The program of change used inside Mountain Ridge Academy is based on criminal personality theory and assumes that young people offend because they habitually make errors in their thinking. "Because That Is the Way You Are" examines the program's more hidden elements, including the assumption that crime is freely and rationally chosen by those who engage in it. Ironically, the intervention modality known as "criminal thinking errors" presumes that criminality is fixed early in life and nearly impossible to change, leading counselors to predict failure for the young people they seek to reform. Embedded even more deeply is a cultural perspective that views urban street culture as evidence of innate criminality. Acting "street"—walking with a swagger or strut, using slang, allowing pants to sag, wearing urban clothing labels, listening to or writing raps—is interpreted by white, rural counselors as a sign that residents are continuing to engage in criminal thinking patterns. As urban residents are stripped of all the outward symbols of their cultural group membership, they feel a strong stigma attached to urban black identity. Blackness is criminalized and therapeutic parlance is used to disguise the racialized nature of the program of change.

"You Can Take Me Outta the 'Hood, But You Can't Take the 'Hood Outta Me" shifts the focus to the ways in which the young men I studied responded to the facility's efforts to induce change. Contemporary reform schools ignore the structural causes of offending such as poverty, instead emphasizing youths' personal shortcomings. The program sends its inmates a discouraging set of messages: you are "a criminal" (read: bad), you are the same as every other criminal found inside the facility's walls, you are here because you suffer from distortions in the way you perceive and respond to the world, and you will likely always be that way. The manner in which these messages are received by young inner-city men of color is complicated by the fact that the counselors are almost all white and from backgrounds very different from their own. When young men experience what they perceive as a cultural assault, they resist, challenging the legitimacy of staff members to affix stigmatic labels and strip them of their sense of self. They reject the messages offered by staff members and focus on ways to maintain the integrity of their identity. Nevertheless, the stigma of these labels is painful and lasting.

The next chapter, "Nothing's Changed but Me," documents the young men's first few months in the community. Why did things unravel in so many ways and so quickly for most of them? Tony's story richly exemplifies the challenges young men face when returning to the city after a period of incarceration. Tony, who had grown up with a drug-addicted mother, was hoping to follow in his older sister's footsteps and become a nurse. While at Mountain Ridge, his counselor and community reintegration worker encouraged him to join Job Corps, which would provide him with housing while he went to nursing school. But this well-intentioned plan quickly crumbled. The criminal background check required for Job Corps turned up an outstanding arrest warrant for a charge of disturbing the peace, which took five months and hundreds of dollars in court fees to clear up. Giving up on Job Corps, Tony enrolled in a private technical school near his home and looked for a job that would work around his school schedule and help him pay his tuition. After doing day labor under miserable conditions, he returned to selling drugs, work that was easy to get and allowed him the freedom to hang out with his friends and meet young women. He was arrested five months after his release and stopped attending school, although a tuition bill continued to arrive each month. Undeterred by his arrest, he graduated from hand-to-hand sales to running his own block with a partner. After accumulating multiple arrests, for robbery, assault, and statutory assault, Tony was sentenced to state prison within two years of his release from Mountain Ridge.

Leo's story, "I'm Not a Mama's Boy, I'm My Own Boy," sheds light on the relationship between work and adulthood. Leo never felt more like a man than when he was fifteen years old and selling large quantities of drugs for his "old head," a man from his neighborhood who took him under his wing to teach him the drug game. As he returned home from Mountain Ridge Academy, he had to weigh the status and respect he had enjoyed as a drug seller versus the very real risk of being locked up as an adult the next time he was arrested. While he looked for work, he felt infantilized because he had to rely on handouts from his grandmother and mother. Leo's work trajectory after his return to Philadelphia exemplifies the findings of many studies of employment among inner-city young men. He had to commute to the suburbs in order to find a job; his coworkers frequently made racist comments; and relying on family and friends for referrals was the only way to secure work at all. Leo continually compared the reality of low-paying, degrading work to his ideal of a job that offered autonomy and a sense of competence, even mastery. Disappointed that he could not become a car salesman or stereo installer, Leo eventually moved from engaging in small quasi-legal hustles to occasional drug selling in order to meet short-term financial demands.

"I Just Wanna See a Part of Me That's Never Been Bad" follows Sincere and Isaiah, two young fathers who set up independent households with their babies' mamas. Both wanted passionately to become better fathers than their own fathers had been, but their inability to provide steady financial contributions placed them in a precarious position within the household. Sincere's girlfriend, Marta, frequently kicked him out for days at a time, reminding him of his failure to be a breadwinner. Isaiah's girlfriend, Tamika, was even more insistent that he secure steady employment as their family grew. Ashamed at their inability to provide for their fledgling families, both occasionally turned to selling drugs, which addressed acute financial crises and enabled them to feel like competent adults who knew the rules of the game. Both relationships were characterized by constant "baby mama drama," struggles for control and conflicts over infidelity. Both Sincere and Isaiah resorted to domestic violence to reassert their masculinity, although Isaiah's outbursts were more frequent and extreme and eventually led Tamika to request a protection order. Sincere and Marta's relationship was somewhat more stable, but he rarely felt like he was living up his own and others' expectations of him as a man.

"I'm Finally Becoming the Person I Always Wanted to Be" asks what enabled a few young men to make successful transitions to adulthood and fall back, or stop offending. The experiences of James and Gabe, two young men who settled into law-abiding, adult lives after their stint at Mountain Ridge, could not have been more different. While James's life was filled with constant upheaval and complete uncertainty from one day to the next, Gabe's was marked by stability. James viewed falling back as an unceasing struggle that involved active maintenance and renewed commitment each day, much like a recovering alcoholic. Gabe made it look easy, perhaps because he enjoyed substantial advantages before he went to Mountain Ridge that he reclaimed after he returned. Unlike every other young man I followed, Gabe had grown up in a house with two parents and returned to an older girlfriend who was steadily employed and pursuing a college degree. Moving out of the city to live with her, he quickly landed a stable job. He lost his job only once and was soon able to secure another. Most important, his job offered full-time hours and paid a living wage.

Despite these important differences, their formulas for success shared some important similarities, including the importance of masculine identity. For James, falling back hinged upon successfully performing the roles of "good father" and "working man." He cut ties to those who refused to believe that he was a changed person and established new social networks with people who never knew him as a hustler. At first glance, Gabe's life looks like a case study in deterrence; after being incarcerated for selling drugs, he was determined never to have his freedom taken away again. Upon closer inspection, however, identity was also important to Gabe's process of "aging out" of delinquency. He viewed Mountain Ridge Academy, especially the emasculating experience of having "another dude" get in his face to give him "feedback," as inconsistent with his self-concept as a man. For both James and Gabe, external and internal sources of change worked together as social ties to meaningful people allowed them to develop law-abiding identities.

The contrast between Gabe and James, as well as the other young men who did not fare as well, suggests that the deterrent power of incarceration may be limited to those with enough reliable social resources that they can make the rational cost-benefit analysis of involvement in crime that deterrence theory assumes guides all offenders.

I returned to Mountain Ridge Academy for the annual graduation ceremony with five of these young men several months after their release, a story recounted in "I Got Some Unfinished Business." I wondered why they were so invested in returning to the facility they hated and what other functions the ceremony served. The ritual recognizing their new status allowed graduates to reverse the identity-stripping process they had experienced while confined, temporarily erasing the moral boundaries between them and their counselors. With their mere presence as evidence that they were "doing good" in the community, they strove to disprove their counselors' negative predictions about their future, to demonstrate they "ain't all bad and shit." However, unlike most rites of passage, Mountain Ridge's graduation ceremony failed to confer the concrete privileges of a new status. The graduates' claims to be "doing good" were based on ties to legitimate institutions that were not as tight as they attempted to portray. Staff members were invested in the fictions and exaggerations making up the ceremony because the ritual affirmed the value and effectiveness of their work. Ultimately, the ceremony was successful for the staff, not the graduates.

The conclusion highlights the broader implications of these stories for young men of color and considers the questions that originally inspired this work. Reform schools such as Mountain Ridge do not prepare their graduates to use a different calculus in future decision making because they do not alter the structural sources of crime, especially lack of opportunity to enact adult roles. Moreover, these coercive programs of change do not facilitate social bonds that will lead young men in a more positive direction. Instead, the messages that young men of color receive in reform schools are frequently negative and stigmatizing. The counselors' dire predictions about their futures become reflected self-appraisals, messages that make change even more difficult to accomplish.

The disconnect between what youths experience inside reform schools and the settings in which they must put their new skills and achievements into practice contributes to a high rate of failure on the outside. This contradiction is built into the structure of these institutions, which work by removing the juvenile offender from his environment but do not teach him the survival skills he needs when he returns. In the inner city, engaging in illegal forms of income earning, particularly selling drugs, is too often the only way a youth can achieve the social status of adult manhood. These men's engagements in employment, fatherhood, romantic relationships, and housing were all characterized by constant flux, not the linear model of progress employed by most programs of change, as well as most who conceptualize transitions to adulthood. Many who would appear from official records to have stopped offending are simply "selling smarter," using techniques that make arrest less likely. The struggle to fall back involves both masculine identity and social bonds, which—for better and for worse—are mutually reinforcing.

The conclusion offers thoughts on better methods of addressing serious youth crime, including judicious use of reform schools, keeping young people closer to their homes and communities when incarceration is the only option, using interventions that have strong empirical support and holding institutions accountable for the outcomes of their young charges, and building what sociologist Victor Rios calls a "youth support complex."[17] I discuss the advantages of conducting long-term ethnographic field research, including the ability to represent the socially situated meaning of key concepts (such as fatherhood), the capacity of the researchers to portray the day-to-day and intermittent nature of desistance and the transition to adulthood for urban youth, and the depth of understanding offered by close relationships with research participants. The chapter concludes with brief updates of the men's current status as they enter their mid-twenties. Although most still strive to fall back and become productive, law-abiding citizens, their day-to-day experiences often represent them falling back into old ways of making ends meet and forging masculine identities.

CHAPTER 1

No Love for the Brothers

YOUTH INCARCERATION AND
REENTRY IN PHILADELPHIA

PHILADELPHIA IS OFTEN CALLED the city of brotherly
love because its name combines the Greek terms *philos*, love, with
adelphos, brother. For the twelve years I lived in the city, I found
it exceptionally easy to strike up conversations at pubs, on buses
and trains, and at dog parks. Urban sociologist Elijah Anderson has
described places such as Rittenhouse Square and the Reading Termi-
nal Market as "cosmopolitan canopies," public spaces where people
of different colors and social classes come together and interact with
civility and even pleasure.[1]

The rest of the city, however, is deeply divided. Indeed, Philadelphia is one of the most persistently racially segregated municipalities in
the nation. Although 43 percent of its residents are African American,
middle-class whites and poor blacks rarely have more than superficial
encounters. Most white residents have no reason to travel into Kensington in North Philadelphia, Kingsessing in Southwest Philadelphia,
or Gray's Ferry in South Philadelphia. Largely forgotten by everyone except the police, these and other impoverished neighborhoods
belong to the "hidden Philadelphia," an economically devastated and
physically blighted urban area that contrasts sharply with the visible
city. The young men whose lives I documented came from the hidden
Philadelphia and returned to it after being released from Mountain
Ridge Academy.

In this chapter, I introduce the young men whose stories unfold in
this book and offer details about their lives before and after their incarceration. Their stories contradict Philadelphia's depiction as a city that
loves its residents. The inner city they inhabit is marked by poor public

services, which are constantly under threat by budget crises; a rising murder rate; aggressive attempts by the police to curb drug sales; vanishing or
absent job opportunities; old and deteriorating housing; failing schools;
and increasing property taxes. Paradoxically, or perhaps because of these
characteristics, Philadelphia has a state-of-the-art juvenile justice system,
complete with a wide array of private correctional programs, an outcomes tracking system designed to help judges and program administrators improve services, and a system of reintegration that pairs probation
officers and reintegration workers to support young people returning
from reform schools.

   Philadelphia's residential landscape has been shaped by the clustering of
racial-ethnic groups near the industries that employed them. As black migration from the South and immigration converged and precipitated white
flight, African Americans found themselves in the "ghettos of last resort,"
crumbling communities filled with abandoned houses and factories. In 1993
sociologists Douglas Massey and Nancy Denton identified Philadelphia as
one of several cities where the white and black populations were "hyper-
segregated."[2] An analysis using 2000 U.S. Census Bureau data demonstrated
that Philadelphia ranks fourth in the level of residential segregation between
blacks and whites and ninth in that between whites and Latinos.[3]

   Figure 1.1 illustrates this point. The most heavily shaded census
tracts, with 75 percent or more African American residents, are clustered
primarily in North Philadelphia west of Broad Street, West Philadelphia
from the western edges of the University of Pennsylvania's campus to the
city boundary at Sixty-ninth Street, and Southwest Philadelphia, with
a small pocket in South Philadelphia, west of Broad Street and below
Washington Avenue. As figure 1.2 shows, white Philadelphians are concentrated in Center City, Northeast Philadelphia, working-class neighborhoods on the Delaware River such as Fishtown and Port Richmond,
and upper-middle-class communities in Northwest Philadelphia, such as
Chestnut Hill. Many white neighborhoods are ethnically distinct, with
Greeks and Italians concentrated in Fairmount (the Art Museum area),
Italians in South Philadelphia, and Polish in Port Richmond, although
this pattern is changing as these neighborhoods become gentrified.

   Philadelphia's recent history is best understood against the backdrop
of strained relations between racial and ethnic groups competing for a

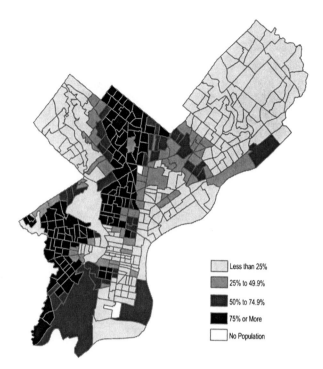

Less than 25%
25% to 49.9%
50% to 74.9%
75% or More
No Population

1-1. Residential segregation of the black population.
(Source: Jeaneé C. Miller.)

declining number of jobs. Racial-ethnic tensions were exacerbated by patterns of immigration that are specific to Philadelphia. Because of its reliance on smaller-scale industries, Philadelphia never drew the massive waves of immigrants experienced by other similarly sized seaport cities such as Boston with firms producing durable goods. Between the restriction of immigration in 1924 and the lifting of these restrictions in 1965, the city's composition shifted in three meaningful ways: southern blacks poured into the city, looking for work and improved living conditions; whites began fleeing to the surrounding suburbs; and the Puerto Rican population became established.[4]

Immigrants arriving in Philadelphia in the 1980s and 1990s encountered a radically different economy from that of their predecessors. The city's old industrial base had all but disappeared, and new immigrant groups—including not only Puerto Ricans, but also refugees from Southeast Asia and Koreans—had to compete with blacks for low-paying jobs

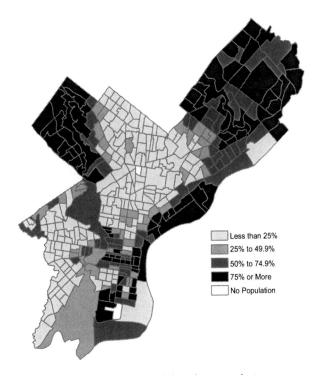

1-2. Residential segregation of the white population.
(Source: Jeaneé C. Miller.)

in the service sector. Recently, the influx of Puerto Ricans has been sur-
passed by that of Central Americans, Mexicans, those from the Spanish-
speaking Caribbean islands, and South Americans. African refugees from
over thirty different countries have settled in the Southwest, West, and
Northeast. Puerto Ricans have maintained a strong presence, despite
their decreasing numbers in cities such as New York and Chicago.[5] As is
apparent in figure 1.3, Latinos, who are predominantly Puerto Rican, are
concentrated in Kensington in North Philadelphia, east of Broad Street.

The young men whose stories I tell in this book lived in neighborhoods reflecting these patterns of racial segregation. Luis, who was Puerto
Rican and white (but whose appearance suggested no hint of Latino), lived
in the Frankford section of Northeast Philadelphia, a white working-class
neighborhood.[6] Sharif, Keandre, Hassan, Akeem, Raymond, Leo, and Isaiah
were from North Philadelphia. Sincere lived in Kensington on a block
inhabited by both African Americans and Puerto Ricans; his girlfriend,

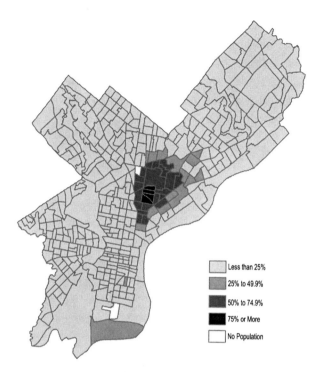

1-3. Residential segregation of the Hispanic population.
(Source: Jeaneé C. Miller.)

Marta, whom he moved in with shortly after his return from Mountain Ridge, was Puerto Rican. Warren and his cousin, Malik, resided in South Philadelphia, Warren in a gentrifying neighborhood not far from Center City and Malik in Gray's Ferry. Eddie, James, and Gabe were from Southwest Philadelphia. Tony lived in West Philadelphia, not far from the campus of the University of Pennsylvania, where I attended classes.

During the course of my research, three young men moved to "better" neighborhoods, which were less racially concentrated and less scarred by violence. Shortly after coming home, Gabe moved to Upper Darby, an inner-ring suburb, with his girlfriend, Charmagne. Isaiah moved into a tidy single-family home in Northeast Philadelphia with his girlfriend, Tamika. He described how the neighborhood facilitated his efforts to fall back:

> My neighborhood is quiet, a lot of Caucasians mixed with blacks. But it's a quiet neighborhood, no violence, no gunshots. Well, there's violence everywhere, but I don't see any. I've lived here about two

months now with my son's mom. I see a lot of drug dealing going on, on the other side, where I catch the bus. I mean, I don't feel safe but I know it's not on my block so I feel safe that my son can't go out there and just automatically get shot or something like that on my block, 'cause it's not happening. I don't know the drug dealers and they don't know me and that's how I keep it.

Sincere and his girlfriend, Marta, moved several times in the six years I knew them, mostly from one poor neighborhood to the next. Most recently, though, they moved to a spacious home in a community some people call "Port Fishington," where Port Richmond, Fishtown, and Kensington come together. Although there are more African American residents on their block than the surrounding blocks, their neighborhood is safer, draws less police attention, and offers more amenities than their previous neighborhoods. Their new home is also a few short blocks from the Fishtown home I rented for my last three years in the city.

Sincere and Marta's new address hints at a meaningful feature of the city: the proximity of living areas inhabited by the rich and the poor. Despite the pervasiveness of racial segregation, gentrification has brought the two groups together in adjacent communities, with clear but often renegotiated boundaries such as Girard Avenue in North Philadelphia or Washington Avenue in South Philadelphia. Watchful eyes and subtle or overt messages sent by white residents prevent poor blacks from patronizing stores and other businesses in white middle-class neighborhoods, and fear of violence prevents most whites from using public space in areas where African Americans shop and spend time. Two Philadelphias sit side by side.[7]

STRADDLING TWO PHILADELPHIAS

Although I was not aware of it when I moved to the Brewerytown section of Philadelphia in 1997, I was part of a larger trend of movement by young urban professionals into the city. This reverse migration had been encouraged by the revitalization of several Center City neighborhoods such as Old City, Fitler Square, and the area near Graduate Hospital, as well as ten-year tax abatements for the construction of condominiums and lofts. According to the *New York Times*, by 2005 eight thousand new units had been built, with over half of the new residents benefiting from tax abatements having moved from outside the city.[8] As middle-class suburban residents began returning to the city and buying condominium units for between $200,000 and $750,000 or even more, long-standing residents of neighborhoods such as Northern Liberties, Fishtown, Fairmount, and Pennsport began feeling the pinch of gentrification as they bore the brunt of property taxes.

Although I suspected early on that Paul and I were gentrifiers, we appeased our guilty consciences with the knowledge that our condo was not new and at least we were contributing to the tax base. Our townhome in Brewerytown, a neighborhood named for its abundant breweries in the late nineteenth and early twentieth centuries, was equal parts North Philadelphia and Art Museum area. We lived a block and a half south of Girard Avenue, a busy commercial strip with trolley tracks running down the middle and low-end stores such as Murray's Meats, a dingy ThriftWay that closed soon after we moved in, Young's Sneaker City, ACE Cash Express, and Thrifty Beauty Supply, which catered to the poor African American neighborhood just north of it—an area our next-door neighbor described as "death and destruction." Most of the crime we experienced was aimed at property, including frequent rashes of car break-ins and vandalism, such as when my potted flowers were ripped up or when we returned home one day to find someone urinating on our doorstep. At night, in the distance, we regularly heard gunshots and saw police helicopters sweep their lights over our roof deck.

I had grown up in the suburbs of south Florida and had just moved from suburban Delaware, so our home in Brewerytown offered my first experience of straddling the two Philadelphias—white and black, rich and poor. Walking out my front door, I often encountered black men who were passing through on their route between the area above Girard and Center City. These men stepped with purpose, knowing that the Art Museum area was known for ethnic whites ready to defend their territory against invaders.[9] In fact, during our first few months living there, a story circulated that a black man had been shot inside Krupa's Pub around the corner because he had the "audacity" to ask for a drink. I never learned whether this story was true or if it was designed to deter nonregulars from entering the bar. From the roof deck of our townhome, on the other hand, we could see the Philadelphia Museum of Art, roof tiles sparkling in the sun like a Grecian temple; Boathouse Row was a short walk from there. It was the perfect spot to view the colossal Fourth of July fireworks show each year. Walking our dogs through the white section of the neighborhood, we passed Greek women sweeping their stoops and dressed all in black, other yuppies with dogs or jogging strollers, and expensive restaurants that drew diners from Center City.

In the mornings, I either hopped on the number 48 bus at the first white stop as the bus wended its way from North Philadelphia into the central business district or, in good weather, walked down the Ben Franklin Parkway to my job at Broad and Arch Streets. On my way, I passed the Youth Study Center (YSC), the detention center that held young people awaiting court hearings or placement in reform schools. Although I soon realized that inside the YSC was a crumbling way station of despair, the side abutting the Parkway featured two well-known public sculptures, Waldemar Raemisch's *The Great Mother* and *The Great Doctor*, depicting adults offering care, comfort, and guidance to the children surrounding them.[10] Next door, on Logan Circle, was Philadelphia Family Court, a beautiful but imposing neoclassical building designed as part of the local version of Paris's Champs-Élysées. Between each set of Roman columns at the building's entrance was a black wrought-iron gate, locked except for the sets nearest the front doors. Here probation officers, police officers, court administrators, and family members smoked cigarettes before entering the building. A line of people snaked out the front door and down the front steps as families of kids in trouble emptied their pockets, removed belts, and passed through a metal detector. In a second line on the other side of the entrance, lawyers, judges, and other court personnel were admitted with little scrutiny.

I spent time inside of Family Court with a team of program evaluators who were working with the city's Division of Juvenile Justice Services, which was part of the Department of Human Services. During my first weeks on the job, several judges allowed me to sit in the jury box and observe the proceedings as part of my immersion course in the juvenile justice system. Our team met with judges and probation administrators to help them build the capacity to use the data we were generating. After I decided to return to graduate school and joined another research project there, I spent hours inside J Court, the specialized courtroom reserved for review and discharge hearings. Here, our research team was charged with identifying and meeting with young people who were slated to return from reform schools to Philadelphia public schools.

Later, when I set up my research project on young men returning from Mountain Ridge Academy, Family Court is where I first reconnected with them. The controlled chaos in the waiting rooms outside the courtrooms was a wonderful site for ethnographic research. The waiting rooms—like the courtrooms and the juvenile justice system as a whole—were filled with a disproportionate share of black and brown faces. Since these families were drawn from a small number of impoverished neighborhoods, they often saw old friends, got updates on each other's lives, and passed the time by commiserating. They shared information about which judges were the harshest and which ones routinely started hearing cases an hour late. Parents usually waited for hours, afraid to leave for a short trip to the restroom or to grab a breakfast sandwich at the food truck parked outside lest their case be called and they lose their place in the queue or, worse, their child be held in contempt for failing to appear.

The waiting rooms at Family Court presented ample evidence of the massive structural changes affecting the urban economy, as well as the continuing history of racial conflict between residents and the police and the mayor's aggressive, geographically based attack on drug markets. The young men I followed came of age during a time when jobs were scarcer than ever but the chances of being arrested for selling drugs were high. The rising rate of violence was concentrated in the hidden Philadelphia. Young men growing up in these neighborhoods were socialized into the street code as a means of survival. Understanding these conditions is essential for comprehending what it meant to these young men to be removed from their communities and incarcerated at Mountain Ridge Academy.

PHILADELPHIA'S SOCIAL AND CULTURAL LANDSCAPE

Like other urban areas that have been historically built on industry, Philadelphia has undergone a profound transformation as manufacturing plants have disappeared to the suburbs, the Sunbelt, Mexico, and overseas. The labor market is now sharply bifurcated, with well-paying positions for professional and technical workers and low-paying positions for less-educated workers.[11] What makes the situation in Philadelphia worse than it is in other cities is the timing and duration of this transformation. Unlike its counterparts, Philadelphia never recovered from the Great Depression or prospered during the post-World War II period. Its vulnerability was rooted in its emphasis on nondurable goods, such as clothing, magazines, and cigars and cigarettes, whose machinery, plants, and equipment required less capital expenditure and were more easily moved to other locations than their investment-intensive counterparts producing durable goods, such as machinery and automobiles.[12]

A defining feature of the economy of Philadelphia and other rust belt cities is the marked decline in manufacturing. As table 1.1 indicates, manufacturing jobs declined by 38 percent in the ten-year period between 1993 and 2003. During the same time, employment in wholesale

TABLE 1-1

Changes in Employment Sectors for Philadelphia, 1993-2003

	1993 (in thousands)	2003 (in thousands)	% change	% of total employment (2003)[a]
Manufacturing	54.9	33.9	–38	5
Transportation and utilities	26.2	27.5	–5	4
Information	18.1	17.4	–4	3
Wholesale and retail trade	86.0	70.3	–18	10
Financial activities	61.0	51.2	–16	8
Services	263.1	299.2	+14	44
Leisure and hospitality	43.4	52.4	+21	8
Construction and mining	10.5	12.5	+19	2
Government	126.0	114.5	–9	17
Total employment	689.1	679.0	–2	

SOURCE: Philadelphia Planning Commission, "City Stats: General Demographic and Economic Data" (January 2005), http://www.philaplanning.org/data/citystats.html (accessed April 25, 2008).

a. Percentages do not sum to 100 because of rounding.

and retail trade declined by 18 percent, and the financial sector shrank by 16 percent. Government employment decreased by 9 percent. The service sector grew by 14 percent to employ a whopping 44 percent of workers. The leisure and hospitality industry grew by 21 percent, and the construction and condominium boom of the early 2000s increased substantially as a percentage change but created only two thousand jobs.

These structural shifts disproportionately affected poor racial and ethnic minorities, who remained in the city while better educated whites and blacks left. The reconfigured labor market offered few opportunities for those with little education to earn a living wage. As stable jobs disappeared, the disparity in family income between whites and blacks increased dramatically.[13] Whites had already moved out of the city in droves starting in the 1950s, when the federal government sponsored highway construction and the GI Bill made home ownership possible for many veterans. After the civil rights movement brought an end to formal housing discrimination, middle-class blacks began to move out to the suburbs, removing an important "social buffer" and concentrating poverty in inner-city neighborhoods.[14] Racial tensions were exacerbated as working-class whites worried that blacks would pose a threat to the shrinking base of decently paid jobs. Neighborhoods that were already defined by ethnicity became defended territories with even clearer dividing lines between blacks and whites.

Philadelphia's color line is also reflected in a long history of strife between its black residents and the police force. During the postwar period, myriad cases of harassment by white students resulted in the roundup and arrest of their black victims. Racial encoding of urban space was reinforced by the fear of white victimization and a lack of police protection, limiting where blacks could travel and spend time. Discriminatory practices and outright violence against African Americans eroded confidence in the police as a legitimate institution. Police inspector (and later mayor) Frank Rizzo earned the nickname The Cisco Kid through his aggressive roundups of black citizens in South Philly neighborhoods in the 1950s.[15]

Several high-profile cases highlight the ongoing problems in law enforcement's interactions with the black community. In 1978, Delbert Africa was severely beaten by police as he was leaving the MOVE headquarters; he was unarmed. On Mother's Day in 1985, police (under orders from then mayor Wilson Goode) dropped a bomb on the MOVE compound in West Philadelphia, destroying approximately sixty-one houses and opening fire on MOVE members as they tried to escape their burning building. In 2000, right before the city hosted the Republican National Convention, millions of viewers watched police rip Thomas Jones, an alleged carjacker, from his car, punching and kicking him fifty-nine times as a news helicopter hovered overhead. In 2008, a similar scene was recorded of a dozen officers beating and kicking three black suspects in Huntington Park. Philadelphia is the only city where police have been sued by the U.S. Justice Department and criticized by Amnesty International and Human Rights Watch.[16]

Philadelphia's crime control strategies have been different from their more successful counterparts in Boston and New York. Boston's Comprehensive Communities Program has received national attention for its collaborative approach to reducing crime. This neighborhood-based strategy brings together criminal justice and social service agencies to offer a wide range of responses to offending, including community policing and support for youthful offenders.[17] It targets gang leaders, urging them to prevent their members from engaging in violence. New York, under Rudy Giuliani, used the broken windows theory as a guide to crack down on public order crime, enhance sanctions, and increase the number of police patrols.[18] The guiding principle was that enforcing quality-of-life offenses sent a message that discouraged more serious crimes. Though New York's approach has its fair share of critics, its comparatively low rates of violence have been sustained over the past decade.[19]

Crime control policies in Philadelphia have involved a series of geographically targeted assaults on known drug markets (Operation Sunrise and Operation Safe Streets), with the goal of disrupting sales. Increased attention to drug markets has resulted in record backlogs in court cases and numbers of Philadelphians who are incarcerated as they wait for trial or after sentencing. According to a report by the Justice Policy Institute, Philadelphia has the highest rate of jail-based incarceration in the country. Its prison-based incarceration rate is more than 50 percent greater than the national average and twice as high as those for Baltimore and Miami.[20]

While rates of violent crime declined nationwide, Philadelphia was among a handful of urban areas where violence surged during much of the 2000s, making its control one of policy makers' top priorities. Despite the fact that overall rates of serious violent crime declined dramatically from the height of the crack trade and the recession of the early 1990s, cities such as Philadelphia, Baltimore, and Detroit actually witnessed sharp increases, particularly in homicides.[21] Detroit's already astounding murder rate rose from 42 to 48 per 100,000 inhabitants between 2002 and 2006, dipping to 36 in 2008, and rising again to 43 in 2010. Baltimore's murder rate rose from 38 in 2002 to a height of 45 in 2007 and declined to 36 in 2010. Philadelphia experienced a sharp increase in rates of lethal violence during this period, from 19 in 2002 to a height of 28 in 2006, before returning in 2010 to 20 per 100,000.

One of the factors that makes Philadelphia (and Baltimore) distinctive is its loosely regulated drug markets. Drug selling is more widespread here than in cities such as Boston and New York, offering underground economic opportunities to a broader array of citizens. This open market may be a result of less organized gang structures. Although Philadelphia had a national reputation for street gangs in the 1970s, today's gangs are smaller and based in neighborhoods, and their memberships are more fluid. It is not unusual for a member to be part of multiple "crews" or "squads" centered on the illegal generation of income.

Former adult and juvenile prisoners returning to inner-city Philadelphia find themselves in a volatile environment of loosely organized drug markets, vigilant but ineffective attention by the police, and a constant influx and outflow of neighbors, friends, and family members who are cycling in and out of jails and prisons. When combined with an economy that offers few legal opportunities to make a living wage or to fulfill the masculine ideal of provider, "the game" beckons as an abundant opportunity. Drug selling is available to a wider array of interested parties than is the case in markets more strictly or effectively regulated by gangs or the police. Given its ease of access, however, it also offers less profitable, less regular income than in more structured drug markets.

The young men I followed grew up watching economic opportunities diminish in their neighborhoods. Many came from families that had been pulled apart by substance abuse, incarceration, or early death. With chronically underfunded schools and dwindling prospects for any job that paid a living wage, they became involved in the drug economy, which offered an alternate way of making ends meet, as well as means of constructing masculine identity.[22] The streets became a primary source of socialization, teaching them survival strategies: how to distinguish a customer from an undercover officer, how not to "fuck up their money" (i.e., to fully repay the person who gave drugs on credit), how to avoid carrying drugs and weapons at the same time, and, above all, how not to snitch. Using the street code, these young men glimpsed an alternate means of achieving manhood that ultimately pulled them into the sticky web of the juvenile justice system and resulted in their incarceration at Mountain Ridge Academy. In the pages that follow, I introduce this code and the young men who explained it to me.

PHILADELPHIA'S STREET CODE AND THE YOUNG MEN IN THIS STUDY

Philadelphia's inner-city neighborhoods are simultaneously dangerous and ordinary, its residents desperate yet resilient. The crumbling walls adjoining weed-choked, trash-strewn empty lots display colorful spray-painted messages of hope or anger. Underfed dogs with no collars and visible mange patches wander freely, while black and brown children escape the heat under the spray of a fire hydrant. Groups of men congregate on corners, drinking beer in paper bags, smoking blunts, and talking to women, under the watchful eye of passing police officers and surveillance cameras installed on the telephone poles. The El train roars by periodically, hip-hop music pours out of the windows of a passing car, and police and traffic helicopters hover in the distance, sometimes swooping closer and drawing everyone's attention upward. Occasionally a man's girlfriend or his baby's mom appears on their front stoop, broadcasting a request for him to pick up cigarettes or some frying oil at the corner store. Cars must park with two wheels up on the sidewalk so passing vehicles can squeeze down narrow streets. Shoes dangle by their laces from telephone lines. Long hours of boredom pass as residents sit on their front stoops and porches, some encased in decorative safety bars. Strangers are regarded with caution.

Leaving the confines of their own street to walk to the bus or train stop exposes young black males to a number of dangers, requiring an intricate ballet of performance management. Police may shake them down, taking cash or drugs from their pockets and daring them to show any signs of disrespect. Passing through a white, racially defended territory, such as the edges of Fishtown or Fairmount, is always a practiced affair, requiring purposeful strides and deferential nods to passersby on the street. Eye contact and perhaps a nod or "what's up?" must be offered to other black males as a sign of respect, but holding eye contact for too long can easily be mistaken as provoking violence.[23] Dark "hoodies" (sweatshirts with hoods) allow young men a feeling of safety and anonymity; in the winter, a puffy coat presents a more imposing physical presence to ward off challengers. A "strut" makes meeting these performative requirements appear casual, nonchalant.

This book draws heavily from Elijah Anderson's notion of the code of the street. I specify here what I mean by the street code, since the term itself seems to have multiple interpretations, both within Anderson's work itself and, later, in its application and critique. When I employ the concept of the street code, I see it as the product of socialization and as "a set of informal rules governing interpersonal public behavior, particularly violence."[24] I also, following Anderson, consider the street code to be a performance: a package of language, dress, and comportment that is unique to urban milieus.

I depart from a third interpretation, which appears to borrow from traditional subcultural criminological theory and which posits that the inner-city poor share a value structure that is oppositional to the mainstream. These theories suggest that while middle-class youth value delayed gratification, poor youth value short-term satisfaction of needs. Moreover, while middle-class youth value civility, poor youth value violence. When taken to the furthest degree, these characterizations crystallize and essentialize these cultural differences, separating them from their structural sources and making them seem natural. Moreover, treating concepts such as "decent" and "street" as real and fixed prevents us from seeing how very mainstream and American the values of the poor truly are.[25] After considering the narratives I present in this book, I can conclude only that even youth who are the most embedded in street culture are well aware of and in fact aspire to mainstream values of work, family, and above all dignity.

Young black men from the inner city take a great deal of pride in their mastery of the street code, which allows them to both regulate and avoid violence in milieus where it is pervasive. Warren wrote a pamphlet titled "The Streetz" to demonstrate his knowledge, including how to find "wifey"—a girl who will "help you raise your kids the right way," how to survive a house party, and how to use street slang.

Now, I'm a get into street slang 'cause I've lived an' visited a lot of places. I've learned a lot of slang, so this is like your ghetto tour of words, code and just names that you will need to know the meaning to understand our talk. A "spot" or "crib" is a house or home. A "bean" or a "buck" is 100 dollars. A "yankee" is 1 dollar. A "dub" is 20 dollars. When someone "got change" that mean a lot of money, not silver unless you're at a parking meter or phone also known as the "hitta."

For my country sistas, if a guy call you a "smut," a "scag," or a "jumpoff," that's not good. That's a girl who sleeps with everybody an' their daddy. If a girl is having a baby, she's either "knocked" or "about to drop a load." To have sex or make love is "hittin'," "smashing," "piping," or "scraping" on the streets. Having unprotected sex is "going raw doggy" or "on their snake back." If somebody has an STI, then they're "burning." AIDS is "A-I-Die slow" on the streets. Someone that "throw that shit on" or "fresh" means they dress nice.

A "weirdo" is someone who is not into the street life like the typical "thug cool tough guy" image that's going around. They be theyself and stay positive, even though they around around a bunch of negative stereotypes, like they supposed to be tough and not show emotions. They express they feelings. I'm versatile plus my own man. An' I don't give a fuck what another person think about me. Basically, be yourself around everybody.

My youngins, if someone offer you "yoke," it's not the inside of an egg, it's crack cocaine. Watch out if someone is offering you work, that a job without any benefits. The only benefit is dead or in jail. Or wishin' you were dead because you are so far out on that stuff. Work on the street is whatever drug or product they're sellin' or basically anything illegal. Get ya 9-5 or legal job and fall back. A "brick" is 36 ounces or a "bird" or "stone." Someone name is J.R., that's because they're a Junior. "Miz" is Mike or Mom. If someone "blicked," "hit up," or "got dumped on," they've been shot at.

If someone "caught a body under their belt," then they killed someone. If they "did a bid," then they've been locked up. The "bing" or "joint" is jail. A "turnkey" is a CO [correctional officer]. A "burner," "slammer," "gat," "biscuit," "Peggy Sue," "choppa," or "lama" is a pistol. If you "drawin" or "hot," this mean you're bringin' a lot of attention to yourself and the people around you. A "hawk" is a knife. If someone's been "shanked," they've been stabbed. If somebody's a "rider," we're not talking about a person on a horse or a bull. He or she is all moving out on anyone who disrespect them on their "strip" AKA block and get it done by any means necessary, day or night, no matter who, what, where, when, why. They on the front line. When something is "on site," it means it's going down right there, no questions asked. When there's a "beef," it's a disagreement between individuals that's gonna be handled. If you hear someone got "rocked" or "took a dirt nap," this mean killed or murdered, 187.

Someone that "send a kite" means writing or sending a letter to somebody that's away in either the army or jail. To "spit" is to talk or rap freestyle. "Square up," "box," "give me a fair one," or "defend yourself" are all words that indicate that a "rumble" or fight is coming. A crack house is usually where fiends or addicts got to shoot up the "diesel," or heroin using a syringe, AKA "straight" or smoke crack cocaine. A "rose" or car antennae is what the fiend, addict, or piper smoke their crack out of. A "trap house" is where any drug of your choice is sold by the "trapper" AKA the drug hustler.

A "squada" is a car that's not in top-notch shape, and your "crew," "team," or "squad ride in" are people you associate with. A "burn out" is a phone that is usually on illegally, for a couple of months, by people who are selling or using drugs. A "flim-flam man" is a con artist who get over on anybody, even his own mom. And you always got one or two of them in the 'hood. If someone "knocks on you," "dropped a dime," or "ratted," this mean they told on you or snitched. If something "is poppin" then it's exciting. A "whip" is also a car. I'm a get off the street slang because this is only a portion of what this book's purpose is, an' that's a whole book in itself, so if you want to know more about street slang, just "hit me up," AKA call me.[26]

Warren, eighteen, was the first of the young men I met at Mountain Ridge to return home. A stocky, round-faced young man who often squinted because he did not like to wear his glasses in public, he came from a family that was deeply embedded in drugs and violence. His older brother was a leader of a gang called Deuce Deuce. At age four, Warren witnessed his father being shot and killed by a pimp after failing to pay a prostitute. During the height of his drug selling, he told me he earned $6,000 a week. Once the police caught onto him, he was on the run for over a year and a half, referring to himself as the Gingerbread Man. He returned from Mountain Ridge in December 2004 to live with his mother and several siblings in a gentrifying area of South Philadelphia. Warren loved to write raps and short stories. His depiction of the street code in "The Streetz" is downright hilarious, masking many of the harsh realities of inner-city life. At the same time, it illustrates the surprising resilience exhibited by the young people I encountered during my research.

Returning home on the same date as Warren was eighteen-year-old Luis. Luis saw himself as a rap artist and recovering drug addict. He returned from Mountain Ridge to live with his mother, Frankie, in a white working-class neighborhood in Northeast Philadelphia. Frankie had three sons, two of whom—including Luis—had been removed from the home by the Department of Human Services when they were younger. She had spent some time in jail and had a violent relationship with Luis's father, Hernan, whom she had divorced but remained in contact with. I first met Luis at Powelton Aftercare a couple of years earlier when he was transitioning home from a reform school. While working with him in the GED classroom, I became convinced that his habit of smoking "wet"—cigarettes dipped in embalming fluid—had damaged his brain. More than any of the other men I followed, he articulated the challenges of falling back in terms of sobriety.

The next to return to Philadelphia was eighteen-year-old Akeem. He returned to live with his older brother, Jerome, in the Olney section of North Philadelphia. Jerome, who worked as a nurse's aide at Temple Hospital, lived in a tidy apartment with his girlfriend and their newborn son. Akeem was the only one of the young men I followed who wavered about his commitment to falling back on the outside while he was incarcerated at Mountain Ridge. He loved the excitement that the drug game provided and "stuntin'" in front of girls with all the "flash" he earned as a seller. His status in Jerome's house was contingent upon his getting a legal job, following the conditions of his probation, and contributing to household expenses. They often argued. A Muslim and aspiring freestyle rap artist, Akeem was one of three young men I followed who did not finish high school inside Mountain Ridge. He enrolled in the Twilight night school program soon after returning home and was mandated by the court to attend counseling.

Sharif, eighteen, was a stocky, light-skinned young man with a scruffy beard and tattoos on his forearms. One said "Pablo," after the Columbian drug lord Pablo Escobar. The other, which looked like a little girl holding a hair dryer, was supposed to represent a tough guy with his hat on backward, holding a gun in one hand and shooting a bird with the other. Sharif was shorter than most of his peers and often wore a puffy coat to make himself appear more imposing. He returned in January 2005 to live with his father and stepmother in North Philadelphia not far from Temple University. His father, who according to Sharif drank too much, liked to hang out on the corner with his buddies. He and Sharif had an easy relationship. Sharif had a girlfriend who was a cheerleader for the basketball team at a local high school. He came home with plans to renovate his grandmother's house, which had been left to him in her will when she died several months earlier. He told me that he had been promised a job working with his local state representative and that he had plans of painting houses on the side, "'cause it's better to have two jobs than one."

Next to return to the community were Hassan and Keandre, who traveled together on the bus from western Pennsylvania. Hassan, eighteen, was a sturdy young man who was very serious about Islam. At our first meeting at Mountain Ridge during Ramadan, he was fasting and had a prayer rug rolled up in his hand. He seemed nervous as we talked, not making much eye contact and pulling at his pant leg repeatedly throughout the interview. Unlike with most of the young men I followed, I never developed trust with Hassan. Although I gave him my address, he never wrote to me. He was discharged from the facility with plans to move back in with his mother in a row home in North Philadelphia. He had finished high school inside Mountain Ridge and told me that he hoped that his probation officer would help him get a job, perhaps at UPS. He was interested in attending trade school to become a mechanic, but he said that college was out of the question because he didn't like the idea of being away from home. Keandre, eighteen, was a smooth-talking father of twins who spent a mere eight months at Mountain Ridge before being discharged in February 2005. Although he was nearly nineteen, he had not completed his diploma or GED while at the facility and was required to enroll in school upon his return. I spent only one day with Keandre in Philadelphia. After his discharge hearing, I accompanied him to get his DNA test (a requirement for all felons) and gave him a micro-cassette recorder and instructions for the first week's audio reentry journal. I was never able to reach him by cell phone again, although he did call me once and left a message to "suck it."

Two weeks later, seventeen-year-old Malik returned home. A light-skinned, thin young man, he had arched eyebrows and a very alert look about him. His driving force in life was his six-month-old son, Tyrik. Malik felt guilty about missing Tyrik's birth and was determined to be released from Mountain Ridge in time for his first birthday. He told me that Tyrik was going to be his "brain" when he came home, helping him weigh his decisions more carefully. He returned to the city in February 2005 to live with his mother, Shavonne, in the Gray's Ferry section of South Philadelphia. He had finished his GED inside Mountain Ridge and planned to do carpentry work with his father and enroll in community college. Malik was Warren's cousin and had similarly deep ties to the street, although his mother was a devout Muslim and had high expectations for both her son and grandson.

In April 2005, James and Raymond returned to Philadelphia. James, nineteen, was an angry young man while he was locked up and away from his daughter, Maya. Once he was released, he quickly revealed a broad smile and positive attitude that he carried with him everywhere. James and his twelve siblings had spent their childhood moving between family members' homes. At age nine, the uncle whom he considered his father died of AIDS-related illnesses and he moved in with his Uncle Clifton in Southwest Philadelphia. Clifton, in his early thirties, was one of the traditional, law-abiding "old heads" that many said had left inner-city neighborhoods in the 1970s and 1980s.[27] He demanded accountability from James, who chafed at the constant oversight but was himself fully committed to a law-abiding, drug-free lifestyle. James had earned his GED while at Mountain Ridge and, on his first day in Philadelphia, secured a job and started working out a custody and support arrangement for Maya.

Raymond, eighteen, was discharged from Mountain Ridge to live with his mother, a hairdresser, in the Nicetown/Tioga section of the city. Raymond was a most challenging young man to work with because he had shockingly few boundaries and was probably a pathological liar. He made nonstop requests of me for transportation and personal loans and had no compunction about calling my cell phone repeatedly until I picked up. In May 2005, he called me eleven days in a row. Once, when I picked up, I found myself in a three-way phone conversation where he expected me to resolve a dispute with his mother. Finally, concerned that I might be dealing with someone with a mental illness, I contacted his reintegration worker to get his thoughts. "He's a problem child," Todd said. By talking to Todd, I learned that everything Raymond had told me about attending school and getting a job was complete fiction. In June, his mother had grown tired of her son's lying and manipulating behavior and arranged for him to live with family in South Carolina. I lost touch with him at that point and had no access to his criminal records in another state. I used very little of the material generated through interviews and field research with Raymond because I did not trust its veracity.

Eddie and Gabe were released in May 2005. Eddie, seventeen, was one of two young men who were under the age of eighteen when I recruited him, and therefore I had to obtain consent from his mother, Ronnie, who was a staunch advocate for her children and refused to accept any excuses for their lack of success. She had spent eight years of Eddie's childhood incarcerated while he and his brother were bumped around from foster home to foster home. Although Ronnie was blind, she worked at the grocery store down the street and was an active caregiver for her grandson. Bright and outgoing, Eddie had been identified as college material by the teachers at Mountain Ridge. By the time he was discharged in May 2005, he had enrolled in a four-year university in central Pennsylvania and had to make it through only a few short months in the city before leaving for college.

Gabe, nineteen, was tall and extremely mature. He was the only young man in my study to grow up in a house with married parents. His mother, Beverly, worked full-time through his childhood, serving as a model of routine and reliability by waking up at five o'clock each morning to catch the train out to the suburbs. Although Gabe chafed at the lack of freedom at Mountain Ridge, he found the program easy to follow, telling me that the rules were "little expectations . . . for kids." He returned to his parents' home in Southwest Philadelphia. He quickly resumed his relationship with Charmagne, his twenty-seven-year-old girlfriend who lived just outside of the city, had a steady job doing medical billing, and was attending college. By the time he returned home, his family had already gotten him a well-paying job as part of a nighttime crew cleaning office buildings in Center City. He was determined never to get locked up again, pointing to the legal alternatives to which he had access and adding, "Who would wanna live that life?"

The next month, Leo, eighteen, returned to Philadelphia to live with his grandparents, Haywood and Ida, in the Allegheny West section of North Philadelphia. Because he was prematurely developing male pattern baldness, Leo looked older than his age and was compared by many inside Mountain Ridge to Danny Glover. He had already achieved several markers of adult status at fifteen, when he was "moving weight"— selling large quantities of drugs—for an older man in his neighborhood. Becoming a law-abiding citizen, which he badly wanted to do, would require that he give up the income and status associated with the street and take a menial minimum-wage job. Leo had a quick wit and a winning smile, which seemed to hide some loneliness. Even more than a job, he craved the stability of a loving relationship with a woman.

The last two young men to return home (in July 2005) were Tony and Isaiah. Tony, nineteen, was a quiet young man who often felt overlooked and unfairly treated by others. His mother had been a drug addict throughout his childhood and left him and his siblings with various family members. He remembered being dropped off in the street right in front of the drug house where his mother was inside. "Who does that?" he wondered aloud. Regardless of being repeatedly abandoned, he felt a fierce loyalty to family. He longed to follow in his older sister Gniesha's footsteps and leave the drug game behind to become a nurse. He returned to the city to live with Gniesha in her spotless apartment on the top floor of a house in West Philadelphia. His counselor at Mountain Ridge and his community reintegration worker had started the paperwork for him to join Job Corps, a program that would provide him with no-cost medical training and a free place to stay while he was in school.

Isaiah, nineteen, was a tall, light-skinned black man with an athletic build and glasses that made him appear very studious. He spoke clearly and deliberately, pausing to give each of my questions serious consideration before answering them. Isaiah told me that his experience at Mountain Ridge Academy was the first time he had ever viewed himself as intelligent. In Philadelphia, he rarely attended school and never passed the tenth grade. Before being arrested, he was a high-level dealer in North Philadelphia, running an entire block including a crack house, and had several older people working for him. He belonged to two gangs that were based in inner-ring suburbs. Despite the fact that he detested Mountain Ridge, he chose to stay several extra months so he could finish high school. While at Mountain Ridge, he applied and was accepted to La Salle University to start in the fall, with plans to go into the navy afterward. Isaiah lived and died for his two-year-old son, Darius, whom I later learned was not his biological child, but belonged to his girlfriend, Tamika. Although Isaiah had mixed feelings about resuming his relationship with Tamika after his return, he feared losing Darius and viewed falling back as having "ripple effects" that would also help his son. He returned to the city to live with his aunt in the Logan section of North Philadelphia, but soon moved in with Tamika.

As these thumbnail sketches suggest, the young men's personal stories and the story of the two Philadelphias are inextricably intertwined. Poverty, hunger, instability, homelessness, anger, pain, mistrust, and fear are part of the inner-city experience for most young men who have found their way into the juvenile justice system. Understanding this context is necessary to appreciate how young, inner-city men experience juvenile correctional facilities such as Mountain Ridge Academy. At Mountain Ridge, residents are told by white staff that they suffer from a "failure to endure adversity." From the young men's perspective, simply being alive is evidence that they had endured a level of adversity most middle-class people could never imagine. The pride that these young men took in their ability to manipulate the street code and to survive in Philadelphia's poorest and meanest neighborhoods coalesced into a race- and place-based identity, which is often reflected in tattoos that advertise their street numbers and memorials to fallen family members and peers. The notion of leaving the city is both a refreshing fantasy about starting over and a terrifying threat to the core of their self-concept. They simultaneously love and hate their block, their street, and their city.

CHAPTER 2

"Because That Is the Way You Are"

PREDICTIONS OF FAILURE AND CULTURAL ASSAULTS INSIDE MOUNTAIN RIDGE ACADEMY

THIS CHAPTER EXAMINES THE methods and philosophy of change employed at Mountain Ridge Academy. Mountain Ridge's explicit theory of delinquency is based on criminal personality theory and assumes that young people offend because they regularly make serious errors in their thinking. The school's practice is also based on implicit assumptions, including the assertion that crime is freely and rationally chosen by those who engage in it. Embedded more deeply in the way the program is implemented on a daily basis is the conviction that urban street culture is evidence of an innate criminality.

By studying Mountain Ridge in depth, I open the "black box" of reform schools, making visible the inner workings that are so rarely discussed in the public realm. I describe its target population, therapeutic strategies and activities, and guiding theory of delinquency and change. This chapter draws heavily on my years of working with Mountain Ridge Academy as a program evaluator, participation in staff training in summer 2005, and analysis of its staff training manual. I also observed events inside the facility while recruiting young men for the longitudinal study. Finally, I read the original two-volume treatise by Samuel Yochelson and Stanton E. Samenow, on whose research the program's design is based.[1] Before describing Mountain Ridge's program in detail, however, I situate the institution within the array of reform schools to which Philadelphia youth may be committed by the court.

MOUNTAIN RIDGE ACADEMY
AS A SETTING FOR "REFORM"

Mountain Ridge is a particularly good place to study the institutional reform of delinquent youth. Judges and probation officers hold its program in high esteem, especially for treating drug and alcohol problems. Outcomes from the independent evaluation I was involved in confirm this assessment.[2] Juveniles often remain for a considerable period at the Youth Study Center, waiting for a bed to open up at this facility. At the same time, Mountain Ridge is an intrusive intervention, particularly given its distance from Philadelphia and the difficulties that family members experience in traveling there to see their children. Decision makers in the juvenile justice system believe that young people will not be coddled at Mountain Ridge, as they might be at other facilities. For that reason, many consider it the last stop before young offenders move into the less therapeutically oriented state system.

The facility distinguishes itself by its carefully constructed program design. Mountain Ridge's theory of change, explicitly stated in its staff training manual, is based on criminal personality theory, an empirically derived (albeit problematic) explanation for antisocial behavior. The program's theory, short- and long-term objectives, and activities are tightly linked, a relatively rare and highly valued characteristic of program design.[3] Moreover, unlike other facilities, Mountain Ridge generates few informal accounts of physical and sexual abuse. In these ways, the young men sent to Mountain Ridge are given one of the best possible institutional placements for delinquent youth. However, despite the treatment they received, few Mountain Ridge graduates experienced unqualified success upon their return to the community. Just under one-third of all program clients were rearrested within six months of release from the program.[4] The vast majority of those I followed resumed regular marijuana use, continued to employ drug selling as a sporadic means of earning income, and had spotty work histories. Several had chronic housing problems. We can only assume that the graduates of less well-run facilities, particularly those where they experienced abuse or that had lower graduation rates, might encounter even greater challenges when returning home.

In other respects, Mountain Ridge looks like many other institutions. Several historians have argued persuasively that today's reform schools have retained many of the features of their predecessors since the birth of the reformatory in the nineteenth century.[5] Now, as then, young people who are disproportionately poor and members of racial-ethnic minority groups are identified as exhibiting problem behavior, labeled delinquent, and sent to institutions where professionals seek to turn them into productive citizens. Today, as when reformers became alarmed about the waves of immigrants crowding into urban areas in the late nineteenth century, delinquency is seen as arising from the conditions of urban life. Most facilities are located in rural areas, a reflection of the enduring legacy of "sentimental pastoralism," the notion that the country has curative properties. Finally, as the framers of the first juvenile court in Cook County intended in 1899, the juvenile justice system and its reformatories embrace elements of both treatment and punishment, while its adult counterpart has abandoned the rehabilitative ideal. This rehabilitative philosophy is the basis for indeterminate sentencing, whereby young people must earn their release by demonstrating progress.[6]

Young people in Philadelphia's juvenile justice system are likely to have a somewhat different experience than their counterparts from other cities. The juvenile justice system in Philadelphia has a broader array of both community-based and residential providers than most other jurisdictions and relies heavily on privately run programs. Philadelphia is equally remarkable for its commitment to evaluation and planning. Between 1994 and 2004, the city was home to the Program Development and Evaluation System (ProDES), an outcomes-based tracking system for delinquent youth committed to intervention services by the court. I worked on ProDES for almost six years, between 1997 and 2002. The system was designed to facilitate (1) program development through continuous feedback to programs about their short- and long-term outcomes compared to those of other similar programs, (2) informed planning by the Department of Human Services and Family Court, and (3) better matching of youth to programs by eliminating "bad matches," that is, sending youth to programs that had been unsuccessful with clients like them. It represented a significant investment in research-based governance and secured the city's place at the forefront of innovative service delivery.[7] In most other jurisdictions, few programs are evaluated; instead, administrators rely on reactive monitoring by state and local funding agencies and inspect programs only after an incident has aroused public concern. These efforts emphasize compliance with minimum standards for service provision, such as staff-to-client ratios, instead of outcomes such as recidivism rates. Philadelphia's evidence-based approach to planning and evaluation makes the city's juvenile justice system unique; programs are held accountable for their results. Nevertheless, the experience inside Mountain Ridge Academy is shared by youths coming from many different states, as it is a large and growing private corporation with contracts in many jurisdictions.

CRIMINAL THINKING ERRORS

The guiding theory behind Mountain Ridge's intervention is criminal personality theory, which is based on the idea that offenders share a set of cognitive distortions that distinguishes them from law-abiding members of society. Youths must memorize twenty-two criminal thinking errors during their time at Mountain Ridge and practice standard correctives for each. To be released from the program, young people must demonstrate a willingness to accept criticism, called "feedback," and a desire to make a change in their lives. These changes, while ostensibly occurring internally, that is, cognitively, must be demonstrated behaviorally.

The criminal thinking errors consist of the victim stance, seeing oneself as helpless and controlled by others rather than as responsible for one's own actions; the "I can't" attitude, giving up rather than trying to do difficult things; failure to endure adversity, or laziness; failure to assume responsible initiatives, or irresponsibility; failure to put oneself in another person's position, or lack of empathy; suggestibility to peer pressure; misdirected energy; "criminal" pride, or pride stemming from engaging in crime; failure to manage anger or emotional upsets; a belief in one's own uniqueness; lack of a long-term perspective and unrealistic expectations; "power thrust," or intimidation of others; fear of fear, or the experience of fear as a challenge to one's manhood; perfectionism, "an attitude about himself that says he is perfect"; fragmentation, the inability to concentrate or focus on one idea at a time; lying; poor decision making; super or unrealistic optimism, particularly about committing a crime; zero state, or a sense of worthlessness; religion, particularly that which "increases or decreases as the need arises for a person"; loner behavior, or isolating oneself from the group; and pretentiousness, or a superiority complex.[8]

Mountain Ridge's program design is based largely on forensic psychologists Samuel Yochelson and Stanton Samenow's notion of "criminal thinking errors," which they developed during their clinical work with juvenile offenders in Maryland and published in 1976-1977.[9] Frustrated by the ineffectiveness of traditional therapy, Yochelson and Samenow concluded that criminals were distinct from law-abiding individuals because they had well-defined thought patterns that led them to make criminal decisions. They argued that the criminal could be identified by his need for excitement, drive for power and status, tendency to see himself as a victim and blame others for his position in life, and exploitation of others for personal gain. They portrayed the offender as a habitual liar and manipulator, someone with "abundant energy" who viewed himself as worthless but outwardly argued that he was a "good person" and was haunted by irrational fears, particularly of allowing others to see his personal weakness. One moment sentimental, the next violent, the criminal mind moved back and forth quickly between contradictory emotional states, a cognitive pattern they termed "fragmentation."

Yochelson and Samenow viewed criminality as being fixed in early childhood and extremely difficult, if not impossible, to change. After fourteen years of intensive psychotherapy with 240 youths, they admitted to being successful with only 13. For change to occur, they claimed, the personality must be broken down by an assault on the self and built back up. A total rejection of the old self and acceptance of the new identity were necessary for meaningful change to be sustained. A successful "conversion" required "a total destruction of a criminal's personality, including much of what he considered the 'good' parts." Converting involved "surrender" to a "responsible agent of change," such as a counselor, and was most likely to occur during periods of confinement, "when his options are considerably reduced and he is more likely to reflect on his past."[10] However, they believed the criminal should never view himself as an ex-criminal, much the same as with addicts.

Interventions designed to curb criminal thinking errors have a better reputation among practitioners than among criminologists. Clinicians hold the approach in high regard, probably because it confirms widely held, intuitive notions about the differences between offenders and nonoffenders. Yochelson and Samenow marketed their instructional training manual effectively.[11] However, the research guiding the theory has been heavily criticized. The group they studied, youth committed by the court to St. Elizabeth's Hospital for the Criminally Insane, can hardly be described as representative of juvenile offenders. Social psychologist Hans Toch noted that those identified as "criminals" were actually psychopaths.[12] Moreover, the researchers did not have a control group. When they made comparisons between offenders and nonoffenders, they contrasted psychiatric patients to "normal" youth with whom they came into contact in an unsystematic fashion outside the facility. Finally, the approach neglects the important facts that delinquency is a normal part of adolescent development, and many young people engage in law or rule breaking during this period.[13] When confronted with questions about this matter later, Samenow backtracked, saying, "I admit that the title—*The Criminal Personality*—does suggest that there is a different breed; that criminals are different from you and me. That was the publisher's choice."[14]

The "criminal thinking errors" intervention is implemented systematically at Mountain Ridge Academy. Residents are given contradictory messages: that they must change their criminal ways, yet there is little hope that they will be successful. This theory is used alongside the idea of deterrence, that incarceration will prompt them to reconsider the consequences of their actions and make better decisions in the future. To be rehabilitated, young people must learn how to weigh the costs and consequences of offending more effectively. This theory of rational action posits that crime is freely chosen, which contradicts the assumption of the criminal thinking errors approach that criminality is fixed within the personality and controls the mind. Finally, the intervention bears marks of subcultural theory that links street culture to crime.[15] Street behavior, such as using slang or "strutting" around campus, is explicitly forbidden, and any behavior that smacks of street culture is considered to be evidence of criminality. While traditional subcultural theories of delinquency are based on white working-class youth, this adaptation focuses on "street" culture, which is racialized.

IMPLEMENTATION OF THINKING ERRORS
INTERVENTION AT MOUNTAIN RIDGE ACADEMY

Cognitive behavioral therapy (CBT) at Mountain Ridge Academy consists of training clients to recognize thinking errors as they occur in their daily thought patterns and to employ a series of correctives that are intended to deter criminal and antisocial behavior. Residents are required to complete thinking errors reports in which they describe their regular thinking patterns and plans for change. They are given constant feedback on their behavior around their dorms, in school, and during mealtimes. This feedback is the basis of the client's "status," or level, in the program; as he moves up through the status system, he is accorded an increasing number of privileges. Rarely do young people advance through these levels without backsliding, however. Failure to abide by the program's rules results in a drop in status and a loss of privileges. Serious misconduct constitutes a major norm violation (MNV), and all privileges are suspended. To earn home passes and to be discharged successfully, clients must remain on status 3—serving as a positive role model for their peers—for four to six consecutive weeks.

In addition to CBT, Mountain Ridge's program includes a twelve-step component to address drug and alcohol addictions. At the beginning of each day, a morning meeting is held inside the dorms during which counselors announce the day's theme and which of the twelve steps and traditions will be highlighted. No distinction is made between drug sellers and drug users, or among types of drug use. Group counseling sessions are employed both to practice thinking errors correctives and to disseminate information about the dangers of drug use.

Mountain Ridge Academy is a fascinating place to study the way in which young offenders make sense of and address expectations for thinking and behavior that lie far outside their experience. The facility's distance from Philadelphia is not simply a symbolic break from the norms and routines of street life. Freedom hinges directly on the offender's ability to interact with and adapt to the culture at Mountain Ridge, including its isolated rural setting, its nearly all-white staff, and its demand that the offender abandon the trappings of the street as a demonstration of his commitment to conventional values.

Days and weeks at Mountain Ridge are highly structured. Clients have limited time for activities such as showering and shaving and must ask permission to move about the dorm, even to go to the bathroom. Rules of civility are strictly enforced on residents, although not consistently demanded of staff. Baggy pants and clothing labels such as Rocawear or State Property (a clothing line started by South Philadelphia hip-hop artist Beanie Sigel) are forbidden, as is any attire that suggests that a youth is too "image conscious." Handshakes and fist thumping, a common cultural greeting practice of black inner-city youths, are seen as indications of gang membership. Prolonged eye contact with other clients while passing in the hallways and sidewalks is discouraged to avoid the potential for confrontations. Team sports, particularly basketball, are monitored carefully for their potential for posturing, verbal put-downs, and aggression masked as play. Listening to and writing rap or hip-hop music are not allowed except on special occasions. "Strutting" is pointed out continually as young men move about the campus. To regain their freedom, young inner-city men at Mountain Ridge must learn how to either eliminate or conceal the behavioral repertoire associated with street culture.

The people responsible for implementing the thinking errors intervention are strikingly different from the residents whose actions they regulate. During the study period, aside from the program director and one staff member, all counselors, teachers, and staff were white. Most resided in the small, rural communities surrounding the facility and were avid hunters and outdoorsmen. They regarded Philadelphia and other urban areas with suspicion and disdain. Based on my discussions with staff there and at other facilities, I believe this attitude is due in part to a general distaste for urban life and in part to a feeling of frustration that their hard work is so easily undone when clients return to the city. The interventions used at Mountain Ridge Academy tend to identify Philadelphia and other cities as the source of delinquency, to link street culture to crime, and, finally, to make predictions of failure on the basis of criminal personality theory.

"Dogs R Us"

Consistent with the sentimental pastoralism that drove nineteenth-century reformers to establish facilities for wayward youth far away from the pathological influences of the city, counselors at Mountain Ridge viewed Philadelphia and other cities as a problematic site for young people attempting to make better decisions and avoid criminal activity. Leo explained,

> This one staff . . . in my dorm, he call Philly kids "Dogs R Us." He call everybody from Philly thugs. These country people, they all like . . . I don't know what. They think it's like a whole bunch of gangs in Philly. I don't even know if it's gangs in Philly. I know where I'm from there ain't no gangs.

Tony offered a similar story about a conflict with the dorm staff after the Pittsburgh Steelers lost an important game:

> I said, Oh, Pittsburgh lost. . . . And I guess they was all tied up [angry] over that. 'Cause one staff said, "Oh, Pittsburgh lost so please don't get on my nerves." I'm like, "Y'all sittin' here mad over a game?" And so, after that, I talked to the other school staff. And I said, "Damn, so how y'all feel about how Philly lost the Super Bowl, like ain't y'all gonna root for us? We still PA." He talking about, "I don't care about Philadelphia, y'all some slimey, ignorant kids." Like that. "That city don't show no respect." Talkin' about, he said even the players, even the football players, they sneaky, they cheaters and stuff like that. And they dirty and stuff like that. I'm like, "You really don't like Philadelphia." He said, "I hate that city. That city don't got no type of respect or dignity." So I told him, "You displayin' the same attitude that you sayin' the city is actin'." He talking about, "That's my perception on Philadelphia and stuff like that. I'm a productive person, I got a job, I'm workin' here, I'm a productive citizen." [I said] "Alright, alright, so you're here with a buncha people that made bad choices, so that means you either better or you think you unique [a thinking error] or something." He talking about, "In that case, yes." I was mad. I was mad 'cause Philly's not even like that type of city. It only bad when you go in and join the bad people. Like you can go in Philadelphia and be a positive person.

Malik's stories echoed those of his peers:

Seventy-five percent [of the staff] hate [Philly kids]. Because Philly
kids come up here and talk about how staff can't survive in Philly. So,
they really hate us 'cause we got this mentality that . . . they say we
got this dumb mentality, this criminal mentality, that no matter what,
they just see it in us, we are nothing but criminals down there. We
ain't ever gonna be nothing. I think they look at Philly as, Philadelphia got nothing but criminals, they got nobody else that's gonna do
something with life down there.

Responses to these veiled but clearly racist comments suggest how
stigmatizing they are to young people coming from urban areas. Surviving the toughest neighborhoods in Philadelphia is a matter of great pride
for these young men.[16] Race, culture, and geography come together to
compose a key component of their identities. When the staff at Mountain
Ridge associates Philadelphia with gangs, dirt or slime, and unproductive
citizens, youth interpret these insults as a cultural assault.

"Street" Clothing as Evidence of Criminality

Erving Goffman has rendered a powerful account of the mortifi-
cation rituals an inmate endures upon admission to a total institution,
including surrendering his "identity kit, for the management of his personal front."[17] This kit includes clothing, jewelry, and personal grooming
tools, such as razors. In prisons, inmates' heads are shaved, and they are
issued uniforms and numbers, which are used in place of their names.
The goal is to strip away any remaining shred of individuality, erasing
all differences among inmates and reinforcing the moral divide between
inmates and guards or staff members.

In juvenile facilities, these admission rituals are typically less rigidly
adhered to than in adult prisons. Since two of the basic principles of juvenile
justice are individualized treatment and the minimization of stigma, youthful offenders are not forced to resign their names and are often permitted to
wear their own clothing.[18] Long hair, braids, and dreadlocks are shaved down
into a cropped cut; facial hair of any sort is typically against the rules.

At Mountain Ridge, the rules about acceptable clothing revolve
around the idea that residents should not be too "image conscious" and

cannot wear any colors or other signs of gang affiliation. The hustla or gangsta is stripped of his swagger and all the means by which he signals his adherence to street culture. The process of distinguishing "street" clothing becomes entangled in matters of race- and place-based identity in ways that are both confusing and stigmatic for urban youth.[19] Clothing that is deemed acceptable tends to replicate staff members' personal tastes, while any clothing line affiliated with a Philadelphia-based or black-owned or black-oriented company is prohibited. Tony explained,

At one point, I was thinking, alright, maybe they don't like these clothes. Or antagonization would go on 'cause I got better clothes than that person so I will antagonize that person and cause a fight or something. Me specifically, when I came in here I had State Property. They said, Where you from? I said I'm from Philadelphia. And they said State Property, what's that, you committed to the state or somethin' like that? And after that they cut State Property. I think it was because I said I'm from Philadelphia or somethin' like that. But I guarantee if I said I was from another area, they woulda said Ok you can wear it. We can't wear nothin' that's affiliated with our neighborhoods. Like say, if I had an Eagles jersey and it had a number on it. Like [Donovan] McNabb is number 5. They say I'm in a gang. I got a jersey in a bin where they keep the clothes that you can't wear. I got a jersey in there, it's a Green Bay jersey and it say, James Lofton, and it got a number on it and they say I'm in a gang or somethin' like that. But then it said "Made in Philadelphia," and they said No, that's gang material. [laughs] It's a jersey. It's a lotta racist prejudice.

Leo explained,

I like wearing Amici jeans. They said no, I can't wear that 'cause that's image clothes. And the staff come in with $200 silk shirts and Versace. I say, "Oh, that's image clothing." They say "Listen, I ain't locked up." Then they say I can wear my own watch, so I wore my Movado up here. They took that like, "Oh, you can't wear no watches up here, that's image." I'm like, what? What else they take from me? They took my jacket. They said that's image. Everything here is image, image. Just 'cause they wanna see us in Levis and Wranglers and Route 66, Walmart, K-Mart stuff. They said Dickies the only things you could wear, Dickies and sweatpants. To tell you the truth, I'd rather be upstate [in adult prison] than here.

Most striking about these conversations are the double standards invoked throughout. Clothing that is associated with rural areas or even Pittsburgh was acceptable, while clothing made in Philadelphia or linked to an urban or black clientele was considered gang related or evidence of being too image conscious. Tony identified the source as "a lot of racist prejudice" and a pattern of connecting Philadelphia to gangs. (Interestingly, gang activity peaked in the 1970s and has since largely disappeared.) He also pointed out that enforcement of clothing rules varied by dorm so that residents sat side by side in the cafeteria with others who were allowed to wear urban labels. Identity stripping was conducted unevenly, reinforcing urban youths' impression that representing Philadelphia or black culture more generally was symbolic of violence and criminality. The fact that rap and hip-hop music were not allowed but country music was permitted underscored their feelings of disparate treatment.

Predictions of Failure

During his initial interview, each young man was read a series of statements intended to inform him that he fit the profile of someone with a criminal personality. The last of these was "We are aware that you may go through a period of 'monasticism' where you will try to avoid all criminal thinking and actions. You will eventually grow tired of this and start looking for excitement again. Violation equals excitement. You will seek it out because that is the way you are."[20] Many of the young men reported that their counselors had declared that they would likely be back shortly after being released or, worse, would end up in the adult system or even dead.

There may be clinical reasons for taking this approach: to motivate the young men to succeed and to prepare them to deal with verbal baiting by others, such as employers. Failure after the program is quite common. However, the young men internalized these predictions and experienced them as stigmatizing. These negative predictions are compounded because residents of Mountain Ridge Academy often formed close bonds with their counselors. This strategy is doubly perverse given the potential for a self-fulfilling prophecy as when teachers approach students with the assumption that they will fail.[21] Predictions of failure contradict rehabilitation as an organizing principle of juvenile justice. So too the stigmatization of black urban culture contradicts another fundamental principle: the system's desire not to stigmatize young people, which forms the basis of all language and rationale for a separate system of justice (e.g., why, in juvenile justice terminology, youth are not found guilty, but "adjudicated"; that they are not sentenced, but "committed"; and that they are not incarcerated, but "placed" in "residential treatment facilities").

CHAPTER 3

"You Can Take Me Outta the 'Hood, But You Can't Take the 'Hood Outta Me"

THE EXPERIENCE OF "REFORM" AT MOUNTAIN RIDGE ACADEMY

THIS CHAPTER EXAMINES HOW young men of color from inner-city Philadelphia interpreted and adapted to the program of change used at Mountain Ridge, drawing primarily on in-depth interviews conducted shortly before they were released.

Understanding these young men's experiences requires an appreciation of the social and cultural lenses through which they view the world. I show that their mastery of the street code and the pride generated by enduring poverty and violence-stricken neighborhoods shape how these young men perceive and respond to interventions designed to address criminal behavior. I then discuss their perspectives on the various components of Mountain Ridge's program and their views of staff members. Finally, I describe a series of double binds presented by the rules at Mountain Ridge Academy and the strategies they employed to satisfy the program's requirements in order to earn release while retaining their street-based identites.

We might expect that asking young men to share their views of Mountain Ridge Academy would result in a litany of complaints and a summary dismissal of the therapeutic aspect of the program. Although they did make plenty of negative comments, I was impressed by their balanced and rather nuanced view of the facility and program. When describing his counselors, for instance, Warren told me that some were "here for a paycheck," but others really wanted to help. "Staff that's here for a paycheck will let you get away with stuff. They see you doing something, they'll say, don't do it again, but staff that's here to help you, they will punish you. One staff member might tell you to go ahead, the first time on something small, but another staff member will catch you on something small so it won't turn in to something big you get caught in or face consequences for." Here it seems that Warren subscribed to the notion that facing consequences for any infraction was for his own good. Luis shared this opinion of the staff's intentions: "They ain't tryin' to hurt you, they just tryin' to better you."

When I asked the young men to describe the most important lesson or skill they had learned inside the program, most mentioned "coping skills." Eddie differentiated those he thought were inapplicable to urban life from those that he found useful:

> I learned a lot of different coping skills. They got this thing called conflict resolution that I would never use because you gotta get with a person that you got a conflict with and talk with him. I'm like, nowadays people are not trying to talk about their issues they got with you. But I'd say how to control my mouth, how to control what I say to people, 'cause that got me in trouble a lot. It got me in trouble with the police, it got me in trouble with different people in the street, it got me in trouble at home, in school, in public places. And I learned how to control myself. I've matured a lot since I've been here, too. I see the way I think is totally different, I think my thinking is way more advanced than it was before I came here.

Sharif described learning how to handle his anger as the most helpful aspect of treatment: "The most important skill I learned is . . . to me it ain't just one skill, it's just like coping skills . . . that I would never have used when I was home. If I was home and I got mad, that would just lead to something else and escalate the situation to something more worser. But here, now I learned how to deal with my anger, I learned how to cope with stuff. I learned better communications skills than just sittin' there and talking all this slang." Here, Sharif appears to be referring to his appreciation at being required to use language that was not filled with slang. Luis especially appreciated "the fact that you know you got people that's gonna be here twenty-four hours a day that you can talk to that'll help you with your problems." Here, Luis implies an inconsistency in his life before Mountain Ridge that was likely brought about by his mother Frankie's incarceration and her strained and often violent relationship with his father, Hernan. It is a testament to the dedication of some staff members that young people confined against their will demonstrated this level of appreciation for their attention; it also speaks to the lack of consistent support they received at home.

Several others mentioned that Mountain Ridge had "good information" to offer if young people were willing to take advantage of it. When I asked what a person would need to do to get the most out of the program, Gabe responded,

> A person would need to come up here and be really willing to take a look at his past behaviors and he'd have to be open to all the things that they give you up here. They give a lot of good information up here. But you're gonna have to be willing to accept that information. You got to go and apply it 'cause if you're not applying it, then it's a waste of time. You're not hurting nobody but yourself if you think you can make it. So my best advice is to just be open to all the information they got to give you and to be willing to change your ways. Just from the sake of you and your family, 'cause if you go home and do the same thing, it's only a matter of time before you get caught selling drugs.

Similarly, Sharif told me, "The best thing about this program is that they could teach you a lot if you're willing to learn. And when you get home, you're gonna really apply this stuff. If you don't ask questions, they're [staff is] not gonna have nothing to do with you. . . . So there's a lot being offered here, it's just up to you if you wanna take it and use it."

While identifying some worthwhile aspects of their time at Mountain Ridge Academy, the young men expressed carefully considered views of the thinking errors intervention. They told me that they believed that some errors were actually errors, but other supposed errors were just plain silly. Eddie offered a nuanced evaluation:

> Thinking errors, those are some funny things. They [the staff] said that they [Yochelson and Samenow] interviewed people in prison, . . . and

they kind of had the same thinking sometimes. . . . Thinking errors, they're kind of weird to me because some of them relate and some of 'em are just off.

The one I think is stupid is like religion, because it kind of make it seem like people turn to religion just for like wishes and stuff like that. But I looked at it as like I don't think religion, no matter how you use it, is a bad thing. [Other stupid criminal errors include] the "I can't attitude." They say "I can't" means "I won't" and [I say] it's just some things that you really can't do. Some people can't read, some people can't write cursive, some people can't walk. Just because they can't walk don't mean that they're not willing to, it's because they really can't.

But, I mean, but the ones that I really agree with, [laughs] I would say criminal pride, failure to put oneself in other's positions, failure to consider injury to others. The loner . . . I don't know, some of 'em I just really don't pay attention to but others I look deep into. [Criminal pride], that's the one that, like you act like a tough guy, get mad easily, refuse help, don't care about the rights of others, but want your needs or want your wants or whatever. Like that's the one that I relate to a lot because I did all that when I was on the streets. I didn't want help from nobody, I put down others, I got real mad real fast. That's one thing that I worked on a lot, anger. Like I don't know, struttin' . . . I mean everybody got a little strut to 'em, like a little different, unique walk. Don't care about the rights of others, I really didn't, I used to just care about myself. My mom wanted me to stop what I was doin' out there but I didn't want to, I wanted to keep on doing it.

[Failure to endure adversity] is not a thinking error because everyone fails to endure adversity every once in a while. Like it's just some things that you can't accept. Like me getting shot in my eye, that's something that I can't accept 'cause it affected me for life, I'm blind in my eye and now it's all like, it's bigger than everything [it's a bigger problem than anything else]. That's just something that I can't accept, that I hold onto. My mom goin' to prison for eight and a half years, that's something I can't accept because it's not normal that it happened, me going from foster home to foster home, that's just something I can't accept.

With his typical sense of humor, Leo commented,

Whoever made them thinking errors must have been drunk or high theyself, 'cause half them thinking errors don't even make sense. Like criminal pride, everything you do that's breaking the law is criminal pride. If you strut, that's criminal pride. But some people got a walk, like me, I usually walk with my head back, that's strutting, so basically I'm using criminal pride. So I had to work to fix that, you know. One other thinking error I think is a bunch of crap . . . The "I can't attitude," they say "I can't" mean "I won't." Well, what if you really can't do that? . . .

Victim stance [makes sense to me]. 'Cause you just keep saying I got screwed, my PO [probation officer] sent me here, when you're not really looking at like it's your fault that you did it. Like what other? Fragmentation. Like when you just got a lot of thoughts running through your head, you're trying to do things fragmented, like you just got a chain of thoughts in your head. And another thinking error is religion, like some people just use religion when they get locked up so they can get out of this situation. And celebration after a crime, I never knew that was a thinking error. *Everybody* use celebration after a crime. Some people speed [as they drive] and get away with it, they go home, make a margarita or an apple martini and call it a night.

These young men pick and choose from the aspects of the intervention, applying what they believe is useful and discarding the rest. More interesting is the degree to which they resist the program's tendency to dismiss material conditions and reduce all problems to individual pathology. Some forms of adversity, such as losing an eye after being shot or growing up in foster care because parents are incarcerated, are not remediable. From the young men's perspective, acknowledging adversity is not simply a form of making post hoc excuses for one's behavior.

Finally, Mountain Ridge's residents develop well-worn tropes of resistance against the whole idea of criminal thinking errors.[1] Nearly everyone I interviewed pointed out that both law-abiding and offending individuals make thinking errors. In fact, pointing out instances when counselors used thinking errors appeared to give residents great pleasure.

Many critiqued the notion that "I can't" really meant "I won't," arguing that a lack of ability does not equal a lack of motivation. Although I did not spend sufficient time with these young men inside the facility to confirm this, I suspect that they shared these criticisms with one another to help cope with the dissonance that the criminal thinking errors approach provoked.

PROBLEMATIC ASPECTS OF "REFORM" AT MOUNTAIN RIDGE ACADEMY

Lack of Staff Legitimacy

Residents at Mountain Ridge Academy were encouraged to open up to their counselors and work though their problems at home during individual and group counseling sessions. Counselors and other staff members lost credibility, however, when they failed to appreciate the special challenges presented by life in inner-city neighborhoods. Young men from urban areas rejected one-size-fits-all therapeutic strategies and dismissed counselors for never "having walked in my shoes." Leo told me,

> These people [counselors] get paid for making educated guesses, they don't really know people here. [The counselor] is like, "Oh, it ain't no different from [rural town where Mountain Ridge is located]." I'm like, "What you mean it's no different than [rural town]? You understand the things that I've been through in my life?" He said "Yes, I do." I'm like, "Trust me, you're from [rural town] where the population is twelve." [sigh] He don't understand the things I've been through, mm, mm. Then when I try to break it down to him, he don't listen.

Similarly, Gabe reported, "They talk to you about things. They try to get you to be honest with 'em, [to] trust 'em. But it's not something that they can expect to fall right in their hands 'cause we don't know them from a can of paint, then how can you trust 'em? They don't know what we've been through, so how can they help me cook the turkey when they don't know how to cook the turkey? How can they help me fix something they've never been through?" When I asked Warren how he could distinguish between staff members who were "just there for a paycheck" and those who really cared about clients, he said,

Some just think they know everything about the streets, but they really don't know nothing, and they try to put on that front like, that façade, like they know what they're talking about and know what we're about when they really don't. Some staff is cool and some staff is not. [The ones who pretend like they know what life is like on the streets], they're the tough guys. They'll say, "I know what you're about. I probably didn't walk in your shoes, but I walked something close to it." They use the "back-in-the-day" stuff that they used to do. It's not fisticuffs no more, it's guns. We're not playing with fists no more. I never really fought. I always had a gun on me.

From the program's perspective, offenders view themselves as victims of their environment, using poverty and other forms of hardship as an excuse for criminal offending. In contrast, residents see staff members as out of touch with the realities of urban life and unwilling to understand where they're coming from. Ultimately, they dismiss the intervention as useless because it fails to offer a roadmap for addressing the obstacles they will inevitably encounter in returning to inner-city communities and attempting to become productive, law-abiding adults.

Double Binds

Although their knowledge of the street code helped these young men safely navigate inner-city milieus, those skills proved problematic as they attempted to adapt to the program at Mountain Ridge. Many of the behavioral elements of the street code were in direct opposition to the types of behavior that residents were required to exhibit in order to earn release. To comply with Mountain Ridge's rules, the young men had to eliminate or conceal any behavior associated with the street and replace it with behavior that would be risky or outright demeaning in an urban setting. Minimizing friction with the staff and progressing through the level system meant communicating freely about their feelings with staff and other residents, alerting staff members to any instances of rule breaking by others, keeping their cool when counselors disrespected them, and reframing marijuana use as addiction. All of these requirements put urban young men in seemingly inescapable double binds.

Open Channel of Communication, Loner Behavior, and Holding Others Accountable

Street culture teaches young people to mind their own business and keep to themselves. Sharing too much information with others is discouraged by parents and elders out of a concern that opportunists could seize upon it. Most young people told me that, as a rule, they trusted no one except their family members and fictive kin. For example, when I asked each of them to give me the first names of their three closest friends, most named their parents or guardians (usually mothers and grandmothers), their siblings, or their own children. They carefully distinguished friends from associates.[2] They have good reason to view others with suspicion. It is not uncommon for family members to institute house rules about visitors after having cash or valuable possessions disappear. Sincere's close family friend and neighbor Kevin swiped his ATM card and withdrew the maximum amount before Sincere discovered it was missing.

Children growing up in dangerous neighborhoods are taught never to show emotions in public. Displays of fear or pain, especially tears, may brand a young man as weak, inviting victimization. These young men expected their own children to accept discipline without crying. Psychologist Richard Majors calls this the "cool pose," a mask of sorts that is often (though not always, and not exclusively) adopted by black males. The "cool pose is constructed from attitudes and actions that become firmly entrenched in the black male's psyche as he adopts a façade to ward off the anxiety of second-class status. It provides a mask that suggests competence, high self-esteem, control, and inner strength. It also hides self-doubt, insecurity, and inner-turmoil."[3] This description highlights a sense of vulnerability that black males experience as a result of their marginal status in relation to mainstream institutions and the stigmatic messages they receive daily from the representatives of these institutions.

Inside the "safe community" of Mountain Ridge, counselors expect to see evidence of emotional growth in the form of honesty during individual and group sessions. Keeping an "open channel of communication," one of Mountain Ridge Academy's key principles, requires residents to be honest, self-critical, receptive to feedback offered by others, and willing to disclose their feelings. To advance through the level system, clients must admit their mistakes and identify their own failings. From the counselors' perspective, vulnerability is desirable, because only through feeling emotionally exposed can young people accept the need to change. However, this skill has only limited usefulness once young people return to inner-city neighborhoods.

These young men reported that the requirement of total honesty often put them in a no-win situation. "If I tell them that I'm angry about being locked up, then I've avoided one thinking error [closed channel of communication], [but] made another thinking error, anger. I tell them I'm angry, that goes in my file and comes back up again during the status meeting," James told me. This double message contributed to a sense of confusion about which behavior staff most desired. Honesty had to be constructed on the counselors' terms. Leo explained the perversity of the situation: "It feel good to start cursing [during our interview], like just to vent. Everything be bottled up, you can't like speak your mind and if you speak your mind you're inappropriate." He described how frustrating it was to share his feelings with a counselor: "When I try to break it down to him, he don't listen. He's concrete thinking [a thinking error], he's thinking about one thing and just trying to get his point across. And if I could have five minutes longer in the room, whoever I pick and whatever I do to him in that room won't get back [be reported], I'll feel better." After some time in the facility, residents learned that progress was made by sharing enough of their feelings to satisfy the requirements of an open channel of communication while carefully avoiding the kind of honesty that resulted in punishment or withdrawal of rewards. Residents frequently mentioned reading books, one of the few solitary activities that was approved inside the facility, as a way of avoiding the problem of feeling like they could never say the right thing.

Withdrawing from conversation with counselors and other residents was not a viable solution because keeping to oneself was deemed "loner behavior," another thinking error. Residents were expected to interact with other young men from a variety of settings, although in a very controlled manner. In some instances, forced interaction facilitated the development of friendships with young men from other cities and from other racial or ethnic backgrounds. Yet abandoning loner behavior entailed another risk—discipline resulting from others' behavior. By interacting with others, a young man might become aware of rule infractions they committed, and failing to "hold others accountable" brings severe consequences, including a drop in status and possible loss of home pass or other privileges. Clients themselves regard reporting others' infractions as "snitching," which is condemned by the code of the street. Warren discussed his technique for managing the tension between the street code that prohibits snitching and the program's demands that residents hold their peers accountable for misbehavior:

> If they're doing something that's going to get me caught up, of course, I'm going to come to them like a man. I'm not going to go to staff. I'm like look, you're doing this, and you're doing that, and you need to chill, and if they don't fix it, you say, I'm not going to get myself jammed up, I brought it to them first and that's when I've got to say, "Look, he's doing this and I told him. . . ." Somebody else that's going to get brownie points they go right to staff. No, that's not even my style.

If not informing staff carried a risk of severe consequences, however, that changed the calculus.

> They tell you how to hold people accountable and you've got to hold yourself accountable. I looked at it as snitching, so I didn't do it [early on in the program], but then [later, when release is closer] you've got to get to a point where somebody is doing something around you that's going to let you stay here longer and when you think about it, them or my family, you've got to pick, and you're going to pick your family, so that's how I looked at it.

Interventions and Restraints

Respect is valuable currency among the inner-city poor, whose opportunities to earn respect are limited.[4] Before coming to Mountain Ridge, these young men enjoyed the status they gained by selling drugs, displaying their mastery of the street code, and being prepared to use violence whenever someone failed to demonstrate sufficient deference. The sense of masculinity derived from the street code, along with the very real adult responsibilities carried by so many inner-city youth, conferred the privilege of being considered "grown men" at very early ages.

Once arriving at Mountain Ridge, their status as children was reinstated as they were stripped of their autonomy and their words and actions
were regulated. The same behavior that garnered respect on the streets
was likely to trigger direct confrontation by the staff, in the form first of
verbal feedback and then of "interventions" used when feedback failed
to produce compliance. According to Mountain Ridge's training manual,
an intervention can be offered by any staff member at the facility and is
a "method of communication used to modify behavior" and to "teach a
client new skills to prepare him to become a responsible member of the
community."[5] Although the manual forbids staff members from screaming in a client's face or violating a client's body space unnecessarily, nearly
every one of these young men described interventions as "getting in your
face." I witnessed an intervention in the cafeteria once; when I asked the
other residents what had caused the tongue-lashing a resident was receiving from a counselor, they told me he had tied his shoes incorrectly.

Leo avoided any behavior that could conceivably have resulted in an
intervention: "I don't get into trouble. What's the point of getting in trouble and all that's gonna do is keep you here? And then, I ain't one that,
another person in my face yelling, breath smellin' like hazelnut coffee, man,
Folgers—I ain't with all that." Tony declared, "I'm not gonna sit here and
act out and keep my stay here longer and have grown men—I'm a grown
man myself—what I look like havin' you in my face all the time?"

Criminal personality theory posits that criminals need to control
others and respond swiftly and negatively to verbal putdowns. Interventions often take the form of verbal baiting, testing residents' mettle by
making comments that would never be tolerated on the streets. Residents
were commonly told that they were destined for failure after discharge
from the program. These dire predictions of failure were grounded in
the program and the system's high rates of recidivism: approximately 40
percent of young people returning from reform schools to Philadelphia
were rearrested, either while at the facility or, more commonly, during the six months after release.[6] Yet these predictions were profoundly
counterproductive.

James was deeply offended when his counselor announced for the
group to hear that his continued lack of progress was why his young
daughter, Maya, was going to end up at Mountain Ridge's facility for

delinquent girls. Insulting his family was too much for James to take on the chin, and his status dropped after he defended his daughter to the counselor. Eddie objected when his counselor told him that he had spent much of his childhood in foster care because his mother didn't want him. (Actually, she had been incarcerated during that time.)

> They would say, that's why you're here, because you [sold drugs], and that's why your mom didn't want you . . . [and I said] "Oh, time out. Cut it short right there." That's when I start getting real disrespectful back to 'em. They be saying that to some people, people that's here with DHS [Department of Human Services, the child protection agency]. They say you don't love your mom. I be like, Come on, now, you're all taking that a little bit too far.

Eddie also stood up for others whose families were derided by counselors. Insulting someone's family is a severe offense under the code of the street. Despite some ill treatment and neglect, these relationships are characterized by unconditional love from child to parent.

Malik reported,

> When you first come in here you wanna mouth off, they're gonna treat you like a animal. They gonna talk all this type of stuff in your face and see how you gonna act. If you're going to swing [try to hit staff] they are definitely going to treat you like a animal. They gonna start throwing you around. Every day they gonna mess with you to just to see how you gonna act. Just gonna call you all type of stuff . . . dis[respect] your family and that. How you're gonna be nothin', you're not gonna amount to nothin'. You're nothing but trash. You're wasting your life right now. They just talk all crazy to you. I don't know what they're tryin' to do. I think they just doin' it 'cause they have the upper hand. They know we really can't do nothin' [in return].

Sometimes residents viewed this type of provocation as "power thrusting" by staff, which is a criminal thinking error. Many mentioned that it was especially hard to take when another man made that sort of comment, and he could not physically retaliate. Although some young men were astute enough to recognize staff's motivation for doing this,

others saw it as a "cheap shot," as bullying someone who was in no position to fight back without significant consequences. Gabe told me,

> Criminal pride—that's what get most people in trouble up here, they
> let their pride get in the way. Staff start yelling at 'em and then they
> build a shield on 'em. They feel this small when staff start yelling
> at 'em and they don't wanna feel like a sucker. But I think that's
> nonsense because, like me, if you really didn't want nobody yelling
> at you, don't put yourself in that predicament. I never put myself in
> that predicament because I don't like them in my face. Then if it was
> situations whereas criminal pride will come in, I will swallow my
> pride. That's where most people mess up in this program, they let
> their pride get the best of them. And they wanna stay with the smart
> remarks back, and it's not gonna get 'em nowhere, it's gonna keep
> 'em in the situation longer.

When interventions do not produce the required behavior or, more
commonly, when they result in the expression of visible signs of anger or
aggression, which young people refer to as "swinging," the next step is to
use restraining techniques, or "putting their hands on you." These holds
are designed to physically incapacitate residents while preventing them
from harming themselves or others. The resident remains face down on
the floor with one or more counselors holding him down. When the staff
member determines that the moment of crisis has passed, the resident
must ask permission to apologize for his behavior, which staff can choose
to accept or reject. Later, the resident must process what led up to the
incident, acknowledging his errors and promising to respond differently
in the future. Physical assaults that occur inside the facility can result in
new criminal charges, which could lead to longer stays or a transfer to a
harsher institution.

Malik told me that he had frequently been restrained early in his tenure at Mountain Ridge: "When I first came I didn't like none of the rules
here so I was really doin' what Malik wanted to do. Rules didn't apply to
me at first, that's how I looked at it, and that's what I did. So every time
staff would say something to me, I say something back and I tell them
don't come close to me and if they'll come close, I just swing. So they just
dumped [restrained] me." He described the process:

The longest restraint I have ever been in was two and a half hours. In one spot. It's 'cause I ain't cooperate, I didn't say what I had to say: "May I make a commitment that I will not harm myself or any others or destroy any of Mountain Ridge's property?" And they'll say, "Yes you may," and then you gotta tell them everything you just said. That I will make a commitment to not destroy Mountain Ridge property, hurt myself, or harm others, or abscond from the facility. And you say, "Do you accept my commitment?" If they say no, you gotta do it all over. They, sometimes they say yes or no, sometimes they're like, "Let me think about it" and still say no. They just want to keep you down there. You gotta keep sayin' it over. You actually gotta process through what made you get restrained. And then they'll let you go.

Eventually Malik learned that the costs were simply too high. "[Recently] I've been doing good. . . . I think it was me putting myself in situations where they'd be on me. I don't like that 'cause I consider myself as a man, so what do I look like [with] another man on me? Plus they're older. I just looked at them, like no, that ain't me, I can't do that. So, I don't want to get myself into a predicament that I don't like."

Although Malik's testimony must be viewed with skepticism because of its internal inconsistencies, I confirmed the portions quoted here in interviews with other residents and by participating in staff training on restraint techniques. Being restrained is an emasculating experience that most young men say they learned to avoid—some more quickly than others.

Other residents suggested that this kind of trouble was difficult to avoid altogether because restraints could be initiated with little cause. Tony was baffled by the train of events that had led to his most recent restraint:

They said I had threatened a staff or somein' like that and they said that I was gonna jump another peer. In here, I don't know nobody from a can of paint.[7] Why the hell would I jump them? How do I know that they ain't gonna jump on me, how do I know that they not settin' me up? I'm not gonna jump on nobody. So I went around and specifically asked every peer, "Did I ever threaten you?" There's thirty-two of us, I asked thirty-one peers, they said nothing, like clue-less. So I'm thinking the staff settin' me up right here. Tryin' to get me out for somein'. So [my counselor] tell me they said you threat-ened a staff member. I said, "Staff member? When have I threatened a staff member? I never threatened 'em." So I went around and asked peers, "Have I ever threatened a staff member?" Man, look how little I am. Back then there was peers way bigger than some staff members, man, they not scared of me, man. And then they restrained me, sayin' they don't know what you thinking.

Once he was restrained, Tony did not resist.

I just closed my eyes like this while they had me and I was really get-ting upset 'cause I had three men on me, and usually if I was home and men sittin' there tryin' to wrestle me, I'm gonna swing. But the best thing in my interest was to let them go ahead. I'm not tryin' to catch no more charges.

When another man gets close enough for them to smell the coffee on his breath and to have his spittle fly onto their faces or, worse, when he physically dominates them and holds them in a posture of submis-sion, residents experience the ultimate form of disrespect. Interventions and restraints are humiliations that most residents do not want to suffer more than once. It may call up memories of being roughly handled by the police or activate cultural images of black persons being physically subdued by whites. Moreover, the young men worry that when peers see them being restrained by staff members, they interpret it as a sign of weakness. These young men experience great internal conflict as their rage threatens to boil over but is ultimately kept in check by the threat of even more serious consequences.

We may wonder whether verbal baiting by counselors is simply a way to prepare residents to return to the "real world" and respond to put-downs by others in a more productive way than through violence. It may be intended for this purpose. However, some residents saw it as a "power thrust" by staff. It seems likely that some staff enjoyed the power they were entitled to wield over young black men and may have deliberately baited or provoked them. In either case, the lessons young men learn were context specific and not easily translated back into a milieu governed by the street code. In inner-city neighborhoods, failing to respond to insults makes a youth vulnerable to predatory behavior by others. As I witnessed time and again as these young men returned to the community, learning to submit to someone who has the power to have them rearrested or to extend the length of their confinement does not help them manage negative feedback by employers or police officers after they return home.

The Addictions Model

Another way in which inner-city residents found Mountain Ridge's program ill-suited for them involved its failure to distinguish between drug sellers and drug users. Leo summarized the policy: "They mix people up with drug selling and drug using all in one door. They said it's all the same thing. I'm like, how is it all the same thing?" Counselors at Mountain Ridge also lumped marijuana use with other forms of addiction, even though there is no consensus among experts that marijuana is addictive. Marijuana use is nearly ubiquitous in inner-city neighborhoods, as well as on college campuses. In urban neighborhoods, it is common to see or smell people smoking weed in public. The police seem unconcerned with low-level drug use and generally ignore it unless they want to search for weapons or evidence of intent to deliver drugs. Philadelphia-based residents of Mountain Ridge are surprised when they are defined as addicts in need of substance abuse services. Most are required to attend Narcotics Anonymous meetings after their release as a condition of probation. Gabe protested, "They want me to go to NA meetings but I don't need no NA meetings and I'm not gonna attend them. I don't need to give my life to God for me to say sober because I'm not an addict. And that's like that's what they try to hammer on us, like we addicts. I'm not no addict. I agree, some people do need NA and it's a good program, but I don't need it."

Some residents do appreciate the substance abuse treatment and addictions counseling at Mountain Ridge. When I attended the facility's graduation ceremony, I noticed that many graduates used addictions terminology to describe their own struggles, saying that "I have a disease that wants me dead" or "I'm living the sober life." However, using a twelve-step model with residents who only smoked marijuana as well as with drug sellers reinforced the perception that the intervention was of little use to them.

The addictions model had a final problematic element, particularly when we consider the racial and cultural differences between staff members and residents. Residents were encouraged to develop disgust for their former selves. Gabe explained his reaction to this aspect of treatment: "I don't wanna go home and do the same thing I was doing, but I wouldn't say it's a self-disgust. Like I'm fed up with being away from my family and me living that life, putting my family in danger. So that's why I'm gonna change the ways I was living back in the day. But no, I don't got a self-disgust. I'm happy with who I am." Gabe's statement suggests a sense of pride that is more likely to be racial or cultural than to derive from what the program calls "criminal pride." It is reminiscent of a phrase I commonly heard among young people in juvenile corrections, "That's just me," which suggests that people are reluctant to relinquish these aspects of the self despite being pressured to change. Given the legacy of racial stigma and shame endured by African Americans for centuries, it seems psychically damaging for white staff members to suggest that black residents should be disgusted with themselves.

"Fake It to Make It"

Because staff expected residents to relapse, those who sailed through the program without experiencing any setbacks were suspected of "faking it to make it." Outcomes confirmed the staff's skepticism. Keandre was so astoundingly good at faking it that he was discharged after only eight months, which was unusual for an older client from Philadelphia. Within three weeks of his release, he was rearrested for drug selling, the first of four arrests during the three years following his return to the city. Gabe, an unusually mature eighteen-year-old, told me that his stay at the facility was longer than average because his behavior was too good: "I got intervened with on the third day for not saying 'thank you' after I asked the staff if I could go to the bathroom. That was the last time I got intervened with, because I didn't see any reason to act a fool like the other bulls there." "Fake it to make it" is a common adaptation to the performative requirements of Mountain Ridge and other facilities.[8] Gabe's counselors thought he had learned the rules a little too quickly for his behavior to be a genuine reflection of cognitive transformation.

The theme of "fake it to make it" emerged early in the pre-release interviews, so I asked young men to explain what it meant to them and how they could tell when a peer was faking it. Sincere said, "I could tell you what you want to hear, like, 'I'm really feeling bad about stuff I used to do.' I'm basically telling somebody what they want to hear to get [the] benefits of going on a home pass." Leo, who was charged with robbery but who had a history of drug selling, said, "I ain't even here on drug charges, that's the only thing that get me upset. When I tell 'em that, [they say] I'm in denial—why do you deny that you got a drug problem? So I just go with the flow. At least some of the time I tell 'em what they wanna hear. Hey, if it gonna get me home, by all means, tell 'em."

Malik was an expert at detecting—and, perhaps, practicing—the art of faking it. He explained,

> It's clients that come in here, the worst kids on the streets, probably. They probably use more drugs than a little bit. As soon as they come in, they [act like they] got no problems whatsoever. "Oh, I ain't got no anger problems, but I do have a drug problem." But they got anger problems, they [just] don't show it. They hold all of it in; they tell us what they wanna hear. I mean they're not being real, they don't actually act like themselves, they act like a robot. And it's the staff controlling them. And they do everything up to a T no matter what, they don't let anyone take them off their Ps and Qs 'cause they just want gonna go home quicker 'cause they just fake it.

Malik thought that the practice had some intrinsic benefits as well as external rewards: "But I look at it as, you fake to make it, and you gonna learn something through all of this, 'cause in order to fake it to make it, you gotta learn something." Yet some lessons were inapplicable to the street to which these young men had to return: "If you were out there you wouldn't hold nobody accountable to the cops because you know what would happen." The calculations that shaped his own behavior were clear in his description of others:

> You just want staff to look at you like you a good person, or you might just want to get brownie points so staff would just tell them

you're a good kid, I know you want to change and you're gonna be successful. They just want to hear good things so they'll do some things just in front of staff and say things just in front of staff, whereas when they get behind the scenes they are the most negative person ever. I see it all the time, but I keep it to myself. I used to tell people but then they started holding me accountable, so now I keep to myself.

Finally, many young men reported being confused by the labyrinth of seemingly conflicting expectations at the facility. Leo illustrated this confusion with an analogy: "Sometimes I feel like I've been dropped into a video game and there are all these doors, and I don't know how to get out. If I open one door, I get to the end of the game. If I open another, I'm back to the beginning again and I have to start all over." Sincere, who respectfully called me "Miss" during this first interview, was frustrated that he seemed unable to convince staff that he had changed as a result of the program: "I see myself as a completely changed person, Miss. . . . Staff here, they don't know me out in the world, so they just go by what they see me doing here. They want to see the change that I've made inside, they want to see it outside before anything ever happens. Before we can even talk about me going [home], they want to see an outside change. . . . I believe they see the change to the inside, but it seems like the change starts outside. My beliefs changed a lot."

The experience of incarceration at Mountain Ridge Academy involves a set of double binds. Young men must choose between retaining their fidelity to the street code and meeting the facility's behavioral expectations in order to be released. Rationalizing these contradictions involves a tightrope walk: temporarily suspending behavior that is associated with the code of the street while maintaining a sense of identity that is still firmly rooted in the street. For some young men, this tension creates confusion about what is required and how to demonstrate cognitive change behaviorally. Others "fake it to make it," pretending to have a newfound commitment to the "decent" orientation. They do not learn how to code switch between decent and street behavior, which is an important reason why they so seldom succeed after their return.

CONSEQUENCES OF MOUNTAIN RIDGE'S
CULTURE-STRIPPING APPROACH

Although Mountain Ridge's program of change is based on criminal personality theory, its daily implementation contains a significant and damaging cultural element. Staff view street behavior as evidence of criminal thinking. Prohibiting the expression of street culture has three negative consequences. First, it has the unintended result of reaffirming street culture through its challenges to practices with which the young men are familiar and feel a sense of mastery. Moral boundaries constructed by the staff force residents to take sides, and some become increasingly entrenched in an identity rooted in the street. Many of the facility's rules, such as the requirement to "hold peers accountable" for rule breaking, place urban youth in a double bind because of their direct opposition to the street code.

Second, this approach undermines the credibility of counselors, convincing residents that Mountain Ridge staff have not shared experiences that allow them to teach lessons that are useful in urban settings. Young men from the inner city view their counselors as out of touch with urban realities. Finally, especially when combined with regular predictions by staff that residents will likely fail out the outside, criminal attributions to street culture in general and Philadelphia specifically are interpreted as a form of cultural assault. Young men experience these negative messages as deeply painful and stigmatic, as was obvious when several of those in my study returned to Mountain Ridge for their graduation ceremony with the express purpose of proving their counselors wrong.

These young men adapted to the program and endeavored to promote change in themselves. I was surprised by the degree to which they bought into the program's ideology and accepted the idea that they needed to change. When they got home and began to slip back into old habits, many called their counselors and worried aloud that the effects of Mountain Ridge's intervention were wearing off. Young people growing up in poverty-stricken neighborhoods might well want to live their lives differently, but for the most part they did not challenge Mountain Ridge's definition of the problem: poor choices leading to delinquent behavior. Neither the youth nor the staff acknowledged the powerful role that social inequality played in criminal offending.

Nonetheless, the young men did not accept wholesale the program's methods of promoting change. They expressed a nuanced view
of the program's various elements, sorting counselors into those who
had a sincere desire to help from those who were "just there for a paycheck." They picked and chose from the list of criminal thinking errors,
selecting ones they regarded as applicable to them and discarding those
that were not useful or seemed absurd. They wisely pointed out that
everyone, law-abiding citizens as well as "criminals," committed thinking errors. Some found the educational component helpful but resisted
the therapeutic aspect of the program. Only one of the fifteen residents
I interviewed—Luis, who was the only one who regularly used drugs
other than marijuana—accepted the twelve-step substance abuse component and its demand that they admit their addictions. The rest saw
marijuana use as more benign than addictive.

The young men walked a tightrope between conflicting expectations.
They were required to maintain an "open channel of communication"
but were punished for honest admissions of their feelings, particularly
anger. Over time, many learned how to "fake it to make it," concealing
the behavioral repertoire associated with the street code and pretending
to go along with the therapeutic aspect of the program. At no point did
the staff acknowledge that the street code might be a legitimate adaptation to the demands of inner-city neighborhoods, as urban ethnographer
Elijah Anderson's study of Philadelphia contends.[9] As a result, the program
encouraged the young men to push street conduct underground instead of
teaching them how to code switch between behavior that would be appropriate among their peers and demeanor that would be appropriate for a job
interview. We are left to wonder how much more successful young people
might be on the outside if code switching were among the lessons they
learned on the inside.

CHAPTER 4

"Nothing's Changed but Me"

REINTEGRATION PLANS
MEET THE INNER CITY

TONY, NINETEEN, WAS LIGHT SKINNED, thin, and quiet. We met in the cafeteria at Mountain Ridge, where he approached me about being part of my study. His culinary arts coworker, Sincere, had told him all about me, and he was hurt that I had failed to contact him. Although I realized that a clerical error had prevented him from being on the list, I soon learned that Tony often felt overlooked and left out, and for good reason. His mother had smoked crack for the past twelve years and was still an addict. He and his sister had different fathers, neither of whom was present in their lives. During his childhood, they teetered on the brink of homelessness, moving from one house to the next. His relatives took him in for a week at a time, only to return him. "They dropped me off, literally on the street" at the drug house where his mother was at the time. He felt a fierce loyalty to family, even those who didn't care for him in return. His sister Gniesha, also a former drug seller, got her life together and become a nurse. Clearly, she was a role model for Tony. He planned to go to nursing school when he came home, viewing it as a way to pay society back for the harm he had caused while selling drugs. Shortly before he was released from Mountain Ridge, he told me,

I feel, for me just to think how I was so dumb, that school really is power, right? The more education you got, the more power you have. I wish I was still young, like I wish I could do it all again. Drugs made me forget about school but if I woulda just stopped using drugs, man, I woulda been better off. School is so much, so good. That's all I think about right now, go to school, stay in school, I wanna stay in school for at least six years of my life, the next six years of my life. The more school I get, the more power I have, the more money I have, not even the more money, but the more success I will have. And that'll feel so good, like I don't have to worry about nothin', like lookin' over my shoulders or nothin'. And if I wanted to go to my neighborhood and see my friends, and I could look at them sell drugs and look at them like "Oh that's petty, look what I got." Like even if it's a fourteen-hour job I know I got at least eight hundred dollars or ten hundred dollars comin' to me or even fifteen or twelve hundred dollars comin' to me in the next two weeks. I can just look at 'em or tell them like y'all gotta go to school or somein' like that. Basically my letter writin' [to friends] be about, Go get your GED, get your diploma.

Tony appeared very anxious to continue the cognitive momentum he started at the facility, revealing a fear of "forgetting" to pursue his goals when he got home. I asked him at what point in the program his thinking started to change:

When I was on the verge of getting my diploma. Before, I was only lookin' this far ahead of myself, I never looked . . . all the way down the road, like it feels so good to look all the way down that far. Like it feel real good inside. When I'm in here sometimes it take away that [feeling], but every time I think about my far future I think, well, I be outta there, I be this in a couple more years, it feels good. And if [only] I can just start it now, 'cause I get the tendency to get lazy and not do it.

Tony was released after fifteen months at Mountain Ridge with plans to join Job Corps, a no-cost education and training program sponsored by the U.S. Department of Education. Part of the appeal of Job Corps was that it had a residential component; it would provide him a stable, rent-free place to stay and require him to move to Virginia, away from his criminal networks.

Two weeks after his release from Mountain Ridge, I visited him at Gniesha's place. "I saw my PO yesterday," he said. "She wants to keep me on probation, but I'm not hearin' that." He had called the number for Job Corps listed by his counselor on his continuing care plan several times, but got no response. "Those people be jerkin' me around," he said. Tony's reintegration worker, Karen, and probation officer, Lisa, had worked together to recommend that he be given thirty days of probation (instead of the typical ninety) because he needed to be off probation in order to be enrolled at Job Corps. If he had not enrolled in Job Corps by the thirty-day date, though, he would have needed to stay on probation while he looked for work. A month after his release from Mountain Ridge, he had enrolled himself at a Manpower employment agency and spent two abysmal shifts doing day labor, first at a meat packing plant and then at a cotton factory. I cringed as he described how the blood from the roast beef splattered on his face as he packaged it.

By the time the deadline arrived, Tony learned what had been slowing down his Job Corps application. The agency had done a criminal background check and found an outstanding summary (noncriminal) charge for disturbing the peace generated five years before. Unfortunately, the civil court in charge of summary offenses did not share a computer system with the juvenile court, so the matter had to be cleared up by scheduling a hearing at the civil court. Until that hearing, scheduled for five months after his release from Mountain Ridge, Tony was in limbo. "That's on Lisa! How did she not know that I had a bench warrant from that long ago when I been locked up all this time?" he said angrily.

Now that his probation would be extended, Lisa required Tony to attend the Empowerment, Education, and Employment (E3) Center, a community-based program for "disconnected" or out-of-school youth. His experience there only added to his frustration and sense that the system was screwing him over. E3 Centers had been recently added to the repertoire of services for returning youth as part of the city's attempt to "reinvent reintegration" using best practices that are supported by research. Unfortunately for Tony and several of the other men I followed, the centers were just getting off the ground during their reentry period and weren't fully staffed or offering a full range of programming.

While we were enjoying water ice at a stand in West Philly on a sweltering summer day, Tony admitted that he had walked out of the center of his first day. "I told them they were wasting my time. They had me working math problems and I haven't been in school for eleven months!"

He explained that they had given him a pretest and he had forgotten to answer three of the questions, so they put him in a remedial math class. "Why not another class?" I asked. "Because their systems aren't up yet," he replied. "The program just started. They don't even have teachers for most of their classes yet. But they expect us to be there four and a half hours a day, five days a week." Reintegration services often assume that any required activity is better than leaving young people with unstructured time. Tony realized that this program was ritualistic and put his probationary status on the line by rejecting it.

A few days before his discharge hearing two months after his return to Philadelphia, I saw him again and he reported that Job Corps was still giving him the runaround. First they said that they needed to verify that he had received drug and alcohol treatment. Then, when Karen and Lisa had arranged for paperwork to be faxed, the representative from Job Corps said that he personally needed to go to Mountain Ridge to confirm Tony's treatment there. "Forget about them," Tony said, waving his hand dismissively. "I'm getting ready to go up the street to the Thompson Institute. They do nursing."

On his first day of school less than a week later, I picked him up at home and delivered him to Thompson. He was anxious about going back to school, where he had never experienced much success. He worried aloud about whether training to become a nurse threatened his masculinity. Perhaps most important, he wondered how he was going to pay the $75 per month for tuition and find a job on the second or third shift to work around his school schedule.

One of the key problems the men I studied encountered as they tried to pursue advanced education and training was that it required an intricate balancing act among work, school, and, for many (though not Tony), fatherhood. Tony was not an attractive job applicant and was very sensitive to rejection. He and many of the other young men looked for work only sporadically because repeated rebuffs by employers were too great an assault on their sense of self-worth. Tony was also so embedded in street life that he felt like he was missing something when he had to work indoors. As he sold bags of weed outside a major train stop in West Philly, he could hang out with his friends and get girls' phone numbers. He said that he enjoyed the day he spent doing demolition on a house because he had control over the pace of work and he could be outdoors and engaged in the daily rhythm of his community. His knowledge of goings-on in his neighborhood was a form of social currency and an important source of status that he didn't see as worth giving up for traditional employment.

Six weeks after starting school, Tony's best friend was found slumped over in his car, riddled with gunshots. When he stopped by the make-shift grave, the police picked him up for questioning and found a bag of weed in his pocket. They let him go without charging him, but had been following him since. The next month (five months after his release from Mountain Ridge), Tony was arrested and charged with possession of marijuana with intent to deliver. "I was in the Chinese store when the cops rolled in and popped another guy for carrying a gun. I had just shook his hand. We knew each other, but wasn't friends."[1] That had been enough to charge him with conspiracy for the gun charge, which they used as a pretext to search him. When they did, they found a small bag of weed for personal use. He admitted to me later that he was selling drugs that day, but not to the guy they said he was. They also missed a couple hundred dollars worth of coke that was hidden in his jacket pocket.

Tony had stopped attending Thompson Institute. His attendance before the arrest was sporadic, but he didn't return at all after he was locked up. Each month, he received a bill for $75, and he wondered why he had to pay even though he was not attending. All his momentum and enthusiasm about the importance of education that he had felt while locked up was now washed out by the realities of his life. It had been easy to see the value of education in a bubble.

Meanwhile, he owed hundreds in fines and in court fees for the old disorderly conduct offense. By the time we sat down for a formal interview a year after his discharge from probation (September 2006), he had moved from small-time drug dealing to having his own block with a partner. They were selling "weed, powder, and rocks" for a guy who fronted them the money. They paid themselves $200 every three days, provided they had sold that much. Meanwhile, he had spent more time locked up after he arrived late for his court date and the judge found him in contempt. In December he was arrested for robbery and simple assault; in July 2007 he was charged with statutory sexual assault. In January 2008, just over two years after being discharged from juvenile probation, he began serving five to ten years for the robbery charge.

He wrote from a prison facility that is, ironically, located not far from Mountain Ridge,

> I'm doing all right. I'm in a drug program again it's similar to Mountain Ridge with how its structure[d], it's just now it's more freedom, it's less intense. They say once I'm done this, they will grant me parole. Hopefully, if I can stay out of trouble. The bad thing is I didn't even commit this crime. I know everybody that's in jail claim their innocents [sic], but Jamie you know by now I would just tell you I did it. I'm not that bitter, I was in Logan when this suppose [to] of had happen, of course I'm going to know where I was at because it was Halloween when they said I rob the guy. But for some reason, the guy kept on saying it was me and he said whoever rob him was 5'11" to 6'1". I'm know [sic] where near that height. And they arrested me a month after the crime occurred. My public defender didn't fight for me. Well, you know how that go. But I also gotten recharge[d] two years later while I was still in trial for the robbery. I had got a girl pregnant. She was only 15 years old. I was 19 at the time. So her mom press charges, but by the time I went to court for the case the mom drop the charges, but Commonwealth pick it up, saying "I was too old for her." So they gave me probation and then said I don't have to register under the Megan's Law, so I guess that's good. I think you saw the girl before, but you probably thought she was my age as I did.

There is no way to know what would have happened to Tony if he hadn't encountered the problem with the old bench warrant and had been able to move to Virginia with Job Corps to pursue a nursing degree. Perhaps he would have viewed the experience as outside his comfort zone and would have found trouble no matter where he moved. Maybe, with a nursing degree in hand, he would have turned out more like his sister, who had left that old life behind. In the language of desistance scholars, Job Corps might have served as a "turning point," moving him out of a criminal pathway and into a more conforming one. It does seem regrettably certain that this was a lost opportunity for someone who had few opportunities growing up. Moreover, Tony, who had already been profoundly disappointed by the people in his life, felt that "the system" that was supposed to help him succeed upon his return from Mountain Ridge had failed him. More than ever, he viewed the system with mistrust. Due to be paroled soon, I asked if he would be returning to live with his sister, who is his only social support. Sadly, with the sex offense on his record, he would not be permitted to live with her two- and four-year-old children. He was released nearly four months after he was paroled because it took that long for his PO to find a halfway house that would accept someone with a sex offense history.

Tony's story is emblematic of so many of the reentry trajectories of the young men I followed home to Philadelphia. Most encountered a stunning disjuncture between plans and reality. As Tony left Mountain Ridge, he felt simultaneously hopeful that his life would be different when he returned to the city and fearful that he would lose the momentum and social support he had built up at Mountain Ridge. Like Eddie, James, and Isaiah, he strove to pull himself away from the streets by pursuing an education, but like the others, he discovered that his precarious position in relation to the labor market and the criminal justice system prevented him from maintaining his investment. His reintegration worker and probation officer had good intentions, but ultimately forced him to participate in services for their own sake, rather than offering meaningful and appropriate programming or assistance. Their ignorance of his outstanding bench warrants was a function of the size and decentralized nature of the justice system in Philadelphia. How quickly his reintegration plans crumbled is a testament to their shaky foundation, as they were built to compensate for a lifetime of structural disadvantage.

Reentry

Despite the mass of research on the challenges confronting former adult prisoners as they reenter their communities, relatively little attention has been paid to juvenile reentry from residential facilities. Those who have examined the problem point out that the process is different because young people make a "dual transition" from facility to community and from adolescence into early adulthood.[2] We know that young men are particularly vulnerable as they struggle to disentangle themselves from the sticky web of supervision by the justice system. Failure is all too common.

As many as two-thirds of returning youth are rearrested and up to one-third are reincarcerated within a few years after release.[3] Fewer than a third are either in school or employed a year after release. Because young people sent to residential placements present greater needs than their counterparts who remain in the community, they face even greater problems afterward. They encounter significant challenges in terms of family stability, educational attainment, mental health, and substance abuse. The majority (70 percent) are raised in and return to single-parent homes, and just over half (52 percent) have at least one family member who has been incarcerated. These young people are also particularly likely to already have children of their own. Incarcerated youth are more than twice as likely as the general population of U.S. adolescents to have not completed eighth grade (58 percent vs. 24 percent). By the time they reach young adulthood, only 12 percent of formerly incarcerated youths have a high school diploma or GED, compared to 74 percent of their noninstitutionalized counterparts. These youths are three to five times more likely to need special education services than other young people of their age. One in eight is identified as mentally retarded. The majority of incarcerated youth are diagnosed with some sort of mental health problem, including disruptive behavioral disorders, anxiety disorders, and mood disorders.[4] They are significantly more likely than their noninstitutionalized counterparts to consider, attempt, or commit suicide. Finally, they are also more likely to report being drug and/or alcohol involved and at earlier ages than the general population of adolescents.[5]

This chapter explores the reentry period for the young men I studied. Beginning with the ground-level, day-to-day experience of returning home from confinement, it documents the young men's activities and concerns during the first eight weeks after release from Mountain Ridge Academy. Weekly audio journals, combined with field research, provide a window into their attempts to fall back by navigating the conditions of probation, avoiding further contact with the police, and reestablishing relationships with family members. The young men detail their struggles to view themselves in new ways. Finally, they convey the simple pleasures of freedom, including long showers, sex with women, and the personal autonomy to act, speak, and dress as they wish.

The second lens through which this chapter examines youth reentry involves mapping the disjuncture between the young men's plans at the point of release and what actually happened when they returned to their families and communities. It moves back and forth between the intentions they articulated shortly before their release from Mountain Ridge and the realities they faced upon their return to Philadelphia. Few of these young men were able to follow through with the concrete reintegration plans developed in conjunction with their counselors at Mountain Ridge. Time and time again, I witnessed their hopes and expectations for employment, schooling and technical training, relationships with family members and romantic partners, and falling back dashed shortly after their release.

I analyze the reasons why things fell apart so quickly and in so many ways for these young men and why they expected their circumstances to be changed upon their return. I conclude that the problem stems from the tenuous relationships that these men have with social institutions such as the labor market, families, and the criminal justice system, including police. Neither good planning on the part of professionals nor a simple willingness to accept accountability for past behavior and a desire to "do good" is enough to overcome the structural barriers to healthy adulthood among vulnerable youth.

We begin with excerpts from in-depth interviews with the young men shortly before they were released. Despite their skepticism toward many aspects of Mountain Ridge's program of change, these young men bought into the deterrence language used inside the facility and believed that falling back after their return was simply a matter of thinking more rationally than in the past. They expressed a new appreciation for weighing the risks and rewards of their actions and viewed the costs of offending as no longer worth the meager benefits.

REGRETS AND PLANS FOR CHANGE

The framework of criminal thinking errors offers little hope for change because it assumes that the criminal personality is largely fixed in early childhood. At Mountain Ridge, it was translated in practice into deterrence theory, the idea that readjusting the ratio of risks to rewards prevents offending. Once residents were taught to identify criminal thinking errors, it presumed, they would make better decisions when opportunities to offend arose. While the young men were skeptical about this form of therapy, they did understand their process of change in terms of rational choice, or deterrence.

During his pre-release interview, Keandre explained that his view on falling back changed during his time at Mountain Ridge:

[Falling back] ain't somein that I wanna do when I first came up here but, I done took seven months out my life to sit back and just think clearly, and this is not where I wanna end up at or live my life as a drug dealer, so it's all up to me to make that choice. If I find myself getting back into the same thing I just gotta think twice about it and just stop thinking my first thing. You know how people say your first instinct is your best instinct? Well my first instinct always seems to be kinda shaky, so when I think twice the answer's better so the results is better.

Being locked up gave these young men a "time out" to reflect upon their past actions and imagine a different future.[6]

Eddie told me, "You actually got the time to sit and get your head straight, get your head screwed on straight. Rather than in Philly it's a lot of distractions. It's a big city, it's a lot to do, so you can say that you wanna do one thing and then go to a party and just forget all about it. Rather than here, you got time to actually sit and let it sink in and think about things."

Sharif reported,

Once I came here I started looking at that stuff, analyzing it and finding a solution for all that stuff. And it's like now I look at things differently. Plus with things that happened since I've been here with my family, it's like everything just changed my view from negative to goin' positive. And it's like everybody ask me, do you really think you could stay positive when you get home? And I'll say, Yeah, if I'm determined to do that and I'm confident in myself that's what I'm gonna do. And it's easier said than done, I know that's what I got my mind frame set at and that's what I'm gonna do.

Many talked about regretting the past and wishing they had taken another path. Shortly before his release, I asked Gabe if he agreed with the program's assertion that he was locked up because he made bad choices. He replied, "I agree. Selling drugs was bad because I let my instant gratification get the best of me, you know. Like, 'cause I wanted to provide for myself, but I ain't wanna get no job, you know what I mean? That was a bad choice right there, just goin' out there and sellin' drugs to get money when I could have just got it the legal way and I'd a been still home right now, you know. But I ain't gonna say 'what if' 'cause if what if was a fifth we'd all be drunk."

Keandre's pre-release narrative was also marked by regret. When I asked him what he would change about his experience at Mountain Ridge if he could, he told me,

> My life. If I could just turn back the hands of time I [would] try to do everything different 'cause I ain't never had time to think 'cause I was so high and worried about me sellin' this drug and getting that much money and tryin' to be bigger than that next man and if I see all the consequences [that] came with it, I wouldn't even did it. 'Cause it not even worth it just to sell a little bit of drugs to somebody else and that person not even locked up and *I'm* doin' the time, so I see, that's a dumb reason to get locked up.

All of these young men had more or less specific plans for schooling and/or work and housing. All (with the exception of Akeem, who quite honestly said he wasn't sure if he could stay away from the game) appeared sincere when they talked about feeling changed as a result of the program and their plans for falling back on the outside. Some, like Raymond, were probably skilled liars, trained over months at Mountain Ridge to "fake it to make it" and tell adults what they want to hear. I am inclined, however, to interpret their desire to make good as genuine, whether it stemmed from aspirations to better themselves or simply to avoid being locked up and deprived of their liberty again. So we must take seriously the harsh reality associated with returning home to the most disadvantaged and violence-ridden neighborhoods, which has the power to rapidly eliminate all hopes and plans for a crime-free future. In the next section, these realities are described in detail, with a special focus on the vulnerable period just after release from Mountain Ridge.

COMING HOME: THE FIRST EIGHT WEEKS

The First One to Two Days Home

Being released from Mountain Ridge Academy and returning to
Philadelphia prompted a conflicting array of emotions for the young men
in my study. All were excited to reunite with family members and other
loved ones and to regain their freedom. After taking a bus across the state,
most spent their first night at home celebrating. Eddie's mom cooked his
favorite meal, short ribs and cabbage. Isaiah's girlfriend, Tamika, prepared
him a full breakfast after they had stayed up all night playing with their
son. They also managed to get a little private time together, as evidenced
by the passion scratch on his neck I saw that morning at his discharge
hearing. Several of the young men mentioned that they had taken a long,
hot shower to compensate for months or years of three-minute showers
at the facility. Like Isaiah, many also reported spending sleepless nights
with old girlfriends.

Their first few days at home were an opportunity to recover their
former selves by reestablishing their urban identity kit: heading to the
barber for a "shape-up," buying a cell phone so that they could recon-
nect with their friends, and wearing the street clothes that had been
prohibited inside Mountain Ridge. It also was important to announce
their renewed presence in the community by visiting the corner store
and hanging out on their stoop, two key neighborhood staging areas.
Sitting on his grandmother Ida's front stoop with Leo, I observed the
way that neighborhood residents in inner-city communities adapt to the
constant in- and outflow of their neighbors from juvenile facilities, jails,
and prisons.

While we were sitting there, several people stopped to greet him and
ask if he was home for good. A young woman named Candy approached
us, wearing her arms inside her jacket. "I'm going to be a mom," she said.
"No way. Who?" he asked. She smiled. "No one from around here. You
might know him, so I'm not going to say," she said. "Who's this, your
PO?" she asked. "Yeah," he said. She looked at me warily. "Don't say
that!" I said. He laughed. "She's writing my life story," he said. She looked
doubtful. "He goin' to be locked up again by December," she said.

While we sat there, several people who greeted Leo gave him updates
on other neighbors. "Nia's mom died, did you hear?" "Trevon is out of

jail now." "DeShawn got locked up." A short-haired middle-aged woman stopped in her tracks when she saw Leo and exclaimed, "My man!" He stood up and hugged her. "You home for good?" He nodded. She continued on her way to the corner store, and we saw her again in ten minutes, walking back with food in a black plastic bag. A frail, elderly black man wearing a suit jacket, dress pants, and a rain coat stopped to greet Leo. He tipped his hat to me, and I said "How are you, sir?" "I am drunk!" he said, unembarrassed. I smiled. He continued walking and Leo said goodbye. At one point, a dark-skinned thin man stormed toward us, exaggerating each footstep and scowling. He had his hand jammed in the pocket of his hoodie as if he held a gun. "That dude is crazy," Leo said, unworried. I wondered if we should go back into the house, but we were clearly not his intended target. He stormed right by us and stopped in the middle of the block, but I couldn't see who he was talking to because so many people were milling around on the street. Many small children played on the street, riding their bikes. I thought I saw a drug deal in progress and looked away, following the mind-your-own-business principle. A couple of minutes later, the crazy dude stormed right back by us, apparently having gotten what he needed.

Leo and the other men returning from reform schools soon realized that the opportunities for trouble were the same as they were before they were incarcerated. These unchanged circumstances are the reason why CBT in which offenders learn and practice prosocial behaviors inside facilities does not easily translate to their urban neighborhoods. Eddie summed it up when he said, "Mountain Ridge is so far away from reality, it's so different from the street, it's so structured. Here in the streets, there's structure, but we make it ourselves."

When Candy predicted that Leo would be locked up again by December, she was doing what some describe as "hating." In neighborhoods of concentrated disadvantage, signs of personal success may be scrutinized by other community members. If Leo goes to college, then Candy's failure to succeed could be viewed as the result of personal shortcomings. Misery loves company.[7] I observed hating in James's Southwest Philly neighborhood, where the young people who hung out near the corner store attempted to sabotage his efforts to fall back by falsely accusing him of selling drugs. Correctly identifying his uncle Clifton as the cornerstone of his plan to make good, they reported to Clifton that James was back to the grind, which had the intended effect of eroding the trust that the two were building.

These young men's concerns about returning home were a sobering counterpoint to their excitement. A couple of them mentioned that they needed to watch their backs carefully because they had ongoing beefs with other young men. Warren had an SOS waiting for him, which he explained meant that a gangster in the city had warned him he would be shot on sight. Eddie, who lived in Southwest Philly with his mom, wasn't safe in South Philly because he had angered some guy named Estaban by dating his baby's mom.

Young men like Isaiah and Sincere had another reason to be wary about their return. Sincere's mother, Teresa, spent much of his childhood battling an addiction that resulted in her becoming HIV positive. He continued to worry that she would relapse or get sick, leaving the family without a parent. (His father had died of AIDS-related complications while he was at Mountain Ridge.) Isaiah was released to live with his aunt, whom he alternately called "my guardian" and "mom," and whom he blamed for getting him locked up. He believed that she called the police and turned him in so that she could get rid of him and be free to operate an unlicensed day care in her home. When he returned home, he was dubious about her motives. "We'll see. Only time will tell."

Their most common concerns were about returning to their old ways and the consequences that could bring, especially now that they had left the "last stop" in the juvenile system. They worried that their counselors were right all those times they had predicted that they would end up back in the system or dead. Those who worried most about slipping back into old habits, such as James and Eddie, often spent their first days at home looking for work. Others engaged in desistance talk, a kind of self-talk designed to support a narrative of prosocial change.

Desistance Talk

One of the windows through which I was able to view these young men's struggle to fall back was through their audio reentry journals. Many used "desistance talk" as a cognitive and linguistic tool to help reinforce their determination not to return to their old ways.[8]

Luis, the only young man I followed who regularly used drugs other than marijuana and who saw his reentry process largely in terms of sobriety, underscored this point:

Trying to start off another session of some good talking and hopefully see something better than what I was seeing out here. Start off a better relationship with my family and other the people that I know that I love, deep down inside. I gotta do it, do it soon. Trust is something you keep when you gain it. I came between death a lot of time but I guess God gave me a chance and to this day, I'm trying to understand the chance that I got and why I got it. I guess I needed that chance and now I'm doing what I need to do. I thank you, Jamie, for letting me speak into this. I want to do some more speaking about the streets, about my life. It puts me in the space to know that I can talk about my past. I have it on tape, where people can listen to it and understand what I'm going through right now. I think it's good for me.

Akeem reported during his first week home,

The smell of weed it takes me back to the old days. When I smelled that, I wanted to say forget probation and wanted to smoke, but y'know, I wasn't trying to deal with the consequences all over again just for a blunt. I feel like the drug game is calling me. I see everybody out here, makin' all this money. Stuntin' on people and shit. That's what I feel like. Goin' back to hustlin' and shit. But I also know that I don't want to deal with the consequences of that action, so I gotta think real hard about what I want to do. If a job comes in line, then that's a good thing. If not, that's a bad thing. This is my story. And it's to be continued.

I got chills listening to Warren's first journal entry; he had brought it along as he and his buddies were driving around in an SUV at night and were talking into the recorder at the moment when another young man they knew was shot and killed. His account, clearly influenced by what he had just seen, echoed these concerns about the future. "Deuce Deuce gang [from 22nd Street] is everywhere. Everybody Deuce Deuce. It's going down. Everybody got pistols. Y'know what I'm saying? That's how it's happening. And me? I'm going either way, right or wrong. But you know I love my freedom too much." About the shooting, he said, "On the real tip, man, I felt kinda scared, man, because these guys don't give a fuck."

These messages were more tenuous and reveal more uncertainty than the claims the young men made while they were locked up. As they came home and slipped back into old patterns, I was reminded of addicts who are able to clean up inside rehab, but find that returning to people, places, and things associated with their old lives is simply too much to counter.

Young people do not make this transition alone. Although services are not available to all young people returning from reform schools nationwide, all Philadelphia youth receive these services as mandated by the Pennsylvania Juvenile Court Judges' Commission. Juvenile reintegration consists of supervision and support designed to smooth the transition from facility to community. Before release, reintegration workers and/or juvenile probation officers help youth reenroll in school, work with the young person's family to ensure that there is a stable home environment, connect youths to employment opportunities, and locate other community-based services that fit their clients' individual needs. Young people are required to meet specific conditions of their release, such as paying restitution, doing community service, and passing regular drug screens. In Philadelphia, the supervisory role is played by the juvenile probation officer housed at Family Court, and support services are offered by a reintegration worker employed by a private agency.

Conditions of Probation and Interactions with Reintegration Professionals

Returning youth meet with the various professionals to whom they will be held accountable during their probationary period at their discharge hearing, the morning after they take the bus home from their facilities. In many cases, the reintegration worker will have met with clients in person during their monthly facility visits. He or she is supposed to visit the client's home several times to determine whether the household and the parent or guardian living there are conducive to a smooth transition and develop an individual service plan designed to address the client's needs upon return to Philadelphia.

In addition to working with their reintegration workers to develop plans for employment or schooling, youth often meet with their probation officers on discharge day to discuss the conditions of probation. When I took Eddie and his mother to his discharge hearing, I sensed how overwhelmed he was about meeting all the obligations his PO, Lisa, laid out for him. They held a brief conference outside the courtroom while he expressed his displeasure at having to attend NA meetings four times per week.

"Listen, NA isn't for everyone. If you don't feel comfortable there, don't just stop going. Talk to me and I can get you in somewhere else that is a little more in line with the therapy you've been getting," she added. She told Eddie that she expected to see him next Wednesday in her office sometime before noon. His reintegration worker, Karen, calendar in hand, reminded her that they were both scheduled to be at a facility that day, and she said that he should come Thursday instead. He would need to see her once a week to do a urine screen, she said. Karen added that she would be seeing him three days per week. He reviewed out loud with his mom all his obligations over the next week. "Okay, I have to meet Lisa at her office next Thursday before noon. Karen is coming to the house on Friday. I have to find an NA meeting near the house." His mom suggested that he get a calendar to help organize his daily and weekly itinerary. "You're going to be a busy man," she said.

Eddie's was a high-risk case for Karen and Lisa. He had been enrolled in a four-year university while he was at Mountain Ridge and had to make it only through the summer without any new trouble before he planned to move to central Pennsylvania, where it was assumed it would be harder for him to find trouble. No one wanted to allow a kid with real potential to slip through the cracks. Eddie's conditions of probation hint at a mismatch of services surrounding substance abuse needs and resources. Eddie was eventually tempted to smoke marijuana with his friends, despite the possible consequences that hot urines would have for his case and his ability to leave the jurisdiction to attend college. However, Eddie, like the other young men in the study (except Luis), never reported, and their drug tests rarely indicated, using drugs other than marijuana.

Home and Family Life

The young men released from Mountain Ridge trickled back into their communities with varied levels of stability and support at home. Seven (Malik, Hassan, Keandre, Luis, Raymond, Sincere, and Warren) moved in with their mothers; Sharif moved in with his father and step-mother; Leo went back to living with his grandmother; James moved into his uncle Clifton's spare room; Tony stayed with his sister, Akeem with his brother, and Isaiah with his aunt. Gabe was the only one to return to a home with parents who had been married and living together his whole life. Three young men—Sincere, Gabe, and Isaiah—quickly moved in with their girlfriends, retaining their original addresses for the purposes of probation. Gabe's strategy was especially risky since his girlfriend lived in the inner-ring suburbs outside of Philadelphia County. He violated his probation every time he crossed county lines, and his probation officer got angry every time he visited Gabe's parents' home and found him missing. Had Gabe not been steadily employed during the entire period of his probation, his regular failure to meet his PO would have presented a major obstacle to his getting off probation.

Most of the young men had betrayed their family members' trust during their days in the drug game. They stored drugs, money, and weapons in their homes and brought over friends who stole anything of value that wasn't tacked down. They lied about their whereabouts and activities and engaged in behavior that resulted in police raids and other unwanted attention from the authorities. Their involvement in the system had been costly, both financially and emotionally, for many of their family members. Their return was greeted with a mixture of relief at having them home and a nagging concern that they had not changed their ways. This ambivalence was evidenced by the common practice of withholding a house key until a period of trouble-free time had passed. Without a house key, the young men's status was diminished to that of a guest; if they returned home when others weren't there, they had to bide their time elsewhere. I watched as they phoned upstairs to see if anyone was available to drop keys down from an open window.

Many chafed at the new house rules, particularly with regard to visitors. Some felt the rules challenged their autonomy and manhood by infantilizing them in similar ways that Mountain Ridge had. All but two (Eddie and

Malik) had turned eighteen while incarcerated, fueling their expectations that they would be treated as adults when they returned home. This disappointment often resulted in conflict, leading to instability in their housing. Akeem, for instance, battled with his older brother over house rules and his brother's demands that he find work. During his first week home, Akeem reported, "I got into an argument with my brother about the phone. I packed my shit and wanted to go to mom's house, and I was thinkin' fuck him, fuck everyone. The next morning, we worked through our problems. We worked out the rules and what to do and what not to do. His rules are really simple, really easy. I don't know why I don't follow them. I do know why, I just got my own tendency to do what I want."

Within four months of returning home, Akeem had been kicked out of his brother's house for failing to pay his portion of the bills and refusing to meet with his caseworker during scheduled visits. He then moved in with his mother in a neighborhood adjacent to Temple University. I lost touch with Akeem during this period, although I was able to keep tabs on him through his probation officer's notes. Five months after his release from Mountain Ridge, he was still on probation and refusing to meet with the family counselor the court had assigned. According to his PO, he was suffering from suicidal ideation and it was "doubtful" that he was still in school.

Scrutiny by and accountability to parents and guardians paralleled another unpleasant aspect of Mountain Ridge: being treated like a criminal. Criminologist Shadd Maruna and colleagues note that although "a single deviant event or episode can be enough to stigmatize a person indefinitely . . . a hundred *non*-deviant acts may not be enough to earn someone the recognition of non-deviance."[9] This "negativity bias" caused the greatest problems for those like James, who believed himself to be transformed after his period of incarceration. He wondered how, if people who were supposed to be in his corner, such as his Uncle Clifton, didn't believe in him, he could continue to believe in himself. James repeatedly moved out of Clifton's home when Clifton accused him of stealing things from the house or returning to the drug game. When he moved in with his mother, who claimed to believe his story of personal transformation, she pressured him to "pick up a packet" here and there to help her make the rent.

REENTRY PLANS VERSUS REALITY

Table 4.1 provides a snapshot of rearrest and offending activity during the three years following release from Mountain Ridge.

The youths' concerns about falling back into old routines were certainly justified. Within six weeks, at least four had returned to drug selling, and a fifth, Sharif, was dead. Akeem never admitted directly to selling drugs, but within three weeks of coming home he told me that he needed $300 for an "illegal transaction gone bad." Gabe sold drugs only during his first few weeks at home, as he was waiting for his first paycheck, and ended up as one of two whom I identify as having gone straight during the three-year period of follow-up. Keandre and Luis were both arrested for drug selling, at twenty days and five weeks postrelease, respectively. After a stint inside a state-run juvenile facility, Luis established the longest record, with four more arrests for receiving stolen property (twice), carrying a firearm, and robbery. Sharif was brutally gunned down and killed five weeks after his return to North Philadelphia. Although the *Philadelphia Inquirer* reported that he was found clutching thirty-eight bundles of crack, his family and friends believed his death was payback for signing a subpoena to testify in a murder trial less than twenty-four hours prior to his murder. At the six-month mark, six more had resumed offending and a seventh, Hassan, was on the run from the police. By the time three years had passed, seven had spent time in jail or prison, and the group of fourteen had generated a combined total of thirty-six arrests.[10]

These young men were vulnerable to pressures to return to drug using and selling and to violent victimization. Two months and four days after returning home from Mountain Ridge, Hassan was shot in the rear end after he and some young men from his block were leaving a game of pickup basketball against men from a neighboring block. Soon after, his PO, Anthony, received a phone call from a city detective saying that he had been trying to get him to cooperate with the investigation of the shooting, but that Hassan refused to snitch. The detective claimed that several witnesses had seen Hassan with a gun and threatened to file charges against him if he did not give up the name of the person who shot him. Anthony told me he believed the police were trumping up charges and using Hassan's tenuous status as a probationer to coerce him to comply. Later, when the prosecution dropped the charges, it looked like he was

TABLE 4.1

Reoffending, Reincarceration, and Other Criminal Justice Outcomes, Three Years after Release

	< 6 wks.	6 wks.-6 mos.	6-12 mos.	12-24 mos.	24-36 mos. 3 yrs.	Total arrests 3 yrs.	Reincarceration
Akeem	Self-report					0	
Eddie			Arrest	Arrest	Arrest	4	6–23 mos., 1–2 yrs., 6–12 mos.
Gabe	Self-report					0	
Hassan		Bench warrant	Arrest	Arrest	Arrest	5	3–6 days
Isaiah		Report by domestic partner	Self-report	Arrest		2	
James				Arrest		1	
Keandre	Arrest			Arrest	Arrest	4	
Leo		Self-report	Self-report	Arrest	Arrest	3	1–2 yrs.
Luis	Arrest		Arrest	Arrest	Arrest	5	5 mos. juv.; 1–2 yrs. adult
Malik		Arrest		Arrest	Arrest	4	8-14 mos. juv.; 2–5 yrs. adult
Sharif	Deceased						
Sincere		Self-report		Arrest	Self-report	1	
Tony		Arrest		Arrest	Arrest	3	2 mos./5–10 yrs.
Warren		Arrest		Arrest	Arrest	4	jail max 23 mos.

right. Faced with a new arrest and probation violation or the strong likelihood that he would be killed for cooperating with police, Hassan chose instead to become a fugitive. He remained on the run for most of the next three years.

Being embedded in street culture involves young men in a repertoire of activities that are counterproductive to successful transitions to adulthood. When a crisis occurs, usually when money is needed quickly, their reaction is to use the tools that have worked in the past to resolve it. Recognizing criminal thinking errors and employing correctives become inadequate and irrelevant to meet the demands of the situation. This reliance on drug selling to solve short-term financial problems is clearly seen in the case of Malik.

Malik was one of two seventeen-year-olds I followed. His reentry plan involved moving back in with his mother, getting a job doing carpentry with his father, and going to community college. He had already filled out the financial aid forms while he was at Mountain Ridge. Although he did start working with his father, I never heard him mention college again. His first month at home seemed promising; he was working so many hours that he barely had time to spend with his old friends who were still selling drugs. He said, "Carpentry is hard, man! But you should see my check. $5,000 at the end!" All his efforts came screeching to a halt five weeks after returning home, when the money he'd been saving for his son Tyrik's first birthday party was stolen from his house. I ran into him at Family Court, and he told me the story. He looked terrible, his eyes puffy and small, like he'd been crying or up all night. "It's one thing to steal from me, but they stole from *my son*," he said in disbelief. When I asked what he planned to do, his next comment was telling: "Whatever it takes. I'm in debt now." Later he asked to be dropped off at his old drug block, and it was clear he had returned to the game.

The next month, six days after his ninety-day review hearing, Malik was arrested for carrying a gun. After he was committed to one of the state-run juvenile facilities, the last stop before the adult system, I lost touch with him. Just over a year after he was committed there, Malik, then nineteen, was arrested for selling drugs in Lycoming County, in central Pennsylvania. While he awaited his hearing, he was arrested twice more, once for possession of marijuana and once on a firearms charge. In

November 2007, he was sentenced to prison for twenty-two months to five years on the drug charge. Three years and one month after his release from Mountain Ridge, he was sentenced to three to six years in state prison on the gun charge.

Warren, the young man who witnessed the shooting during his first week home and Malik's cousin, was similarly embedded in street culture. He also struggled to manage bipolar disorder, which was diagnosed when he was in detention. A month after he came home, his mother who told me he had visited a local outpatient mental health clinic. They had given him a number of medications, but he didn't like to take them because they made him sleepy. After several discouraging months, he had returned to drug selling, but this time he was working behind the scenes, connecting buyers and sellers in a manner that reduced his risk of arrest. He also drew a new line about what he would sell, saying that crack was just too risky.

Five months after his release from Mountain Ridge, Warren was arrested for drug dealing. Ironically, according to his story (which I believe, since he had already admitted to me that he was selling drugs), he was not actually doing anything wrong at the time of his arrest. He explained that he had been getting Chinese food down on Washington Avenue and had seen some guys inside from his neighborhood that he usually avoided. He had just walked up to the window to pick up his food when a couple of police officers came in and told all the young men in the store to get up against the wall. Warren had been indignant. "I ain't doing anything wrong. I'm not getting up against the wall," he told them defiantly. Of course, this made them angry and they proceeded to search him. When they didn't find anything but money, they searched the store and found a nickel bag of weed in a wastepaper basket. The store owner tried to explain to the police that Warren had just walked in, but they put him in the car, allowing the other two guys to go free.

Warren kept talking smack to them from the back seat of the cruiser. When he heard a 187 called in over the radio, he derided them for wasting time on a nickel bag of weed when there were murders going on in the city. At his arraignment, he was advised that he would likely get only community service if he pled guilty. Refusing to plead, he went to trial and received a jail sentence for a maximum of two years. After spending a short time in jail, he was arrested again for aggravated assault, for which he received two more years of probation.

Isaiah avoided drug selling for a comparatively long period. His first signs of trouble involved domestic violence against his baby's mom, Tamika. After dropping out of college and working sporadically, he, like Warren, set up a "silent partnership" in which he fronted money for a drug operation. He was never apprehended for this business, but was arrested almost exactly one year after his release from Mountain Ridge for simple assault against Tamika and again the following year for harassment and violation of a protective order.

Similarly, Sincere returned briefly to the drug game but was never detected by police. His one arrest during my study involved buying a five-dollar "blunt" (marijuana cigarette) for personal use; the charge was later dropped. Sincere's involvement in the drug game since I've known him has been characterized by what criminologists call "intermittency," moving back and forth between periods of selling drugs or paraphernalia and of nonoffending.

Finally, Eddie, the college-bound Mountain Ridge graduate, illustrates how criminal behavior can become a familiar routine that young people fall back upon in moments of uncertainty. When he went away to attend the university, he quickly established himself as a small-time dealer in the college town where he had moved. By Thanksgiving of his freshman year, he had been arrested for a check-kiting scheme and had been suspended from school. He spent approximately a year in state prison as a result.

The young men I followed were released from Mountain Ridge with solid reentry plans, a desire to make a better life for themselves and their families, a set of decision-making skills provided by the facility, in most cases a diploma or GED, the deterrent effect of knowing their next arrest would likely land them in the adult system, and a network of professionals who were there to support and control them during their first few months in the community. While these ingredients may seem necessary conditions for them to succeed on the outside, they certainly did not prove to be sufficient. Although many reported feeling changed as a result of their time at Mountain Ridge, their material conditions remained the same. They returned to neighborhoods plagued by violence, households prone to financial crises, a legal labor market offering low-paying, degrading jobs, and an illicit economy that beckoned them with the promise of fast cash and masculine pride.

These material conditions, and the cultural and developmental adaptations to these conditions, are the real reason why young men began offending in the first place and why so many continued to offend. Because the juvenile justice system is ill equipped to restructure the labor market to create better jobs, allow young people the financial freedom to invest in higher education, dismantle racial discrimination or residential segregation, or fix families struggling with poverty or addiction, it must recast the problem in terms of poor decision making, as a matter of individual deficits on the part of the young men who are part of the system.

CHAPTER 5

"I'm Not a Mama's Boy,
I'm My Own Boy"

EMPLOYMENT, HUSTLING,
AND ADULTHOOD

SIX MONTHS AFTER RETURNING to Philadelphia, I found Sincere and several male friends hanging out on the stoop, bracing themselves to go into Center City to look for jobs. I flashed back to the moment when, shortly after my sixteenth birthday, my parents dropped me off in front of our local grocery store with instructions for inquiring about a job. I got a cashier position on the spot and, as I worked my way up into the head office, learned that the manager sorted applicants by physical attractiveness. When I informed him that someone had asked about a job, his standard reply was, "Would I fuck her?" If I answered no, the applicant was referred to the deli or told that there were no openings.[1] Observing such blatant discrimination behind the scenes may have been a formative moment in my trajectory as a sociologist. Having arrived that first day with my bright smile and a dressy blouse borrowed from my mother, I had asked for an application with total confidence that any open job would be mine.

Sincere and his buddies, all of whom were African American, knew before they even went looking for work that their chances of being hired were slim. These men had few work-related skills, had spotty work histories, and wore clothing and used language that expressed their adherence to street culture. Entering a business establishment to request an application meant risking their pride, since reactions could range from outright hostility to more subtle visual appraisals. Most commonly, they waited for a callback that never came.[2] In addition to personal experiences of repeated rejection, these men were aware of the larger patterns of black male unemployment in inner-city neighbor-hoods. In 2005, the year in which most of these young men returned to Philadelphia from Mountain Ridge Academy, only about one-fifth of black males their age (sixteen to nineteen) were employed—half the rate of white males in the same age group.[3]

Searching for work involved intense ambivalence, which could help explain why Sincere and his friends were getting high before ven-turing on their job search. We might well ask why they bothered to search at all when the risk of rejection was so high. Despite the dearth of working men in their communities, they experienced both internal and external pressures to get jobs. Although they knew that few men fulfilled the breadwinner ideal, they still believed it was the best way to achieve masculine adulthood and provide for their families. With failure likely, however, they needed a way to explain their lack of suc-cess. By showing up at the Center City Olive Garden as a group—and a visibly high one at that—they engaged in classic reaction formation behavior whereby people protect themselves against the likelihood of being denied something they seek by pretending they did not want it in the first place. In this case, the hostess told the manager in the back that there was a group of guys out front "acting the fool," so they never even got the chance to apply.

This chapter considers the risks, costs, and meanings of work for the young men I followed after they returned to Philadelphia. Since "supply-side" employment barriers such as hiring practices that favor whites and women and "demand-side" barriers such as the spotty work histories of youth who have been incarcerated are well known, I point out some challenges to securing paid work that have been less commonly dis-cussed. One reason why searching for work is so difficult is that the cityscape is racially coded. Young black men feel particularly vulnerable in spaces they consider to be "white," including restaurants, universities, retail centers, and the streets and sidewalks they must traverse as they look for work. To reduce the discomfort of feeling conspicuously out of place, these young men often searched for work in groups of peers, which was counterproductive. New application processes presented an additional barrier to entry-level retail employment. Online applications requiring technical proficiency with computers and Internet interfaces reinforce the digital divide. Job seekers must also take a battery of personality tests whose scores are normed on a white, middle-class population and that contain items that are culturally loaded or outright biased.[4]

As these factors push young black men away from formal employment, others pull them toward involvement in the underground economy. Hustling offers them both income and a sense of masculine dignity. The money can be easily hidden from others who may stake a claim to it, including their babies' mothers and the government, which may seek child support. The ebb and flow of the informal sector best fits the shifting and erratic demands for time experienced by the urban poor. With these pushes and pulls moving in the same direction, the underground economy becomes a logical, although risky, alternative to legal employment.

THE SOCIAL SITUATION OF WORK
AND CRIME IN THE INNER CITY

Low-wage work rarely pays enough for inner-city residents to make ends meet.[5] Work in the formal labor market is located at one end of a continuum of strategies to meet economic demands. Illegal behavior that involves a risk of arrest, such as drug selling, is at the other end. Various other activities fall into an ambiguous middle ground. These shady activities, often known as "hustles," include any remunerative work for which the person does not receive a paycheck or pay taxes.[6] Common hustles include working "off the books" doing construction for family members, washing cars using water from a fire hydrant, selling pirated DVDs, fixing cars in a back alley, doing laundry piecework, and selling trays of home-cooked food. These activities are more or less licit, and in the inner city they rarely attract police attention.

The network of exchanges that make up the underground economy plays a vital role in enabling inner-city residents to survive. Most of the urban poor engage in a mix of strategies, including public assistance, paid employment, and forms of hustling.[7] The line between hustling and outright criminal activity is seldom entirely clear. For example, Leo spent several months engaged as a "gigolo," accepting small amounts of cash from older women in his neighborhood in exchange for sex. Unlike with traditional acts of prostitution, Leo found his Johns—or, rather,

"Janes"—through informal, neighborhood-based interactions. I suspect that this particular form of hustling may have become more common as inner-city communities have coped with the mass incarceration of black men. Leo also burned CDs with music he downloaded online, selling them to neighbors and friends for $5 per album. Sincere also engaged in a mix of drug selling, paid work, and hustles to support his young family. At one point he was approached by a friend who had stolen over one hundred guns from a house where they were being stored and sold by someone else. In exchange for connecting buyers and seller, Sincere received a gun of his own. Later he was involved in a quasi-legal business run by his fictive brother-in-law, providing drug paraphernalia (such as baggies and vials) to corner stores and dealers who were selling large quantities of drugs. Warren combined paid work with hustling when he worked at Wendy's; he sold burgers at a reduced cost to his friends, neglecting to ring up the order and then pocketing the money.

From these young men's perspective, there is a blurry line between hustles in which almost everyone in their neighborhood engages and outright law breaking. This ambiguity is particularly salient for individuals who have made money by selling drugs. Young men who are on probation worry mostly about illegal behavior that would draw a police response—for example, that which is committed in public or on street corners. Neither Leo's nor Sincere's activities entailed a very high risk of arrest. Situating paid employment, hustling, and crime on a continuum helps us to understand how the urban poor view their choices related to criminal activity.[8]

In inner-city communities, behavior is often uncoupled from the responses of the justice system. As the disjuncture between official records and self-report or victimization surveys suggests, much if not most criminal offending goes undetected by the authorities. Conversely, the police subject young black men to special scrutiny when they are carrying out perfectly legal activities. All of the young men I have spoken with during the course of my research, as well as many of their friends, have attracted police attention through such simple acts as congregating with friends and walking down the street.[9] The criminalization of black males in public has become more intense as the Philadelphia police have enacted stop-and-frisk policies. Inner-city residents view the police and the justice system more widely with deep suspicion, largely because of the perceived lack of response to their emergency calls and the heightened surveillance of law-abiding behavior, as well as the failure of the courts to respond justly.[10] This skepticism of law enforcement is one of the key structural features shaping the "code of the street" among inner-city residents.[11]

THE MEANING OF WORK
AFTER INCARCERATION

The code of the street gives us insight into the substantial psychosocial rewards of successful involvement in the underground economy. Drug selling and the concomitant violence are a significant means of garnering respect for those who are unable to gain esteem through more mainstream accomplishments, such as legal employment or academic success in schooling.[12] In addition to respect from others, the young men I interviewed were proud of their mastery of the street code. The streets are likely the only setting in which they ever experienced the pride associated with knowing the rules of the game, which is what made it so problematic when the staff at Mountain Ridge Academy identified street behaviors as evidence of thinking errors.

A common theme in many of these young men's narratives is "love for the streets." Sincere said that the streets were always there for him, even when his family was not. He added that if things did not work out with his baby's mother, Marta, he would turn to the streets to help him recover from the loss. Young men think of the streets as providing both structure and love when family members are unable or unwilling to be there for them. Unlike many of the people in their lives, the streets offer consistency. They are available at any time, day or night. Unlike other milieus where these men feel they constantly come up short, such as fatherhood and legal employment, the streets offer them the illusion of control over their lives.

The meaning that work provided for young men released from Mountain Ridge Academy shifted as time passed. Upon their return to the community, many saw getting a job as their highest priority, along with getting a cell phone and a haircut. Probation officers and reintegration workers emphasized legal employment as a condition of probation or as a marker of successful transition to the community. Many young men agreed, viewing work as the single most important step in achieving their goal of falling back.

During his second week at home, Warren, eighteen, discussed his thinking about getting a job versus returning to the drug game. "This week I talked [to friends] about really going back out there, getting some money hustling. But I was like, nah . . . something's gonna come through for me." Akeem had offered a similar account, when he said, "I feel like the drug game is calling me. I see everybody out here, makin' all this money." Eddie's initial journal entries were filled with concerns about finding work and the fear that an extended period of time without it would drive him back to drug selling:

> Been calling these places where I filled out applications. Trying to get this job. I need one soon, real soon, before I go crazy. I need money. Money, money, money. S'all it's about nowadays, is money. . . . I just really need to start working, man, real soon. 'Cause if I don't, it's going to be real tempting for me to go back to selling, and I don't want to do that. But I really need a job. I'm stressin' right now. I'm about to call my old friend and start doin' some BS. I mean I don't really want to do, I'm not, I'm not going to do it, but I really want to because I need money in my pocket. I can't stand being broke. I was just thinking, man, like if I don't get caught, then I'm cool. That was my whole thinking. I had that whole criminal thinking and, I mean, that felt stupid because I don't normally do something I don't want to do unless I have to. Like, but I really don't have to do that 'cause they's jobs out there. And it's crazy.

Although these young men viewed work and hustling as mutually exclusive in the period shortly following their release, this division broke down after some time in the community. Hustling, broadly defined and including illegal activity, was something most engaged in periodically when the opportunity arose. If they were legally employed, fewer of these opportunities presented themselves, but these young men hustled both during lapses in employment and to supplement income earned through work in the formal labor market. Like the gang members John Hagedorn studied in Milwaukee, they straddled the formal and informal economies.[13]

If they were stably employed in a job where they could earn a living wage, they would choose to avoid hustling. Gabe, the only young man I followed who had steady employment at a living wage, chose work over drug selling. However, even James, the most outwardly committed to being a "working man," had almost ten different employers in two and a half years, with relatively long periods of unemployment and job searching in between. The jobs these young men occupied included fast food preparation, dish washing, car washing, demolition, security, grounds keeping, and maintenance. Like the factory work that African Americans found after the Great Migration, these were "the meanest and dirtiest" jobs available in Philadelphia, often seasonal, temporary, or susceptible to large fluctuations in hours.[14]

Their changing perspectives on the meaning of work and the viability of hustling suggest that incarceration was a powerful short-term deterrent from returning to full-time drug selling. Its influence began to weaken, however, as their period of confinement faded from their memories. They returned to hustling tentatively, as if they were testing to see whether illegal activity had any consequences. Once successful, they became more daring and more reliant on hustling to generate income. Several—Tony, Eddie, Malik, and Luis—took bigger risks involving high-profile dealing, carrying weapons, or involvement in a check-forging scheme and were relatively quickly reincarcerated. Those who managed to avoid confinement were those who merely "dibbed and dabbed" in the underground economy and began "selling smarter."[15]

PUSHES AND PULLS OF THE FORMAL AND UNDERGROUND LABOR MARKETS

Young black males, particularly those with a history of incarceration, are deeply disadvantaged in the labor market.[16] Employers engage in a variety of sorting techniques designed to select a workforce that is compliant, dependable, and viewed as likely to provide friendly and efficient customer service. Statistical discrimination; a lack of human capital, including "hard" skills such as computer literacy and "soft," or "people" skills; a spatial mismatch between job seekers and available jobs; employee drug testing; and criminal background checks all combine to systematically disadvantage urban job seekers.[17] My time spent searching for work with young men points to at least two other factors that serve as barriers to searching for and obtaining jobs.

Pushes: Electronic Applications and Prescreening Questionnaires

People looking for entry-level employment are increasingly likely to encounter arduous application procedures involving electronic applications or lengthy questionnaires designed to measure the candidates' attitudes and values and assess their prior history of drug use and employee theft. Several of the young men I followed were discouraged by such applications. My field notes from a day of job hunting with Warren document these problems. We began at Whole Foods, a high-end grocery store specializing in organic food. I thought it might be a good place to start since the store had a largely black work force and there were several young men serving as cashiers.

The application took about forty-five minutes to complete. To my surprise, short essays were required. Warren was asked to say what he was looking for in a job, to name a specific instances when he was rewarded for good customer service in the past, to identify a time when he solved a problem at work and whether his suggestion had been taken, to say what sort of performance measurement system his former workplaces had used and, if so, how he was evaluated and, finally, to describe what about Whole Foods seems different from other grocery stores. We worked on the essay responses together and I spelled several words for him, although he misspelled several words such as "environment" that he failed to ask me about ahead of time. He seemed nervous as he filled out the application. One question asked the start and end dates of his last employment and he put 6:00 and 6:15. Then he realized what he'd done and scratched it out. On several occasions, he wrote words on the wrong lines or in the wrong spaces. On one of the essays, they asked what was his greatest accomplishment at his last job. He wanted to say "learning to not think of myself negatively" and "overcoming adversity." I wasn't sure those were the responses WF was looking for.

After completing applications at two Whole Foods locations, we visited several other retailers, all of which had electronic applications: Target, Modell's Sporting Goods, Best Buy, IKEA, and Walmart.

Our last stop was Walmart, where the lines at the customer service counter were unbelievably long. We asked the greeter and she
pointed us to the layaway department, where there were two employment kiosks that looked considerably older than the modern ones at
Target. We sat down and started entering Warren's information. The
interface was stubborn and hard to navigate. The keyboard had sticky
keys and even I had a hard time typing into them. We tabbed through
the various information points until we got to the education section,
where I looked for a place to record Warren's GED. All the education
fields were for people who had attended college. I couldn't believe all
the stupid drop-downs for people who had various law and medical
degrees. Who the hell would work at Walmart if they had a medical
degree? Nowhere could I find a place to enter information about
high school or GED. I tabbed back to a button that said "certifica-
tions," but that was for people who had Certified Drivers' Licenses.
We stayed stuck on that page for over ten minutes. I asked one of the
employees who was headed back to the break room, and she said she
didn't know anything about it.

We gave up and tabbed forward to the next sections. Before long,
we found a place to enter his GED, which didn't distinguish between
it and a high school diploma. As we finished up it was around 5:00
and we both were exhausted from a long day of job searching. We
were shocked to see a seventy-six-item attitudes and values survey
at the end. It was set up as a series of statements to which applicants
needed to respond on a Likert scale. We looked at each other in exas-
peration, and Warren started answering "strongly agree" to each one
just to get through the application. I told him I thought that was a
bad idea and decided to quickly answer the questions for him. Some
were very transparent, such as "I think most people work a little better when they're high" or "I used to be late to work a lot but that's
a thing of the past." Others were less straightforward, and even I had
little idea of what they were supposed to measure. Examples were
"Education is as important as experience" and "Managers deserve
the respect they get because they have worked their way up the lad-
der." I answered somewhere in the middle of the scale here, hoping
to wash out the score.[18]

We submitted the application online, and the interface simply said that it would expire in two months. We were not told if there were any jobs open at the moment or when we could expect to be contacted. I dropped Warren off at home, utterly exhausted even though I was not the one searching for a job. It was clear that these lengthy questionnaires discourage many people from applying. Our day's work generated no responses. Moreover, in all the time that I served as a reference for these young men, I was never contacted by a hiring agent.

An extreme case involved James. One spring I went with him to a fancy seafood restaurant that had just opened in Center City Philadelphia and was hiring for all positions. We filled the application out together while sitting at the bar. The first half of the application was pretty standard, but the second half involved what they called a "quick quiz." This included five geography questions (e.g., "What states does Pennsylvania border?"), five math questions, five spelling and grammar questions, and an untitled section at the end that could have been called "cultural capital." They asked him to list three other Center City (read: pricey) restaurants, name two airlines, and identify Bill Gates. I could not see how any of this information was relevant to the position of food runner, for which he was applying. Despite my assistance, he was never called to interview for the job. On another occasion, James was told that he wasn't hired by a large drugstore chain because he had rated himself as "mostly honest" instead of "always honest." Ironically, he told me later that he thought his answer would be perceived by the employer as more honest.

As a result of these experiences applying for low-wage jobs, Christopher Kelly and I systematically documented the application procedures for entry-level jobs in the retail sector in Philadelphia.[19] We found that almost half of the 113 employers we examined had an Internet-based application process, and nearly a third had an exclusively computer-based process. Furthermore, nearly three-quarters of these retailers asked for the applicant's consent to conduct a criminal record check, 40 percent said they did drug testing, 55 percent asked for a release to conduct a credit check, and 44 percent involved a questionnaire based on or similar to a personality test. We posit that many of these procedures serve as an additional disadvantage to inner-city job seekers because they are less likely to have access to computers, less likely to be familiar with online environments, and sensitive to coded questions such as "It angers me when the courts let guilty people go free."

Pushes: Everyday Race Making in Job Searching

Searching for work is complicated for formerly incarcerated youth of color because most public and private spaces reinforce and reproduce racialized and gendered boundaries. Because few jobs are available in inner-city communities, looking for work requires young men to leave their familiar neighborhoods and traverse public space. Here, they are constantly reminded of their position in the racial and class-based hierarchy.[20] These micro-interactions where racial hierarchies are expressed and reproduced are examples of "everyday race-making."[21]

Young black males are conscious of the meaning these interactions hold. At times, they may choose to wield the power derived from generating fear in others, engaging in what urban sociologist Mitchell Duneier calls "interactional vandalism."[22] I saw an example of this when Eddie and Isaiah went to a professional job fair and forced several white job seekers to acknowledge them by staring and offering an aggressive greeting. Most of the time, however, these young men go out of their way to signal to others that they mean no harm, crossing the street when they notice a woman clutching her purse or moving over so that a white passenger does not have to sit next to them on the train.[23] Following these rules and extending these courtesies, young black men earn at most a tenuous acceptance in common spaces.

These young men expressed extreme trepidation about traveling into spaces in the city that they consider "white." This concern seemed to arise around the consequences of accidentally stepping out of place in these settings. Before one of his guest lectures for my class, I left Sincere sitting in Penn's Sociology Department office while I made photocopies. When I returned ten minutes later he looked mortified, saying that everyone who walked through the door stared at him like he didn't belong there. He was so badly shaken that he did not recover for the next couple of hours. Warren automatically declined to apply for certain positions because they carried the potential for stigma. He told me that he would never be a cashier again after being falsely accused of stealing from the till at Wendy's.[24] When I asked if he would consider a grocery bagging job, he commented that no one would want a guy like him to follow them out to their car. These comments reveal the extent to which young men in my study have internalized racial stigma and suggest ways in which it might affect their job searches.

One strategy for mitigating this fear of encounters with white people is searching for work in groups, typically with other young black males, as Sincere did when he went to the Olive Garden. Leaving the comfort of their home territory behind and venturing into the "white world" of downtown Philadelphia, young men seek the protective company of their peers. Looking for work with friends can relieve the tedium involved in waiting for and traveling on public transportation and can turn an otherwise unpleasant activity into something more fun. More important, young men in groups can defend against the racial stigma involved in traveling into "white" spaces and interacting with potential employers, many of whom might be more concerned with preventing theft than considering them as potential hires. But entering a place of business with several of his "homies" might make a young person appear more like a gang member than a desirable candidate for employment.

Inner-city youth are discouraged from searching for work in the suburbs, where jobs are more plentiful and pay more. This spatial mismatch of inner-city residents and suburban jobs adds to the cost of searching, and urban residents are unlikely to be successful without a personal referral.[25] However, my observations and interviews suggest that this reticence to travel into white spaces may also have a psychosocial component. Because of the cumulative effects of poverty, racism, and lack of mainstream success, inner-city black males are left with "deeply painful feelings of frustration, disappointment, humiliation, and shame" that alter the ways they look for work.[26]

Pulls: Financial Autonomy and Instability

The underground economy offers several advantages for the urban poor. First, doing "off-the-books" work of any variety leaves no paper trail that can be monitored by others. Several of these young men were fathers and, upon their release from Mountain Ridge, had established households with their babies' moms. These partnerships were largely controlled by women, whose income stream was steadier because of their use of public assistance and subsidized housing. When a man received his paycheck, he was often expected to turn it over to his baby's mother, whereby he lost control over how it was spent. Earning money through hustling or drug selling offers an opportunity to mask income and retain control of spending.[27]

Work in the informal economy better fits the structure of time in urban communities. Schedules and time demands are often erratic as individuals must respond to the daily crises, large and small, stemming from poverty. For example, James never had a stable place to live in the time that I followed him. As he tried to balance paid work and school to advance himself, he continued to shuffle back and forth between friends and family members' homes, offering a small amount of money to help with their bills in exchange for being allowed to sleep on their couch. In 2008, the woman whose house he lived in became enraged and stabbed him twice. As he called the police, she began shredding his clothing with a kitchen knife. This emergency call resulted in both of them being arrested, after which James again had no steady place to live. The lives of these young men are characterized by intermittency in offending, work, relationships, and housing.[28]

Pushes: "Selling Smarter"

Warren was the first to openly admit that he had returned to drug selling several months after his return to Philadelphia. However, he explained, there was a qualitative difference in how he was earning illegal income. Before he was incarcerated, he sold whatever was available, including crack. He used to work on the corner, exchanging cash for drugs and keeping a weapon nearby. His new enterprise involved connecting buyers and sellers, limiting his physical contact with the product. Instead of accepting cash as payment, he was paid in marijuana for his personal use. He avoided dealing in crack, fearing the increased risk of arrest or injury.

Several others told me about "working smarter, not harder" after being incarcerated. Isaiah worked as a "silent partner" in someone else's drug business, taking a weekly cut of the profits. Sincere, who mixed small-time dealing with legal employment, explained to me that selling smarter required selling only to people you know and never carrying more product on your person than the buyer had requested. Cautious sellers may hide the "work" in a garbage can or behind the tire of a parked car until they receive payment, avoiding a direct exchange of cash and drugs.[29]

Many of these themes, especially the movement back and forth between the formal and informal economies, the role of masculinity in various forms of work, and the erosion of the deterrent effect of youth incarceration, are seen in Leo's story.

LEO'S STORY: "DOING WHAT I DO BEST"

Leo lived in the Allegheny West section of Philadelphia, which is located just above Lehigh Avenue in North Philadelphia. The area is characterized by a large number of empty lots with overgrown weeds, trash, and trees that have engulfed many of the crumbling, graffiti-covered houses. Although he and his mother were very close, he stayed with his grandmother, Ida, and his grandfather, Haywood. Leo enjoyed taking care of his grandparents; Haywood had advanced diabetes and needed to be driven to dialysis several times a week. Leo took charge of cooking family meals. He hoped to join his mother one day, but she couldn't or wouldn't take him in unless he was able to share the rent.

When I met Leo inside Mountain Ridge, he had worked at Burger King and had been a successful drug seller. These two experiences set the stage for his attitudes and expectations of employment. Of Burger King, he said,

My mom is a manager there, but she got a manager over her [the General Manager, or GM], and I was supposed to get a raise being as I was a kitchen manager and they wasn't tryin' to give me no raise. I was supposed to be makin' like eight dollars an hour and I was making six. So I went to the GM quite a few times like "Look, man, something gotta give with my check, you know what I mean? The numbers ain't adding up and I know I'm supposed to be getting a raise." [He would say] "Oh, yeah, your raise will be on the next check." [I would say] "All right, I'll wait." Two weeks later the next check rolls around, "Hey, where my raise?" "Oh, something must have got mixed up."

I let it slide three times, the third time told 'em, "Look, I'm tired
and the next time you jerk me around with my check. . . ." He [said]
"Do what you wanna do, hey, that's your life." Okay. So my mom gets
sent to another store, told me the combination to the safe, so I went
in the safe and took a deposit. I worked there for a year and a half but
the only thing they did was not give me my last check. I got away
with $3,000. It was like hey, that was back pay money.

He described his foray into the drug game as growing out of his
friendship with old heads in his neighborhood.[30] They took the fifteen-
year-old under their wing, helping him buy a car at an auction and signing the paperwork for him. They generously shared the profits of their
drug business and conferred their status upon him.

I was the only young boy on the block fifteen with a car. And people,
it's like people looked at me, people used to call me old head, like
"What's up, old head?" [And I would say] "Hey, what's up young
bull?" And they older than me, I'm callin' them young bull just 'cause
I had money like that. It felt like, it was fame and glory. It felt like I
was on top, I was having money, cars, jewelry, phones. People thought
I was like actually rich, from selling drugs. To tell you the truth, [my
old head was] the one who taught me, he schooled me on the game,
like "Hey, all that nickel and dime stuff, it ain't what it's hitting for. I
mean start moving weight, that's where your money comin' back." I
said "All right, put me on that."

Leo returned to Philadelphia with a commitment to falling back
and finding a legitimate job, saying that he would be happy to give up
drug selling if it meant that he would no longer have to look constantly
over his shoulder. He also talked at length about never wanting to
be locked up again. However, his history of success in the drug game
meant that he would need to scale back his aspirations. Most available
jobs for which he was qualified would require him to make somewhere
around minimum wage and would never grant the status he attained
while selling drugs for his old head.

Mountain Ridge Academy had offered classes in job preparedness
and had worked with Leo to help identify a career that he might enjoy.
He had a knack for electronics and had been hired by several of his

neighbors to install their car stereo systems in the past. Using Mountain Ridge's computers to search for training programs, he found only two, in New Jersey and Florida. Disappointed, he concluded that he would rather work at Best Buy or Circuit City, or "just save up my money and open up my own shop."

This desire for entrepreneurship was a common theme in my discussions with young men who had been released from Mountain Ridge about their ideal employment situation. Although none had the resources to open his own business, most appreciated jobs that offered them autonomy from constant supervision. As someone who entered the academic world because I don't respond particularly well to authority, I understood their desire for freedom to carry out their work in their own ways and not to be micromanaged. Few entry-level jobs offer this sort of flexibility. Construction or demolition work was one avenue, while landscaping seemed to be another. For several months, Sincere had enjoyed working at the city's recycling plant, where he was the sole person responsible for traversing the lot's various piles to make sure nothing caught fire.

Leo recognized the stereo installation career as a long-term goal; in the shorter term, he said he would take anything as long as it was legal. "In the meantime, my job is gonna be lookin' for a job." His reintegration worker, Ephraim, piqued his interest and made some promises to put in a good word for Leo at his own second job, where he proctored medical school entrance exams, but had never delivered on those promises. Disappointed, Leo told me, "Ephraim is a BS-er, a straight-up BS-er." In the months leading up to his release from Mountain Ridge, he had also talked about getting a job with Pennsylvania's Department of Transportation or as a sanitation worker. I never heard him mention either of these again after his return to Philadelphia.

Upon returning home, Leo put in applications at various shops, both in his neighborhood and at K-mart and Walmart in the suburbs, where a cousin had promised him she had some pull. He also used his mandated time at the E3 Center to search and apply for jobs online. Nothing materialized from any of these efforts. As the weeks passed, Leo became exceedingly frustrated by his lack of success. He was particularly concerned with having enough money to get a car, saying, "I'm really tired of walking and shit, 'cause walking ain't my steel-o [style], know what

I'm sayin'? I can afford to walk, but I dislike to walk." Having to walk or rely on public transportation wherever he went was a constant reminder of the benefits of his former life as a drug seller.

In his weekly journal, Leo spoke regularly of his disappointment at not having a job. Even more than not having a car, he was concerned about having to rely on members of his family to pay for his cell phone, cigarettes, haircuts, and food from the corner store. During his second week at home, he said, "I put out a lot of job applications this week, trying to get myself a job because I'm not with asking my family for money, Can I have this, can I have that? I'm not with that. But I'm hungry." The next week, he said, "I'm getting older, it's like I don't be feelin' all that, asking them for money and shit, 'cause that's not me, I don't like asking people for money. But I really hope that this job comes through, 'cause I just need a job right now. I got bills to pay, I gotta pay my cell phone bill. I'm not trying to ask none of my family to help me out. And, I don't know, I'm just trying to get money the right way. I'm trying to work two-three jobs if possible." During his sixth week at home, he expressed his anger about his situation:

> The most difficult thing for me since I been home is trying to find me a fucking job, man. Everybody talk about, they gonna pull some fucking strings for me, and shit, sayin' Leo, yeah, don't worry about it, I can see what I can do, I got pull there. These motherfuckers ain't do shit yet. You know what? I'm about to stop waiting on those mother-fuckers, but I'm not really waiting on them because I've been filling out applications on my own and I'm just saying like the jobs people be sayin' they gonna hook me up with, some well-paying jobs, and the jobs I filled out applications, they like some bullshit ass jobs, like old minimum wage and shit. And minimum wage ain't even go the fuck up yet, man. When minimum wage goes up, I'm going to fuck it, Burger King, McDonalds, any damn thing I can find to work at, man, because I'm broke. I need that money.
>
> Something that I want is a well-paying mother-fucking job so I won't be asking my people for money, 'cause I don't really like doing that shit. That's like being a mama's boy, man. I'm not a mama's boy, I'm my *own* boy."

The next week's journal assignment asked the young men to discuss spending. That week, Leo's only source of income was the $25 I gave him for his previous week's journal. He invested $10 of it to buy some CDs and began the hustle of burning music off the Internet and selling albums to friends and neighbors. He was able to purchase a pack of fifty CDs for $10, which he could burn and sell for $5 apiece. "The rest of the money, what I did with it, I took my grandma to Denny's and I put the rest to the bill so that she wouldn't have to throw out the whole thing to the bill."

It was during this period in which his cousin got him a job doing demolition, earning $50 to $70 per day. He spoke of what he planned to do with his earnings:

I wasn't really expecting no money, [so] I don't know what I'm planning to do with it. I'll probably just save it because I gotta pay my phone bill, I gotta buy me clothes, I gotta buy a lot of things. But the next week, I'm saving every bit of my money. And I don't know, the main thing I'm really saving my money for is a car, an apartment, and pay my bills because I'm trying to be independent, live on my own.

The final journal assignment, during the eighth week at home, asked about plans for the future:

In the future, my goal is to have my own car sale business, 'cause you know I would like to be a businessman, 'cause I have the gift of gab. And I'm very convincing, I can convince a person to buy a car that don't run. 'Cause then I'd be able to afford any car that I want, and that's what I really want to do with my life. In the next year, I see myself having me a nice car, my own apartment, being independent, and doing things for myself. The next five years, I see myself having a house, probably starting myself a family, once I get financially stable. And I can't make no definite plans 'cause, most of the time I really live my life day by day. 'Cause you know, they say tomorrow ain't promised today.

When the demolition job ended two weeks later, Leo was interviewed for a job as a grocery stocker that offered thirty-five hours per week and the opportunity for overtime. The interviewer told him to be there at eight o'clock the next morning, but when he arrived he was told that someone else had been hired instead. This story demonstrates the precariousness of low-wage work for inner-city black men, especially in retail, where a large surplus labor pool waits ready to be called upon at the manager's whim.

Leo seemed so willing to work and so frustrated by his inability to find a job that I wondered if I could do anything to help. I had recently run into Rick, a friend of mine who had gotten a huge contract with a builder to install bamboo floors in an old building that was being renovated into condos in Center City. He needed reliable people and offered to provide all tools and training. Leo seemed excited at the prospect, and I took him over to meet with my friend for an interview. They agreed that Leo would report to the work site early next week, on Tuesday at ten o'clock in the morning. Tuesday night, I asked Leo how it had gone. "For the most part it was good," he said. He had shown up at ten o'clock and worked laying down and cutting planks. He said that he had gotten off work at two o'clock in the afternoon, which surprised me. He also said he wasn't planning to return to work until the following Monday because he didn't have transportation money to get down to the job site that week.

The story didn't sit right with me, and after a phone call from Rick I knew why. Apparently Leo had just taken off at his two o'clock lunch break and had never returned. I was really embarrassed because I had vouched for Leo. I promised to get to the bottom of the matter. I called Leo, told him what I'd learned, and asked him what had happened. "I had to go do something with my mom," he said.

ME: You know you can't just leave a job without telling anyone where you're going, right?

LEO: No, I didn't know that.

ME: Listen, Leo, if you don't want to do this job, just tell me and I'll let Rick know.

LEO: No, I want to do it.

ME: And you got permission from Rick not to return until Monday, right?

LEO: Yeah, he said it was fine.

ME: When I call him, I'm not going to find out that's a lie, am I?

LEO [sounding a little defensive]: No.

ME: Okay, I'll talk to you later, then.

Rick called me the Tuesday of next week to tell me that Leo had never showed up at work. "I don't blame you, though." Still, I told him that I really felt badly for misjudging the situation. "I can speak frankly with you, right?" he asked. I wondered what was coming next. "Sure," I said. "I just haven't had any luck with African American workers," he said. "Really," I said noncommittally. "They just don't seem to want to work," he said.

I felt sick. This was one of those defining moments in field research. I had gotten involved with one of my participants and worried that I was contaminating the phenomena I was studying by altering Leo's work trajectory. Instead, I learned something by accident. Despite all Leo's lamenting his inability to get a job, it had become apparent that it wasn't as simple as a lack of access. I will never know what happened during the few hours that Leo worked on Rick's crew. Perhaps Leo had been confronted with racist comments based on the crew's previous experiences with African American workers. Maybe cutting and installing planks was hard work and Leo had gotten some early feedback that he was not very good at it. As hard as I pressed, Leo would never talk to me about the reasons why he never returned. I had unintentionally called his bluff by getting him a job that he didn't want, revealing that his claims to wanting "any work that's legal" had their limits.

Three months after his release from Mountain Ridge Academy, Leo was scheduled to return to Family Court for his discharge hearing. He was an excellent probationer, giving neither his PO Lisa nor Ephraim any trouble. He had passed all his drug screens, packing up and leaving each time his friends began smoking around him. In order to be discharged, however, he had to pay restitution to a victim's fund. I knew he had been in bad financial straits, having had his cell phone service disconnected, and I asked aloud how he had gotten the money. Evasively, he said, "I did what I do best. . . . It's nothing bad," he added. Upon further probing, he admitted to "being something like a gigolo" with several older women in his neighborhood. He had started this little business when he was fifteen and had recently gone back to it. As far as he was concerned, this situation was ideal: he was getting paid to do something he enjoyed and believed he was good at. He admitted to doing a lot of sexual role playing with the women, saying that he liked to be the "mailman."

In January, six months after returning to Philadelphia, Leo and I went out to eat at the Penrose Diner in South Philly. "How's business?" I asked. "A little slow," he replied. "It could be better. I'm thinking of starting an escort service." He had been talking with several of his friends about it, and they were on board. "If I take a call and I don't feel like going out, I can send one of them and they would give me like 15 percent for looking out for them." Clearly, Leo's entrepreneurial spirit was still shaping his thoughts about work.

Nevertheless, he was starting to see the benefits of formal employment, telling me that he needed to get a real job. His mom was setting her new house up, and he was planning to move in with her, but she needed him to contribute to the rent. Given the earned income tax credit, he thought he would make more in a legitimate job. These tax refunds appeared to be a meaningful source of income for the young men in my study; James had used the $2,000 he had gotten from working at Popeye's and Au Bon Pain to rent an apartment of his own. Leo planned to look for a job at Restaurant Depot, a membership-only club that sold restaurant supplies.

Leo had gotten rid of his Nextel after it had been turned off. He hated the service anyway and found a cheaper plan through T-Mobile. It was $40 for fifteen hundred anytime minutes. They required only a $30 deposit and that he buy the phone. He still owed Nextel something in the neighborhood of $500. "I'll pay on it when I can," he said. "I don't want to mess up my credit. I think about the long-term like that," he said proudly. Leo's cell phone was absolutely essential to him:

> I won't even come out of the house without my phone. If I don't have my phone with me I go there and right back, I wouldn't take no detour. Who knows, I may get pulled over and be stuck in East Jablip without money in my pocket?[31]
>
> When my phone is shut off, I'm shut off. I can't keep in contact with nobody. I stay in the house. My phone is everything to me. When some bull got shot on my block, my friend called me and said It's hot, that's shit you need to know. So they getting me to be on point when I come home, so I can focus on my surroundings.

That month, Haywood finally succumbed to diabetes and Leo's plans to leave his grandparents' house faded as Ida needed the company. Ida and Leo took good care of each other, with Ida sharing her monthly benefits and Leo making sure she got out of the house to play bingo with friends.[32]

By May, Leo had given up his male escort business and had started working at Chuck E. Cheese in a distant suburb he referred to as "East Jablip." I took him out there one day to pick up his paycheck, and we shared a pizza with his employee discount. The staff there was primarily black and from the city. The restaurant itself was on a busy commercial suburban strip lined with multiple big-box shopping centers and all the standard middle-class restaurants and shops. Many of the restaurants had signs up indicating that they were hiring, and according to Leo, these jobs paid more than those in the city. He made $6.75 per hour, though it took an hour and a half and three buses each way to get between home and work. After a couple of months, he tired of the commute. "I'd still like to work with food, 'cause I like to eat!" he told me. He knew the manager at McDonald's at Twenty-ninth and Allegheny and had heard that they were hiring at $6.50 an hour. However, a job there never materialized.

Before long, his stepfather got Leo a seasonal landscaping job at one of the city-owned golf courses. There he earned $8 an hour and had substantial autonomy. He liked working outdoors and was able to put in a good word to get Sincere hired there, which made the time go by even faster. However, after about four months Leo left the job. "One of my coworkers always had a black joke early in the morning," he explained. "Talkin' 'bout, 'I almost got robbed by two black guys last night and I looked back and realized it was my shadow' and I told my boss and my boss thinks the shit is funny. I came in one morning and decided I'm going to finish this cigarette and tell my boss what I think." When he got no support or sympathy, he quit, saying, "Fuck everybody. I figured I'd better quit before I do something dumb and they press charges."

Besides losing Haywood, three other significant things had occurred in Leo's life before we sat down to do a formal follow-up interview in September 2006. He had returned to regular marijuana use, reviving his neighborhood nickname "Weedy Pots." He had also "made some moves for my man" in the drug game, earning about $1,000. He thought of selling crack as a short-term activity that he had to engage in to "get a couple of dollars in my pocket. I was addicted to money then. I was paper chasin'." But he wanted to avoid that in the future because "I'd rather get it the right than the wrong way."

The other significant event that occurred during his first year home was establishing a romantic relationship with his neighbor, Gwen. With financial support from Gwen and Ida, Leo wanted for little and eventually stopped talking about work. Within a few months he was arrested for drug selling, telling me that police had caught him with fourteen bundles, or about $85 worth of crack.

Before that case was resolved, Leo was arrested and charged with attempted murder. According to Leo and Gwen, Leo broke up a fight between two other men, one of whom pulled out a knife and the other a gun. The gunman had pulled the trigger once or twice and everyone scattered. A month later, Leo returned home to find the police out in front of his house, where they arrested him. Ida called everyone she knew trying to raise the $5,000 bail that had been assigned, with no luck. Leo had to spend the next four months in jail.

In May 2008, almost three years after his release from Mountain Ridge Academy, Sincere and I hung out with Leo on his front stoop in Allegheny West where he waited to be sentenced. Although he was found guilty, his attorney assured him that he would probably get only probation. I doubted that, given the seriousness of the charge. Leo was wearing an ankle bracelet and could go only as far as the sidewalk in front of the house. He seemed strangely happy, though, having revived his CD business. It seemed to be a fairly vibrant enterprise, given that two or three people drove up and requested CDs, in addition to Sincere's constant pleas to have one on credit. (Leo eventually gave in.) He told me that he was also recently involved in credit card fraud. He and some friends had found a lost credit card and ordered a bunch of phones and PlayStations they sold to neighbors. In fact, he sold one while I was sitting there on the stoop. Eventually, Leo was sentenced to one to two years in jail, where he spent less than a year before returning to live with Ida.[33]

Leo's story offers several important takeaways. For Leo, the meaning of work revolved around financial independence. Having achieved adult status so early in adolescence, he longed to once again be his own man, not to have to rely on Ida, Gwen, or his mother for smokes, weed, food from the corner store, or his regular pedicures ("there's nothing wrong with a man tryin' to have nice feet, is there?"). His experience in the formal labor market involved a lot of searching and rejection, a confrontation with coworkers making racial epithets, a job offered and then taken back the next day, a long commute for higher pay out in the suburbs, and short stints in which he found personal autonomy particularly rewarding. He was creative in his hustling strategies, capitalizing on his ability to navigate the Internet to download music for free and "doing what he did best" in his sex-for-money business. His return to the drug game was characterized by a great deal of caution and hesitancy, as he continued to maintain that "slow money was good money," but he found himself dibbing and dabbing more and more to earn independent income. His goal of moving into his own apartment never materialized, although he was finally able to buy a car four years after his release from Mountain Ridge. He continues to serve ten years on probation and has lost at least one job opportunity because of the attempted murder charge on his rap sheet.

The "Own Man" and the "Mama's Boy"

From Leo's perspective, he never felt more like a man than when he was fifteen years old and was "moving weight" for his "old head," the adult man from his neighborhood who took him under his wing to teach him the rules of the drug game. As he returned home after a stint of incarceration at Mountain Ridge Academy, he had to weigh the status and respect he enjoyed as a drug seller against the very real risks of being locked up as an adult the next time he was arrested. While he looked for work, Leo felt infantilized because he had to rely on handouts from his grandmother and mother. He often reminisced about the freedom that owning a car had given him and chafed at the indignity of having to walk or rely on public transportation.

Leo's work trajectory exemplifies the findings of many studies of employment among inner-city young men. He had to commute to the suburbs in order to find work at all, his coworkers frequently made racist comments, and the only way to secure work was by relying on referrals from family and friends. Leo continually compared the reality of low-paying, degrading work to his ideal of a job that offered the benefits of an adult career—autonomy and a sense of competence, even mastery. Disappointed that he could not become a car salesman or stereo installer, Leo

eventually moved from engaging in small, quasi-legal hustles to occasional drug selling in order to meet short-term financial demands.

It is clear that structural forces shaped Leo's opportunities and experiences. Declining work opportunities, racial discrimination, residential
segregation, mass incarceration, failing schools, and rampant gun violence
all define how these young men view their place in the labor market.
With opportunities for steady employment that allowed them to support
themselves, this story would be vastly different. These youths' first-person
accounts offer insight into how these social forces are translated into
individual-level experiences, meanings, and constructions of self.

These young men's stories show a strong connection among masculine identity, employment, and offending. They referred countless times to
the fact that employment in the formal economy "is just not me." Their
view of themselves and their place in the economy is based on feedback
from people in formal workplaces and in the underground economy.
After working at some of the "meanest and dirtiest" jobs available, suffering verbal abuse and other indignities from customers and managers, and
experiencing blatant racism in hiring and in the workplace, many have
given up, concluding that the "working man" image is simply "not them."
Urban sociologist Elliot Liebow's insightful analysis of street corner men
comes closest to this reaction-formation response: "the jobs fail the men,
so the men fail the jobs."[34] Earnestly searching for and holding down paid
work entails a vulnerability to failure that many are unwilling to risk.

The widespread availability of work in the underground economy
and the sense of manhood and affirmation it offers are powerful forces
that, over time, can weaken a young man's fresh resolve to fall back after a
period of incarceration. Inside the drug game, his position is less precarious; his grasp of the rules is firmer. Even when family members support
their sons and grandsons to keep them out of the game, the dual images
of the "own man" and the "mama's boy" reinforce young men's desire to
achieve financial independence in the only job that is always available.

CHAPTER 6

"I Just Wanna See a Part of Me That's Never Been Bad"

FAMILY, FATHERHOOD, AND FURTHER OFFENDING

THE YOUNG MEN I followed were only marginally connected to the formal labor market and consequently were vulnerable
to the pulls of the underground economy. Few were willing or able to
become full-time hustlers, however. Without a consistent income from
either legal or illegal work, these young men sought dignity, autonomy,
and a sense of mastery in other realms, often by becoming fathers. This
is not to say that all planned their children carefully, although few were
displeased to learn that their failure to use protection had resulted in a
pregnancy. A surprising number eagerly anticipated taking on a father
role, in contrast to popular accounts of young black men who shirk all
responsibility for their children.

We might then ask if, as some research suggests, settling down to
assume the role of an involved father might be a "turning point" leading
young men into adult and thereby more law-abiding roles.[1] This relationship among fatherhood, employment, and offending was complicated,
however, when these young men attempted to form fledgling families
with their babies' mothers. While parenthood and romantic commitments can serve as a protective factor against returning to the drug game,
the additional financial pressures stemming from having children create immediate needs that can sometimes be met only by "picking up a
packet" of drugs.

Throughout their incarceration and after their return to Philadelphia,
romantic relationships and fatherhood emerged as vital meaning-making

activities for many of these young men. Of the fifteen I met at Mountain
Ridge, six already were fathers at the time that they were incarcerated
and at least six were responsible for a pregnancy after they were released.
Two others assumed roles as social fathers to their babies' mothers' children.[2] Close inspection of their daily routines and concerns reveals a
complicated picture of their desires to be active fathers and romantic
partners. Ultimately the young men's marginal position in the labor market, coupled with their ambivalence about romantic commitments with
their babies' mothers, undermined their ability to form stable families.[3]
Moreover, their precarious status within the family often led to further
involvement in the underground economy, where respect was earned
more easily and their masculinity was less likely to be challenged. This
response did nothing to cement their place in the household, however.
Ultimately, their attempts to straddle the two worlds were unsuccessful
on both fronts.

   As the young men allowed me access to their worlds, I encountered
a new terminology to describe their relationships with women. "Baby
mamas," or BMs, were women with whom they had children. They may
or may not still have been romantically involved, but calling someone
a BM suggests an ongoing link through the children. "BMD," or "baby
mama drama," describes intense, immature responses to relationship
problems, such as when BMs refuse to share custody of their children,
try to circumscribe men's activities, or accuse them of infidelity. Interestingly, men's behavior was never referred to as "drama," although it was no
less immature. Drama was a near-daily occurrence in the relationships I
documented, with the exception of Gabe and Charmagne. I was so put
off by the tumultuous relationships of the young men I followed that it
took me months to realize that they talked about them nearly constantly.
"Wives" were long-term girlfriends, even though none of them were
legally married. "Wifey" was the ideal type of woman who made a suit-
able marriage partner.

   I present case studies of two young fathers who attempted to form
families with their children's mothers. Sincere struggled to find a balance
between "being there" for his new family and providing financial support.[4] His daily interactions with his BM, Marta, were marked by bitter
conflicts that often turned on money, her derision at his lack of steady

employment, and mutual distrust of each other's fidelity (which seemed well-founded on Marta's part). Since Marta's public assistance was the cornerstone of the family's budget, these conflicts often resulted in Sincere being kicked out and then grudgingly allowed to return. Sincere's lack of success on the job market coupled with the easy availability of underground opportunities made a return to drug selling more attractive. Moreover, he viewed the streets as the only place where he felt familiar with the rules and the means to achieve dignity.

Like Sincere, Isaiah constructed his identity primarily around fatherhood and setting up house with his baby's mother. Isaiah's relationship with Tamika was characterized by a great deal of conflict and even violence, with daily arguments focusing on his infidelity, sporadic employment, and failure to meet Tamika's expectations for good fathering. Whereas Sincere's role as a father diminished but did not eliminate his involvement in drug selling and other underground activities, Isaiah continued to earn income by using a "smarter" approach to the drug game. Although Isaiah did not abandon hopes for getting a good-paying legitimate job, drug selling was a means for simultaneously asserting his independence from the family unit and staking a financial claim to more permanent position in the household. Unlike Sincere and Marta, whose tenuous relationship limped along over many years, Isaiah and Tamika were unsuccessful, and Isaiah lost all contact with his children.

FATHERLESS FATHERS

Sincere, Isaiah, and all of the other young men I studied approached their own family lives in ways that were shaped by their families of origin. The vast majority either never knew their fathers or had minimal contact with them as children. Many of their fathers died early or were incarcerated throughout their childhoods. Several also had mothers with a history of incarceration and lived in homes where every one of their brothers and sisters had been in trouble with the law. Many witnessed their fathers or other men assault their mothers on a regular basis when they were children. These men strove to be better fathers than their own dads had been.[5]

Warren lost his dad in a shoot-out at age four. His father and his uncle had gone into a bar in North Philadelphia with a well-known brothel on one of the upper floors. His uncle invited his father upstairs to partake in some cocaine while young Warren waited in their van outside. When the two abruptly left without paying, the owner of the brothel came after them with a gun. The uncle made it into the van and squealed away in time to miss the bullets. He made a U-turn to pick up his brother, but he and Warren watched him get murdered at point-blank range.

Eddie's father, who had a turbulent relationship with his mother, took custody of Eddie, his younger brother, and two older sisters when their mother was incarcerated. A crack addict, his father disappeared for weeks at a time, leaving the children to clothe and feed themselves and get each other to school. Child Protective Services removed the children from the home for neglect on three occasions during their mother's eight-year stint in prison. After moving with their mother from Ohio to Pennsylvania, they had little contact with their father.

Luis's father was marginally involved in his life, and rarely in a way that made his mother, who also had a history of incarceration, happy. His parents, Frankie and Hernan, had a stormy relationship. Frankie needed skin grafts on her chest and arms after Hernan threw a pot of hot water on her. She blamed herself for the trouble her kids were in with the police, because she failed to end their relationship earlier. When Luis was on the run from the police, he holed up at Hernan's place, also in Northeast Philadelphia. Hernan turned Luis into the authorities shortly before the mortgage was foreclosed on and the house closed up.

Both Isaiah and Sincere strove to be better fathers than their own fathers had been to them. Sincere's father, a former drug addict and notorious drug trafficker, died of AIDS-related illnesses while Sincere was at Mountain Ridge. Isaiah's biological father disappeared after his mother remarried when Isaiah was very young. After that, Isaiah began to call his stepfather, Andre, his dad. When Isaiah was released from Mountain Ridge, his family told him that his father was working in Altoona, but he later learned that he was incarcerated.

SINCERE'S STORY

I liked Sincere the minute I met him. He had a quick smile, a broad nose, and a theatrical presence. At six-foot-four, he dwarfed the chair in my borrowed office on the facility's campus and reminded me of an overstuffed teddy bear. However, he quickly informed me that it would be a mistake to "take his kindness for weakness." Several times during his pre-release interview, he leaned forward into the micro-cassette recorder to make a shout-out to some invisible audience: "Yo, this your boy, Sincere. Coming to you from [rural town where Mountain Ridge is located]. This the *exclusive* jawn [joint]!"

Family, loss, and drugs are recurring themes that have been interwoven throughout his life, with meaningful consequences for how he approached adulthood. His desire for a family of his own was an attempt to impose order and stability on an otherwise tumultuous existence, as well as a way to "do right" as his father had never done. Sincere grew up in northern New Jersey and moved to Philadelphia when he was fourteen. His mother, Teresa, sent him there when he began getting involved in a gang; she arranged for him to live with his godfather, who ran a faith-based halfway house. Teresa spent most of his childhood in a cycle of recovery and addiction to crack cocaine. At some time during her binges she contracted HIV, which she passed on to Sincere's little brother, Caesar, who was sixteen years old when I met him.

Sincere described his primary motivation for gang membership and drug selling as a way to get back at his mother for treating him as second best to his brother.[6] "All my life, my mom been makin' me feel like Doughboy. You ever seen *Boyz n the Hood*? He was the brother who never got anything. His brother got all the attention. That's how I feel."

> I hated my mom for sending me [to Philadelphia] 'cause I thought she was just trying to get rid of me, 'cause I was the problem child, the outcast or whatever. So I already put it in my mind that I was going to come out here and get worser. Once I got to know people . . . I started dealing drugs real heavy, dealing with guns and stuff like that . . . I ended up getting locked up for two guns, a sawed-off shotgun and a nine Smith and Wesson, two pounds of weed and some heron [heroin]. I was only fourteen when that happened.

Sincere became even more embedded in the street life after suffering the loss of two people very close to him. During a trip to California, Sincere and the members of his church group were involved in a gruesome accident when the van they were driving veered off into a ditch and rolled over. Teresa told me, "He held Manny [his godbrother] in his arms as he died. He and the other people in the van literally saw brains smeared all over the highway. They had to undergo crisis counseling while in California and by the time he got back, he had just missed Manny's funeral. Over the next couple of weeks, we went to funeral after funeral. After that, Sincere [then fifteen] just snapped. His thinking was so messed up. He was crazy."

Sincere explained how the accident affected him, linking his drug dealing to his new role as the man of the house.

> My pop was never around and my godfather was like my dad. So he was gone and all that male guidance that I had was gone for good and I wasn't getting that back. So I figured I had to be a man on myself, so the streets was all I knew. So I was thinking by me selling drugs, making a lot of money, handling my business, my mom ain't got no food in the house, I'm puttin' food in the house ... and I got a little brother, he look up to me, so I got to make sure he stay fresh [have stylish clothes and regular haircuts]. I thought that was being a man.

The survivors and family members sued the auto manufacturer for the malfunction in the van, which had caused the rollover. During that time, Teresa moved to Philadelphia to deal with matters related to the lawsuit. In the wake of the accident, Sincere began using and selling drugs more frequently. He was soon arrested for selling crack.

Sincere was incarcerated at Mountain Ridge for nearly two years, during which time his father died. While still inside the facility, he talked about how he had changed since his time on the street:

> When I first got locked up, I was sixteen and I'm eighteen now and time do mature you. . . . It was like weed was my best friend and wasn't nothing in the world going to change that. Now all that's changed. Freedom is my best friend now. I'm trying to get it back. If I was that kind of person, I could return back to all those negative behaviors I was involved in, but me being here and away from home for almost eighteen months and missing my family, losing my pop, putting my mom through it, hear her crying on the phone, my little brother back and forth to the hospital, my little sister having a baby, and my older sister about to have twins. It's just missing everybody

grow up and having people miss me. It's not worth it, me doing all that stuff I was doing out there.

Sincere's choice of a pseudonym was emblematic of a genuine desire to make good and redeem himself in his family's eyes. As he soon discovered, however, desire alone hardly was sufficient to avoid trouble in a neighborhood where trouble was a daily reality.

Sincere's Neighborhood

Sincere returned home to Philadelphia in March 2005, during one of the most violent weeks in the city's history. Between Monday, March 7, and Monday, March 14, forty-two people were shot. Eleven people were killed over the weekend alone, including a child who was sitting in a car waiting for his father. Sincere moved into a crowded and messy apartment on the second story of a three-level row home in Kensington with Teresa, his younger sister, Lakisha, and Caesar.

That spring, Sincere was my guide to Kensington, one of the poorest communities in the city and a neighborhood that seemed to be filled with contradictions.[7] A bright mix of colors adorned the side of the family's rented house, a painted scene of a tropical island, strangely juxtaposed against a crumbling wall and an abandoned, weed-choked lot. Sitting on his front stoop, I caught a glimpse into this community, vibrant and moving in concert with the salsa beats pouring from the open windows of passing cars, yet heartbreakingly neglected.

Sincere's connection to his neighborhood, despite the fact that he did not grow up there, was based on feelings of safety and familiarity. It may be difficult to believe that a neighborhood like Kensington could make any resident feel safe. However, Sincere's mastery of the street code made navigating its environs a rather comfortable endeavor.[8] His community was populated with family and friends who were ready to "ride or die" in response to threats made by outsiders.[9] Here, on the street, his readiness to use violence when necessary accorded him a sense of respect not easily found in other milieus. By contrast, entering white, middle-class settings made him profoundly uneasy. When he visited my mostly white neighborhood, he commented, "everybody's cops."

An important frame of reference for Sincere and the other young men I followed was the all-male peer group.[10] Congregating outside the domestic domain on stoops, front porches, and street corners, groups of men construct masculine identities by sharing stories, joking, and testing one another's mettle verbally and sometimes physically. Manhood is often posed in terms that oppose anything related to femininity, including domesticity and fidelity to one woman. Men who are deemed to be under the thumb of their woman may be derided as "pussy whipped," while those who regale the group with stories of sexual conquests earn heightened masculine status. Commitment to the peer group comes at the cost of commitment to children and babies' mamas.

As a woman, I rarely got more than temporary access to these male peer groups. When I did, I noticed two things. First, these young men were often unabashedly sentimental, openly declaring their love for one another and demonstrating a physical affection that I rarely observed them share with their female partners or children. There were prescribed rituals for doing this, through an urban masculine embrace or fist thumping. Warren's fictive brother, Roemello, who had been in a wheelchair for eight years after being gunned down in the street, spilled tears down his cheeks as he described Warren's long-term loyalty. Instead of shying away from these declarations, Warren reciprocated with his own stories of how Roemello had his back.[11]

The second and contradictory quality of these relationships was their instability. Their much-celebrated loyalty to one another was often broken. Sincere's close friend, Kevin, stole his debit card and withdrew $500 from Sincere's bank account. Interestingly, Sincere later resumed his friendship with Kevin, reframing the incident as his own fault for setting up a PIN number that was so easily figured out. A couple of weeks after Roemello's tear-filled proclamations of love for Warren, Warren said that he wasn't speaking to him "on some personal stuff. It's cool, people just not who they say they are anymore," he said disappointedly. Sociologist Elliot Liebow, in his timeless account of urban black men, stated that "extravagant pledges of aid and comfort between friends are, at one level, made and received in good faith. But at another level, fully aware of his friends' limited resources and the demands of their self-interest, each person is ultimately prepared to look to himself alone. . . . One moment, friendship is an almost sacred covenant; the next, it is the locus of cynical exploitation."[12]

Seeking Employment

Sincere returned to Philadelphia with plans to get a job as a technician at a local cable company and having earned acceptance to culinary school for the fall. Few things went as planned, however. Weeks after he came home, Sincere got a pit bull puppy who exacerbated the already crowded living conditions at his mother's house. He and his younger sister, Lakisha, resumed their tumultuous relationship, fighting to the point of violence on several occasions. He felt Teresa was constantly "coming at" him for not helping more around the house or taking care of the dog. Eventually he stopped going to church with her, formerly a part of their weekly tradition.

Things on the job front were not going well, either. The human resources department at the cable company delayed an interview, and Sincere learned that he lacked both a driver's license and the required job experience to become a technician. Though he was required to fill out job applications as part of his probation, he never turned them in, saying, "I'm not tryin' to work no minimum wage. I got my diploma, so I'm tryin' to get something better than that."

Two months after release, Sincere finally interviewed at the cable company for a customer service position. Although he passed the required math, reading, and ethics tests, he failed the last part, testing him on scenarios he would need to deal with as a phone service agent. He was back to square one. His brother-in-law worked to get him on a construction crew, but Sincere lost interest, having gotten into a daily routine that did not involve work.[13] He used the job offer letter that his brother-in-law had written to meet the employment condition of his probation and was discharged from probation without incident after three months.

Sincere expressed ambivalence toward employment. Stinging after his rejection by the cable company, he was hesitant to risk his self-esteem again by seriously pursuing work. He was also conscious that a low-paying job would not lead to real social mobility.[14] A paycheck from McDonald's, he realized, would never be sufficient for him to purchase his own home, a fantasy he often spoke about. Nevertheless, he was conscious that healthy young men were expected to work, even in a community where unemployment was high.

"I'm going to move out to Western PA," he told me one day, explaining that one of the counselors at Mountain Ridge had offered him free rent if he worked as a chef at one of his family's restaurants. I never heard him mention it again. Similarly, he never pursued culinary school, even though he told me while he was incarcerated that opening a restaurant was his dream. As I noted in the last chapter, he occasionally looked for work in groups of male friends, often getting high beforehand. Looking for work continued to have the ritualistic flavor of a man who felt like he *should* be working but was able to get by day-to-day without very much in his pocket.

The demands for financial contributions upon Sincere and other young men I studied were sporadic. Mothers and grandmothers were often wary of pressuring men to work out of fear that they might push them back into the drug game. Demands by babies' mamas fluctuated over time. Men were sometimes asked to contribute for special occasions such as a birthday or in cases of emergency such as when the cell phone was shut off or when diapers ran low. These short-term calls for support were often most easily met by a quick drug transaction. When resources grew scarcer, often as families grew, the demands for support intensified and required more steady income.

Women in inner-city communities may wish that their partners provided more regular support, but they are reluctant to become dependent upon men because of their unstable employment and the ever-present possibility of being sent to prison. With a few exceptions, the women I documented in the course of my field research combined multiple streams of public assistance, including Temporary Assistance for Needy Families (TANF), food stamps, Supplemental Security Income for the disabled (SSI), state-provided health insurance, and housing subsidies. Even when men worked, they typically made less than what the women could generate using public assistance, creating a power imbalance and offering men only a provisional status within the family.

Fatherhood and Romantic Partnership

Sincere told me on the first day that I met him that he wanted a child, a "mini-me, a part of me that's never been bad." He believed that having a son would redeem his past misdeeds and compensate for his father's failure to be involved in his own life.[15] "[My father] never was around and it was the love I missed growing up. The stuff [Teresa] did to us as kids would make us mad and make us hate her as adults, but bein' as though kids' love is everlasting. There's no limit to a child's love for his parents. I never had that. Word up! I never really had nobody to love me."

The fatherhood Sincere craved soon arrived. By the time he returned home, his former girlfriend, Marta, was pregnant with a child they had conceived during his last home pass from Mountain Ridge. Marta was twenty-four, more than five years older than Sincere, and they had met at the church where they were both members and their mothers were best friends. Marta lived above a pharmacy, a short walk from Teresa's house, in the center of Kensington. She was an intelligent young woman who could have excelled in college if she had had the opportunity. However, she suffered from debilitating rheumatoid arthritis and years later had both knees replaced. Because she lacked mobility, her bed was her command post. She taught her oldest daughter, Mercedes (who was four when I met her), to prepare food and take care of the younger children because she was able to do so little. Most of her days appeared to be consumed with watching television and movies and talking on the phone, in addition to supervising her children from her bedroom.

Marta's inability to get outside and engage with other adults caused her to suffer from malaise. She frequently looked tired and cared little about her appearance. As a result of the steroids the doctors had given her, she had gained significant weight. Marta approached me with suspicion at first, thinking I might be out to prey on her man. Once her fears were allayed, however, we discovered that we enjoyed each other's company, and I frequently found myself taking her side (at least internally) as she reported the details of her disagreements with Sincere. She looked forward to my visits and demanded I bring pictures of my travels because "you know I live *vi-curiously* through you." I had to smile at her clever word artistry.

Sincere was unequivocally excited about having a baby and certain it would be a boy. He planned to give his son the family name, making him the fourth in line to share it. In the weeks after he learned of the pregnancy, he and I became quite close. We endured a number of crises, including his aunt's death, Sharif's murder and funeral, a late-night trip to the emergency room when Marta thought she was losing the baby (she was diagnosed with ovarian cysts), and his shameful abandonment of his dog at a local park when he realized he was unprepared to care for her. Nevertheless, I was floored when he asked me to be the baby's godmother. "Why me?" I asked, honored and terrified at the same time. "Because I know that if anything happened to me, you would take good care of him," he said. In the months that followed, Sincere taught me that godmothers were a critical part of the extended kin system, expected to provide financial assistance and child care when called upon. I began paying attention to how Sincere interacted with his nephew, Lamar, who was one year old.

Lamar was obsessed with the ball, or "ba" as he called it. Sincere and I spent many afternoons throwing the ball back and forth with Lamar. Each time I threw the ball, I said clearly "ball!" When he said "ba," I parroted back "yes, ball!" Sincere did not talk as much to Lamar and interacted roughly with him. Whenever he cried, Sincere chastised him, saying gruffly, "Stop it!" Lamar usually did. As they played, Sincere frequently restrained him, causing him to struggle. Sincere often play-smacked Lamar and demanded that he fight back.

I began to understand my role as godmother during these afternoon play sessions. Sincere and his family took responsibility for teaching Lamar lessons that they believed would serve him in a neighborhood like Kensington: to fight, not to show emotions too eagerly, and to endure struggle and adversity. Involving me in his son's life, Sincere believed, would open up the possibility of learning other lessons and provide him with a window on the white, middle-class world. Sincere hoped that I would help his son learn how to read, encourage him to go to school, and maybe help him get into college someday.

As excited as he was to become a father, Sincere was less enamored with the idea of being tied down to Marta after spending two years without contact with other girls. During her pregnancy, they broke up and reunited more times than I could count. She destroyed his cell phone, the center of his social life, when she found too many girls' names stored as contacts. She threatened to move away and have the baby, even spending a few days outside New York to give the threat some weight before returning home to Philadelphia. On more than one occasion, she warned him that she might not give the baby his name if he continued to talk to other girls.

I wondered about his tenuous role in this newly forming family. As the baby's due date drew near, would he feel increased pressure to contribute financially? If those demands did eventually surface, would he return to drug selling to provide for his son? And given the reality of a baby, would he want to be as involved as he intended?

Back to Broke

Three weeks before the baby was due, Sincere was awarded a cash settlement of $25,000 for the auto accident. The case had been drawn out over several years, but the money came just in time. He moved into Marta's second-floor apartment and got it set up for the baby. Shortly after her baby shower, he proudly showed off the beautiful hardwood crib and all the clothes, diapers, and other supplies he had purchased in anticipation of his son's arrival.

This was the first time in his life that Sincere felt like a man. He was generous, treating everyone around him to the little luxuries that they rarely if ever enjoyed. He gave Marta a hot pink Victoria's Secret nightshirt, one of the only items of clothing that did not strain at her waistline. Her daughter, Mercedes, got a brand new Rocawear jacket and matching purse; Caesar got two pet iguanas; he scheduled and paid for a photo session for one of his friends and his new baby; and he bought Teresa a plane ticket to attend a church retreat in Tennessee. He bought a high-end camera phone for pictures of the baby. And he purchased materials that were going to allow him to work from home doing something related to the stock market and real estate. When I dusted the books off months later, it was clear that this was a scam.

Late one night, Sincere phoned me to announce that Marta was in labor. His son, whose sex was confirmed by an ultrasound, was finally on his way! When I arrived at the hospital, the baby had been taken to NICU because his breathing was too rapid. Marta's eyes were weary and ringed by dark circles after hours of difficult labor; she watched Maury Povich with her mother Olivia, Sincere, and Caesar. Sincere directed me to the spot outside NICU where I could see my new godson. He entered and put on a gown, smiling broadly and pointing proudly to a tiny bundle with a disturbing array of tubes coming out of his mouth and nose. The nurse came over to check his breathing rate and Sincere gave me a thumbs-up, indicating that he was stabilizing. When he rejoined me outside, I said, "He's white!" Sincere laughed. "Yeah, but he's got my nose." Curious, I asked about the baby's name. As a sign of her hope for their future together, Marta had given the baby Sincere's name.[16] Olivia and Teresa maintained a friendly battle, however, over whether he would be called "Little Sincere" or "Sincere Junior."

Within two weeks of the baby's return home from the hospital, five weeks after receiving the settlement check, Sincere went through his online bank statement with me, incredulous that he could be overdrawn already. We added up all the withdrawals to ensure that the math was correct. It was during this time that his friend Kevin stole his debit card and took $500 from his checking account, which was later verified and refunded by the bank. Two months after the baby was born, Sincere was back to broke. His cell phone service was shut off, and he had to pay the wireless company $700 to have it turned back on again.

Nevertheless, at that time, Marta did not appear to expect that Sincere would contribute anything financially to the family. He was as actively involved with the baby as he had promised, taking the night shift and spending so much time with Little Sincere that Marta sometimes envied the visible connection they had already formed. For the moment, "being there" was enough of a contribution, since Marta's public assistance and SSI disability payments covered most of their expenses. With Sincere taking day-to-day responsibility for the children, Marta was able to supervise his activities and ensure that he was being faithful.

Though he intended to continue living with Marta and the baby as a family, he felt ambivalent about the notion of marriage.[17] Soon after the baby was born, Sincere told me that marriage was too serious a commitment for someone his age. Two months later, as we waited for hours in a community clinic for Little Sincere's checkup, he and Marta announced their plans to get married. "Mercedes, you're going to be the flower girl," Marta told her eldest daughter. Outside, during a smoke break, he told me that Marta should feel lucky that he helped with the baby so much, especially given the uncertainty that surrounded the baby's paternity. "You mean because the baby was white?" I asked, surprised.

The baby had since darkened up, and his complexion was a shade darker than Marta's light cocoa skin. "Yeah, I mean. Well, I knew he was mine as soon as I saw his nose." He trailed off here, suggesting a hint of doubt still remained. Although this doubt may have been real, it more likely reflected his deep ambivalence about cementing his role in the family.[18]

"A Broke Guy"

By March, three months after Sincere Junior was born, Sincere was feeling increased pressure from Marta both to make a public commitment to her and to start bringing regular income into their household, which she saw as related. Her sister, Marisol, had recently moved into the apartment with her one year-old daughter, Betony, fostering more stress stemming from increased household demands for resources. Marisol openly criticized Sincere for not bringing in a paycheck, and their arguments drove Sincere to spend more time on the stoop or the corner with his male friends. "It just felt like everybody started lookin' at me like a *broke guy*. Like I was *broke*, and there wasn't gonna be *nothin'*. I remember when, before my son was here, people used to say you ain't gonna be a good father. Two of my sisters told me that, my girlfriend's sister said that. My little sister's friends used to say that. It was just in they heads 'cause they never grew up with a father." His insight about why the women in his life had low expectations of his fathering abilities did not stop him from being deeply affected by how they viewed him. He had his own concerns about his ability to be a good father and worried that these predictions would come true. Unfortunately, these predictions of failure mirrored those that were made inside Mountain Ridge.

Spurred on by the fear of being thought of as a "broke guy" and a bad father, Sincere began to pursue a two-pronged approach to bringing in income. He knew that finding a job was the best long-term solution to being broke. In the short term, however, the drug game seemed a viable option. In fact, he admitted small hustles here and there after completing probation.

> I didn't do it big. I didn't do it like last time, I was just doin' small stuff so I won't get caught up or in trouble. But that wasn't workin' so I stopped. . . . It's rules to the drug game. I was tryin' to make enough money to do my thing, but not hustle too much. But the drug game

was put here for underclass people to support their families. That's how Pablo Escobar did it. He had a poor country. They had a lot of coke and America was big on coke and that's how he did it, and he probably got in trouble for it, but oh yeah, that's part of this game. That's another rule, you shall get locked up.

Sincere viewed selling drugs as a form of employment, although it brought increased risk of violent victimization or arrest. He also noted that there are grades of drug selling with differing levels of risk. Most important, he suggested that hustling requires a full-time commitment that is incompatible with being a family man. Young fathers living in impoverished communities may "pick up a packet" occasionally to meet short-term demands but cannot draw a steady income by selling drugs unless they are prepared to face a high risk of arrest or violence and long hours away from their families.

He later described this period of his life as the time when he was "building a work ethic." "Work, it's still kinda new to me. Now I'm get-tin' to the point where I wanna do it, whereas before, I did it because [it made] everybody else happy. . . . A work ethic [is] like you wake up on time, go to work on time, and do the same thing the next day and the next day after that." He added that work ethic typically is built around the age of sixteen to eighteen, when he was incarcerated. "So me learn-ing how to be a man starts at sixteen, y'know what I mean? And that was going out the window 'cause I was incarcerated, so when I came home, it was like real hard. I didn't have a job for like the first year. And I was doing like part-time jobs, like my brother-in-law, he had his own carpentry/construction business and I been doing that with him, lightly. Taking it lightly, just trying to build a work ethic or something. But I didn't like how the money was coming in. It was coming in too slow." Many young men who at one time earned a steady income selling drugs feel that legal money "comes in too slow." Part of "building a work ethic" for Sincere meant adjusting expectations for his earnings downward. The jobs he held were largely seasonal or temporary and did not produce a steady paycheck, no matter how small.

Employment also posed a double bind. Although Marta and the other women in his life criticized him when he did not have a job, Marta rarely supported his employment either. He often returned at night to find her tired and lonely, castigating him for leaving her alone in the house with three kids. She worried that his long hours outside the home would lessen his commitment to the family and give him opportunities to meet other women. In turn, he felt he just could not do right by her. He could either be there at home for the family or spend his days working, but no matter what he did, it never seemed to be enough.

Glimpses of a Happy Family

At times, Sincere and Marta interacted like a couple in love, or worked especially well as a family unit. Without these times to sustain them, their relationship would have ended long before. Between spring and fall of 2006, Sincere was looking for work and helping around the house; a job at a car wash had been short-lived. Although boredom and cramped quarters caused irritation, there were also many moments of love and playfulness. The tenor of their relationship during the good times is evident in field notes written in May.

I plopped down on my knees next to the bed and said hello, remarking at how different Sincere Junior looked than the last time I saw him. "He just turned five months, but he's already wearing clothes for nine-month babies," Marta said, proudly. "He's eighteen pounds!" Not only did he look bigger, but he was clearly interacting with his environment more than ever before. Sincere placed him in the bouncy chair and he happily sprung up and down, whimpering a bit whenever we stopped looking at him.

"He's showing off," Marta said, rolling her eyes. She seemed to have more energy than she'd had in a while.

Sincere sat on the edge of the bed, playing on the computer. He was playing with a trial version of *Fish Tycoon*, which kept interrupting his game and asking him to upgrade to the complete version. I put Sincere Junior back down on the bed and he rose up into crawl position. "He crawls backward," Sincere explained.

"Yikes," I said, blocking his back end from falling off the bed if he did indeed crawl backward. "Oh, yeah, he's fallen off the bed a few times," Sincere said, still playing his game.

Sincere asked about Isaiah and I said he was doing okay. I said that he was still with Tamika, but that they fought all the time and that he was constantly getting kicked out of the house. "That sounds like us," Sincere said to Marta.

"When's the last time you got kicked out?" I asked. "Yeah, when is the last time you got kicked out?" Marta said, teasing. "Um . . . it's been a while," Sincere said, leaning toward Marta and smiling wickedly. "It's definitely time for a kick-out," he teased. She smiled. Affection was in the air. Despite their money problems, they seemed to be settled and getting along pretty well.

Sincere and Marta continued to scrape by through the summer until Caesar finally succumbed to AIDS at the age of nineteen. During this period, Marta's and Sincere's families rallied together as a unit, helping support each other through the heartbreaking loss. Teresa, not wanting to live by herself in the house where Caesar had grown so ill, moved in with Olivia. Their two families became completely enmeshed, increasing both mothers' involvement in Sincere and Marta's relationship. This had ill effects on the couple, whose family members became involved in the conflicts and took sides whenever they disagreed.

Infidelity and Jealousy

Sincere's stance toward marriage appeared to be a function of his ability to offer financial support and fully trust Marta. He enjoyed the family man role but continued to struggle with his own desires for outside sexual conquests and concomitant fears that Marta would do the same. Sincere openly admitted to having several flings, one of which resulted in an unplanned pregnancy and abortion and another that ended in his catching a sexually transmitted infection. When I brought him onto campus to guest lecture in my classes, he mortified me by offering lewd compliments to my female students and asking for their phone numbers.

Meanwhile, any evidence that Marta was flirting with other men in public threatened his sense of manhood and demanded an immediate response. He didn't want to go to the community pool, knowing there would be flirting. "I mean, I see this before it happens, right? I'm gettin' my Cleo on [like a psychic].[19] We're gonna go down there, and she gonna see her sister talkin' to all the dudes and she gonna want to be a part of that. I'm not gonna put myself in that predicament." When his prediction came true, he yelled at Marta for everyone to hear, "That nigga not your man! That nigga not gonna go home and whoop your ass! I am! So you need to get up outta this pool!" Later, he explained to me,

> In the 'hood, the code is, you can't go out with your girl, you can't go out with your man. 'Cause you bring your girl to the bar, you already know somebody gonna try to talk to her. 'Cause that's how bar fights start, people get shot. . . . Outta the 'hood, we go partyin' and dude go, "Oh, you wanna dance with my girl? Go ahead." That's the type of dude I want to become. I want my girl to be able to live her life, to chill, to say somethin' to a dude without me gettin' mad. But in order for that to happen, the female have to show, "I'm only on [with] you."

Sincere and Marta's relationship was marked by a constant struggle over control, which became heightened whenever they were in public. Here he attempted to assert authority over Marta, solidifying a sense of masculinity. Marta, however, resisted; she publicly reminded him that he was expendable, that he had failed to live up to the traditional model of masculinity.

Sincere had complicated motives for undermining the family he was building by cheating on Marta. Sexual conquest made him feel more like a man. When he "came at" (flirted with) my female students, he imagined the possibility of romantic relationships that were not defined by his status as an underemployed former hustler. Sometimes he felt that he could do better than Marta or worried that she was holding him back. When his younger sister, Lakisha, broke up a relationship he was having with a college student by revealing it to Marta, he said ruefully, "She made me want to *be* something." Because she viewed him as having potential, for the brief period that they were together he saw himself as having potential. Sincere's cheating also reveals his ambivalence about being tied down at such a young age. Immaturity explains much of the cheating, jealousy, and insecurity that characterized most romantic relationships of these young men.

Christmas without the Kids

Sincere and Marta's struggle for control was played out against a backdrop of relentless material hardship. That fall, Sincere started working with a group of men from his church, doing demolition work on hotels up and down the eastern seaboard. This work took him away from the house for several days at a time but did not result in a marked improvement in their standard of living. Bills piled up, collection agencies called at all hours, and the phone service was cut off periodically. It was not clear how long they were going to be able to sustain the household on their own, although there was no room for additional residents.

Shortly before winter break, I called Marta to ask when I could come by to see the kids. In a mere twenty-four hours, Sincere and Marta's fledgling family had completely unraveled. First, Marta learned of Sincere's infidelity when Lakisha revealed that he had paid for an abortion for another woman. This secret had been especially difficult to hide, given that Marta paid such close attention to his income. He had had to borrow money from friends and lie to Marta about how many hours he worked in order to cover the expense.

To make matters worse, the kids, even Marta's niece, Betony, had been removed from the home by the Department of Human Services. Betony's mother, Marisol, was on one of her regular jaunts to New York to party with her friends, leaving Betony in her sister's care. When the police entered Marta's apartment to investigate a noise complaint, they found her hobbling around after three children and the house in total chaos. Sincere described the scene: "I went upstairs and I saw all these cops and I saw Marta hobbling all around, y'know her knees are bad, and that upset me. I said 'What's the problem, officer?' and they said that they was taking away the kids because the house was so messy. Marta was screaming. I didn't know what to do."

As he told this story, I looked around the apartment. Clothes were strewn all over the floor in the bedroom and hallway. It looked like a laundry bag had exploded. Marta was balled up in bed under the bedspread. When I came in, she sat up, wiping her nose with a tissue and adding it to a small pile on the bed stand. Her face was red and swollen. She snuffled,

> They came up in here and took my kids. They came in and started writing down all this stuff, like the kids had urine-soaked Pampers, like my bed is up on milk crates and everything, the kids is dirty. They asked Mercedes if she had eaten anything and she was scared. She said she hadn't eaten, but she had gone to school that day. She ate at school

and when she came home, I made sure she ate some SpaghettiOs. My kids are fat and healthy. There's always food in the refrigerator. So my bed's up on milk crates? She's got her own room, all those toys. Those kids are my life, and now they won't even be home for Christmas.

Sincere motioned for me to come back out into the hallway. He whispered, "Last night, after the police left, I thought we should clean the place up. When the DHS lady came, she wouldn't have anything to write down. But Marta wouldn't help me and I wasn't going to do it alone, so when she came this morning, it still looked like this." The DHS caseworker told them that the kids were going to have to stay with their grandmother for the next two weeks and that she would be coming by regularly to check in on them.

"After this, we're just going to keep to ourselves," Sincere said. "This is what happens when you have people in your life who don't have your best interests at heart. We're going to save up some money and move away from here, be on our own." His family's interdependence with Marta's family was both a blessing and a curse. They relied on each other as inner-city families must do in order to survive, sharing resources such as food, money, and information about available jobs or better housing. However, their enmeshment tied Sincere to Marta more permanently than he was always comfortable with. Moreover, it was a deep betrayal when his sisters took Marta's side, choosing gender solidarity over kinship. I wondered why Lakisha got so involved in his relationship with Marta. Was she trying to keep them together by eliminating his relationships with other women, or, like the haters in James's and Leo's neighborhoods, did she take satisfaction in creating drama and chaos?

A New Level of Commitment?

Before long, the children were returned and the apartment was monitored by a social worker who made weekly visits. Sincere finally saved enough money to buy Marta an engagement ring, and they became formally engaged. Despite this display of commitment, he still felt ambivalent toward marriage.

I wanted to do it [get engaged] because I love her and I always wanted to make her family my own, but it was like the pimp side of me just wouldn't let it go down. I decided it was time for me to grow up, be a man. If I really love her like I say I do, she want to get married and I do too. But I'm not the right away type. I know enough to marry her, but let me see if over time, she show me her true colors.

Sincere valued marriage highly, not wanting to make a mistake by rushing into the decision.[20] He associated marriage with growing up, something he both desperately wanted and feared. Caught between a desire to create some stability for himself and a desire to experience the freedom that many people in their twenties enjoy, he moved back and forth between defining manhood in relation to his young family and in relation to the "swagger" of sexual conquest.

Shortly after they got engaged, Sincere's demolition crew job ended when his brother-in-law's truck died. Since they could no longer afford their apartment, they moved into the house that Teresa and Olivia had been sharing. Sincere steeled himself for what he expected would be a constant barrage of criticism, being the only adult male in a house filled with women. He began looking for work in earnest, and through Leo, whose stepfather worked there, he found a seasonal job as a groundskeeper for a public golf course.

His dire predictions about the living situation were quickly realized. He and Olivia clashed over his discipline of Mercedes. It was midnight and he told Mercedes to go to bed. Olivia said, "You aren't her father. You don't have any say over what she does." Sincere replied, "The hell I'm not her father! Look at all this stuff she has. I bought her that. She calls me dad." During all this conflict, Olivia suggested that she get a paternity test to make sure that Sincere Junior was his biological son. Sincere was enraged. A couple of nights later, he and Marta got into an altercation and Olivia called the police on him. He left, going to stay at Teresa's new house near Temple University. He and Marta broke up, and he pawned her engagement ring for cash.

In August, Sincere's family, including Marta and Sincere Junior, congregated on his older sister Latoya's back patio for a barbecue to commemorate the anniversary of Caesar's death. They had made T-shirts with his photo silk screened on them. Because Sincere had been somewhat evasive about what had provoked Olivia to call the police, I asked Marta her side of the story. She confirmed my suspicions that Sincere had assaulted her that night in the heat of the exchange. It was not the first time either, but it was the worst and had resulted in a black eye. "It's going to be hard to stay away from him, because I love him," she explained to me. "But I can't have my son growing up thinking it's okay to put his hands on females."

For many months afterward, Marta and Sincere lived separately and Sincere's financial contributions to his son's support were sporadic. His landscaping job ended at the end of summer. His commitment to the job, which required him to get up at three thirty every weekday morning, was impressive. Although his boss promised to hire him back in the spring, his financial prospects were bleak. I got periodic phone calls from Marta saying that Sincere Junior and Betony were out of diapers. Sincere and Marta continued to see one another, though not exclusively. Olivia continued her threats to call the police whenever Sincere was around, though he seemed to wear her down as Sincere Junior's second birthday approached. Marta, Sincere, Marisol, and I threw a party in his honor, and Sincere mugged with his son in front of the camera. In the picture I took of Sincere and Marta, their arms clasped around each other, neither was smiling.

The Significance of Fatherhood for Sincere

Popular accounts of "deadbeat" dads in ghetto communities do little to help us understand why Sincere's attempts to build a family with his son and his baby's mom were so precarious.[21] Instead of abnegating his responsibility for his son, Sincere relished the idea of being an active and loving father. Moreover, he saw fatherhood as the defining moment of his becoming both an adult and a man. "People say, when you turn eighteen, you become a man. You don't become a man until you reach fatherhood. A man make a choice within himself, it's like, an unconscious choice that a man makes when your child is born. It's like, either you gonna be there, take on the responsibilities, or you're gonna keep livin' for the moment. You can live for the moment, or you can live for the future."

Sincere saw his son as his legacy, creating a sense of permanence in an otherwise transitory life.[22] "Not only do he got my name and whatever go on with me, but he's me, whenever I leave this earth. And that's why I told my son mom, long as he got my name, you always got a place to

stay, a roof over your head, food in your stomach. I just love having my
son, because I know he a part of me, and I know what I'm leavin' behind.
That's why I'm moldin' and shapin' him now to be whatever he want."

On several occasions over the years, Sincere turned to the drug game
to meet the expectations accompanying fatherhood. Mostly, he maintained an aversion to the risks drug selling entailed. With a two-year
stretch of incarceration behind him, he clearly saw how a future prison
sentence would affect his family, especially his son. Moreover, he was
cognizant of the lessons his son might learn from watching his father
engage in the underground economy.

At our two-year follow-up interview, I asked Sincere how he would
grade himself as a father. He replied: "I'd give myself a A-. First of all, the
minus is because there's always room for improvement. Second of all, I
grade myself on the good view 'cause I'm there. I'm there, 24/7. It's not
a lot of fathers that's there and there's not a lot of people my age that do
what I do. And I think that first should be respected from anyone who
look at me. It's not a lot of young fathers that put everything down to do
the family thing."

The street may always be a draw for Sincere. There, he knows the
rules and feels a sense of mastery and manhood. He explained, "I show
love to the game, 'cause the game show love to me." The sense of accomplishment he got from being a father, by contrast, was transitory and
partially dependent on his status in the labor market. When he could
not provide for his son's material needs, he was happy to offer his time
and affection, something he never got from his father. However, sharing
a household with his baby's mother involved constant reminders of how
he failed to measure up as both a father and a partner.

ISAIAH'S STORY

Of all the young people I met during the course of my study, Isaiah
was the most clearly in search of a family. Because he was so smart, he
was impossible not to like. He was also the most adept at code switching and lying, two closely associated behaviors. These qualities made my
heart go out to him (particularly when he called me Mommy), but they
also made me skeptical of the things he told me. Because of his ability to
anticipate what he thought I wanted to hear, I had to work extra hard to

confirm the stories Isaiah told me, using other sources such as his court records and, more commonly, his baby's mother, Tamika. When she was angry with him, which was often, she spoke candidly about his lies to her and other misdeeds.

Inside Mountain Ridge, Isaiah relished the role of the scholar. He spoke quietly and deliberately, eyes blinking repeatedly behind his wire-rimmed glasses. He took pride in being able to play the piano for the staff and told me that, for the first time in his life, the program allowed him to feel intelligent. During our conversations while he was incarcerated, Isaiah was consumed with thoughts of his son, his baby's mom, and his future on the outside. Determined to attend college and get a business degree, he voluntarily stayed at Mountain Ridge for longer than necessary so that he could complete his high school diploma. Meanwhile, he contemplated his future with his girlfriend, Tamika, and her two-year-old son, Darius, for whom Isaiah had taken responsibility, even though he was not the biological father. He was more committed to Darius than to Tamika.

Isaiah's Return to Philadelphia

After thirteen months of incarceration at Mountain Ridge, Isaiah returned home to Philadelphia in July 2005. I found him early that morning waiting in the courtroom of J-Court, the court exclusively reserved for review and discharge hearings. He was wearing a white T-shirt, khaki Bermuda shorts, white socks pulled up to his knees, and black rubber flip-flops. He stood up and I approached. "Isaiah, welcome home!" I said. "Can I give you a hug?" He nodded, looking a bit dazed. He proudly showed off his high school diploma to me, and later to his reintegration worker, Soledad, and the judge who discharged him.

He was given ninety days of probation with services provided by Mountain Ridge Reintegration Program and outpatient drug and alcohol services through a local reintegration center. After the two-minute hearing, we headed upstairs to the probation offices, where a PO sitting in for Isaiah's PO helpfully printed out several job leads. One was a UPS job fair that was going to be held the following Monday at the Career Link in South Philadelphia. A couple of Boston Markets were also hiring, but Isaiah was dead set against working in fast food. "It's too hot," he explained. "I want something better."

Early Signs of Trouble

My first meeting with Tamika, Isaiah's BM, had gone well. I was prepared for her, like Marta, to be suspicious of my motives, but she welcomed me with open arms. She was short and boisterous, wore fashionable clothes and a Mohawk, and complained about Isaiah's incessant playing of rap music. I found myself thinking about how good an influence she might be on Isaiah. She seemed to have her act together, especially for a young woman of nineteen. I later learned that she had been incarcerated at thirteen at a school for delinquent girls. During the year that she had waited for Isaiah's release, she had lived in a women's shelter.

Tamika was clearly proud of the house that she had recently secured through Section 8, a federally subsidized housing program that caps rent at a fixed proportion of household income and pays the balance to private landlords. Though the house had little in the way of furnishings during my first few visits, she made some sort of improvement each time I came by: a kitchen table and chairs, a new TV stand from IKEA, some dried flowers in a small vase in the picture window in front. More important, I sensed, was the street outside. Grove Street, in Northeast Philadelphia, had a very different look and feel from the other addresses I had visited during my field research. The street itself was quiet, with no one loitering on the corner or on their front steps. The cars parked outside the modest homes did not appear to be expensive, but were clean and well cared for. Unlike the prototypical Philadelphia row homes, the houses were set back from the street a little, and many of the patios out front were filled with signs of summer: kiddie pools, barbecues, and lawn chairs. It was a small slice of the American dream.

During Isaiah's first couple of weeks home from Mountain Ridge, he moved between his aunt's house in the Logan section of North Philadelphia and Tamika's house in the Northeast. Tracking him down by phone meant always going through a female gatekeeper. Tamika kept close tabs on the weekly $25 he was making through his reentry journals, appropriating it for diapers or groceries as soon as I dropped it off with his next assignment. In fact, I soon became aware that she was monitoring his activities by listening to the taped journal entries before he submitted them to me. Less than a full week before he had been home, she phoned me to inform me that she had kicked him out because she had overheard him talking about going to see another woman, although he quickly smoothed that argument over. In addition to having a blowout with Tamika about the tape, he had that week learned that the two-year-old girl we had gone to visit in Darby was not his daughter after all. His ex-girlfriend had an abortion after getting pregnant with his child, and her two-year-old was from another father. Apparently, this information was at the heart of why Tamika had gotten upset. His first week home had been "nothing but drama."

Despite the drama, Isaiah and Tamika's drive to live together as a family was powerful. During his first month home, Tamika seemed to be testing Isaiah's commitment to the family, in terms of both personal involvement and his willingness to share his meager financial resources. As I dropped off his first payment for the journaling assignment, he asked me to take him to the grocery store. "All I have is this," he said, pulling out the $25 from the assignment. Tamika handed him a list, which she asked me to help him with. "He doesn't know how to shop," she said, and I figured she was exaggerating. I went through each of the items with her, making sure that I knew exactly what she wanted. The list included two cucumbers, two lemons, mayonnaise ("if you can"), a bag of baking potatoes, honey turkey, white American cheese slices, chicken wings, fruit ("if you want to get nasty—lol"), eggs, a half gallon of milk. At Pathmark on Aramingo Avenue, we were able to get everything on the list except for chips and soda, which were in a separate part of the list titled "if you have enuf." We did not. We had spent exactly $24.26. "Why do women always want to spend other people's money?" Isaiah wondered aloud. "Tamika has plenty of money." "Where does she work?" I asked, curious. "She doesn't." Tamika stayed home with Darius and kept house. In the past, she had worked at a record store and had been prosecuted for taking money from the till. Since then, she explained, she couldn't get work in retail again. She looked for work intermittently and occasionally talked about college, but she saw running the house as her primary responsibility.

Looking for Work

A security job that Isaiah wanted had not come through yet, so I took him and his good friend, Eddie (the college-bound Mountain Ridge graduate whom I was also following) to Citizens Bank Park, where

Isaiah's PO had said there was going to be a job fair that day. Although most of the businesses were advertising for jobs that required a college degree, they ran into Eddie's neighbor, who directed them to apply for maintenance jobs at the park. Within a couple of weeks, they both were doing cleanup after games.

Now that Isaiah was employed, he seemed to be on more solid ground. He started attending classes at Community College of Philadelphia and moved into Tamika's house. As a sign of devotion, he got a tattoo of her name in script on his chest. Throughout August and September, they were thriving financially, having enough money to take the kids to Dave and Busters (a family entertainment center), to go bowling, and to go out to dinner several times. When Tamika got her assistance check at the beginning of the month, the fridge was full and the household celebrated the abundance. She spent whole days cooking for the family and sometimes made extra cash by selling trays overflowing with delicious comfort foods like fried chicken and macaroni and cheese. Everyone in the house had little treats she had purchased just for them.

Signs of trouble continued, however. Isaiah stayed out all night without calling, claiming later that he had been asked to stay at work late. Another woman called the house, telling Tamika that she was having Isaiah's baby, which seemed to be disproved later. When Tamika accused him of cheating on her, Isaiah's temper flared quickly and he took his anger out on the new TV stand. The next time I visited, the TV had returned to its original spot on the floor.

One day in late September, Isaiah and I met under the El tracks on Girard Avenue, near my house. He was running late because he and Tamika had gotten into another nasty argument right before he left. He seemed despondent and for the first time talked openly about returning to drug selling. I had my suspicions, based on some small lies that he had recently told me, that he already was. We sat at McDonald's and, as he dipped his French fries in barbecue sauce, he opened up to me about the stress of living with Tamika.

He explained that she had just opened a $124 bill from the phone company and was really stressed out because she was behind on bills. The situation had been made worse because Isaiah had quit his job the week before after a confrontation with his boss over his paycheck.

They argued about who was responsible for the bills. "I'm going to school. What are you doing?" he had asked accusingly. "I take care of the house!" she had retorted. "The house is taken care of. You need to start working!" he had said.

Isaiah felt trapped; his aunt had since told him that he was not welcome to move back in with her, and he had nowhere else to go. "She has all the power," he said. "You work so hard for something and then you realize you don't even want it any more. All I wanted was to come home and to live with my girlfriend. I thought that was going to be the best thing in the world. I can never do right by her. There's always something she's criticizing me for," he said. That day's argument was about Darius, an ongoing source of tension. Tamika had asked Isaiah to take him with her, but he refused. The weight of the world was pressing down on him. "Sometimes I just think it would be simpler to go back to selling drugs," he said. "It's just so easy. I could talk to someone and get them to front me the money. Get a big bag and bring it home, separate it into little bags, get someone to move it out on the street, give them a little for it. It's just so easy." Within a few weeks, I suspected he had resorted to exactly that.

Another Baby on the Way

Despite these setbacks, Isaiah and Tamika pressed forward as a couple. They spoke of getting engaged, and Isaiah began regularly referring to Tamika as his "wife." In October, Tamika and Isaiah learned that they were expecting another child, Tamika's third. "Congratulations!" I said, but Isaiah seemed a little less than enthusiastic. I wondered what the new baby would mean for his college career. Within a couple of weeks, he phoned me at home, asking if I had any bus tokens. He had missed school for several days, he said, because he did not have a way to get there. This sounded like rationalizing to me. Tamika confirmed this later when she explained, "He just had too much on his plate, with the baby coming."

During the first few months of the pregnancy, Tamika and Isaiah seemed to be working well together as a family. He got the job as a security guard and the couple began preparations for the baby. Isaiah went on a shopping spree, spending over a thousand dollars on clothing and shoes for each member of their family. He had discovered he could use his debit card as a MasterCard, not caring that it would ruin his credit.

Thanksgiving was a festive occasion. Tamika was cooking up a storm, preparing her first turkey. She seemed very happy in the barefoot and pregnant role. They had an abundance of food for the holiday.

A month later, at Christmas, they were broke. Their phones had been shut off, and Tamika worried aloud about keeping the heat on. They had not purchased a tree or any presents. "It's better to have no Christmas in a home than have a Christmas in a shelter," she said wisely. She and Isaiah were getting along well on Christmas Day, though she reported that she had just come back from staying with her sister for a few days after they had gotten into a fight. When I got ready to leave that evening, Tamika walked me out to my car, confiding that Isaiah had "put his hands" on her. "Wow, Tamika. As much as I love Isaiah, this is not something you can tolerate." "I know, that's what everyone says to me," she said, shivering in the cold.

The baby was born ten weeks prematurely, in mid-March, and had to stay at the hospital for an extended period until he was healthy enough to go home with Tamika and Isaiah. Since I saw them at Christmas, they had broken up, supposedly "for good," reunited, and gotten engaged. In the months after Baby David was born, things seemed to be going smoothly. On a trip to the hospital to visit him in the NICU, I commented, "It seems like you and Isaiah are getting along well." "Yeah! We haven't had one fight since the baby!" she said, sounding surprised. "Wow, how long do you think that will last?" I asked. "I don't know, but I keep telling Isaiah if it's not broke, don't fix it. We have our ups and downs, like any relationship. But we both want control and we butt heads. We work against each other instead of coming together as a family," she said, gesturing first with fists butting and then with interlaced fingers. She explained that Darius's godfather was giving them a break for the whole week by taking Darius off their hands. That was allowing them to spend lots of time together; now that she was no longer pregnant, she could go out drinking with him again.

Tamika and Isaiah were both actively searching for jobs. "Don't tell him I told you this, but he got fired," she said, explaining that he had been reprimanded for lateness on several occasions. She discouraged him from looking for low-level work, saying he would be miserable and, with "some college," he should be able to get something better. Meanwhile, she was hoping to get a job with the city that offered security and benefits.

A month later, over dinner at my house, Isaiah admitted that he had returned to drug selling. He was a "silent partner" in an ongoing drug business, providing up-front money and taking a cut of the profits. During his confession, Tamika made eye contact with me and covered her mouth with her napkin. She did not seem surprised, but she clearly disapproved. I knew that she viewed her housing as easily compromised by Isaiah's illegal activity, as well as his mere presence in the house. She called me the next morning to say he had hit her in the face as they were on their way home from dinner.

Tamika

Tamika was an extremely intelligent young woman who was highly motivated to make a better life for her family than she had as a child. Childbearing and childrearing were central to her self-concept as a nurturer and allowed her to demonstrate competence as a mother, although outsiders might view her as having failed in other domains.[23] There was no denying her ability to care for and discipline her children. I also always had a sense that Tamika knew how to get things done. She had found a women's shelter, gotten a nice house in a safe neighborhood through Section 8, and sought out free couples' counseling for herself and Isaiah. An excerpt from my field notes about a visit to the NICU demonstrates this quality even more clearly.

> Tamika directed me to the guest sign-in sheet, clearly enjoying her sense of familiarity with the place and being my guide. We took the elevator up to the third floor and wound our way around to the NICU. She directed me to two wash basins just outside the NICU and handed me a package containing a sponge with antibacterial soap inside. "Can you buzz me in?" she asked the person behind the Plexiglass. David was just inside, in a clear plastic bed with plastic tenting over him. He was so small and his skin was shriveled and dry; he reminded me of ET. He had a sign over his bed with his birth date and name, his birth weight and "25 weeks" in large print. "Look, he's got Isaiah's nose!" she said. "He sure does," I said, thinking he looked more like a shriveled old man. "You can hold his hand," she said, reaching under the tent and placing her finger inside his tiny hand.

"Excuse me," Tamika said to one of the staff who was passing by. "Can you get my baby's nurse for me?" The nurse, Megan, answered all of Tamika's questions and demands kindly. "How has he been today?" Tamika asked, acting much older than her nineteen years. "He's been good. No problems," Megan said. "Is he still taking 1 cc every 6 hours?" Tamika asked. "No, the doctors took him off food for the day because his stomach was sticking out a little bit more than normal. We did a CAT scan and it wasn't anything but air," Megan explained. "That's because someone gave him formula yesterday even though I didn't want him to have anything but breast milk," Tamika replied firmly. "It gave him gas because he was switched to formula." Megan nodded, not wanting to disagree with Tamika. "Is he crying much?" Tamika asked. "No, he seems content," Megan said.

The way that Tamika spoke with Megan was fascinating. Like a very rich person speaking with a waiter in a fancy restaurant, Tamika felt entitled to good service from the nurses in NICU. Megan seemed very deferential. "Did you bring milk?" she asked, nodding toward the plastic bag filled with bottles. "Yeah, I need some labels though," Tamika said, not looking up or away from the baby as she spoke. Megan nodded and disappeared, returning later with labels.

We were approached by a middle-aged white woman with salt and pepper hair and dangly earrings that made me think of an aging hippie. "Hi!" she said brightly, introducing herself as the lactation specialist. I sat down to avoid being in their way and Tamika resumed touching David's hands and feet, barely acknowledging the woman. Tamika was clearly proud of how much she had been pumping and the lactation specialist seemed to think it was too much. "All he needs is 35 ccs a day and you're pumping up to twice that much. Can you slow down?" she asked. "This is my third [child]," Tamika said authoritatively. "I've always pumped that much milk." The woman pressed on, careful not to offend Tamika. "Wow, I've never met anyone who's pumped that much!" Tamika explained that she didn't want to slow down because she wanted to have enough for the baby when he came home from the hospital and because she thought pumping would make her "uterus go down" (get less swollen) sooner.

"Excuse me, Megan," Tamika interrupted. "His mouth is getting really foamy," she said. Megan came over and looked at David, explaining that he was mouth breathing and it was making his feeding tube foam up. "Can you wipe it off?" Tamika asked, not wanting her baby to look bad. "He's got donut mouth," she said to me. I laughed. Megan came back with a moist towelette and attempted to wipe his mouth, but explained that his lips were so delicate, she was afraid that wiping the foam away might take some of his skin off.

We said goodbye to little David and collected our coats. The lactation specialist came out of the front office area with Tamika's file, asking about her insurance information. "You said you were Keystone, right? This says [some other company]." "It's wrong. I'm Keystone," Tamika said a little sharply. "Oh, I believe you," the woman assured. "I just wonder why it's in here wrong." "I don't know. The social worker asked the same question," Tamika said, softening a bit. I noticed that at no point did she thank any of the staff who had helped her.

Isaiah wavered between pride in Tamika's strength of personality and role as a good mother and frustration at how it undercut his authority and ability to make independent choices. Even when Isaiah was regularly bringing in a paycheck, it was clear to everyone that Tamika was the head of the household. Tamika viewed Isaiah as immature, as unwilling to make the sacrifices necessary to be a good father. Isaiah only felt like a man on the rare occasions when Tamika recognized him as one, and when he spent time with his male peer group, drinking and "coming at" girls. Torn between wanting to be an involved father and to build the happy family he never had and craving the freedom that seemed natural for any nineteen-year-old, Isaiah often felt emasculated and angry. Lashing out in violence against Tamika temporarily leveled the playing field, until she again reminded him of his place by kicking him out of her house or calling the police (well within her rights as a domestic abuse victim). This struggle for power and control over the family, also visible in Sincere and Marta's story, characterizes many romantic relationships among the young men in my study, leaving them vulnerable to dissolution, continued violence, and the male's involvement in the underground economy.

The Beginning of the End

In summer 2006, Tamika got a job as a camp counselor with the city's Department of Recreation and left for a five-week stint in the center of the state. She left Isaiah with a sizeable sum of money and careful instructions about how to care for the kids. "You don't need to take them to McDonald's every day. You can get some spaghetti, get some ground meat. You can make it work." Within two weeks, however, she felt compelled to return home, giving up her position because he was not taking good care of the kids. On one occasion, he admitted to leaving them with a thirteen-year-old neighbor whom Tamika did not know. On another, he drove around in their car with them, visiting friends until two o'clock in the morning.

Many of their struggles that summer surrounded the car they had recently purchased together. Tamika had bought the car with her own money, but they registered it in Isaiah's name because she was not eligible for auto insurance. They constantly fought over whose car it was and how it should be used. One mid-July night, Isaiah returned home late after joyriding with his buddies. As he pulled up to the curb outside their house, she flew outside, jumped on the hood, and started attacking the car, ripping the windshield wipers off in frustration. In response, he assaulted her and was arrested for domestic violence. She filed a restraining order soon after.

At the time I left Philadelphia, Isaiah and Tamika had another child together and reconciled for several months, though they continued to live apart. During that period, he worked with his father in the center of the state, clearing trees for cell phone towers. While he was gone, she discovered that he was expecting a child with another woman who lived around the corner from Tamika. "On top of lying to me, he must've slept in my bed with this other girl while I was working," she said. Nevertheless, with a one-year-old, a two-year-old, and a five-year-old at home, she was hesitant to cut him loose. As his lies and violence continued, she eventually left him and moved to Atlanta, where they could afford a bigger house and her children could attend better schools.

FAMILY AND FATHERHOOD AS A TURNING POINT?

Sincere and Isaiah's experiences have much in common. Although family and fatherhood were central to their identities, neither could say that he had lived up to his own or others' standards of fatherhood or romantic partnership. Despite having a sincere desire to build a family and to compensate for a lack of love provided by their own fathers, both chafed at the expectation of monogamy and fathered children by other women after their return to Philadelphia. Perhaps most notably, both resorted to physical violence during altercations with their partners.

The trajectories of their relationships are characterized by chronic infidelity and subsequent lack of trust, a reaffirmation of commitment shortly after the birth of a child, and an eventual unraveling of the romantic relationship and their involvement with children.[24] These relationships can best be described as a struggle for power.[25] The women's control stems from the regular income they receive from public assistance and their tenancy of the home. When Sincere or Isaiah disappointed or angered their partners, their living privileges were revoked and their partner's authority reinforced. Without steady employment, these young men did not have the social capital to exercise more power in their relationships. With their manhood threatened, they attempted to reassert themselves physically.

Sincere and Isaiah's cases illuminate and complicate the relationship between family and reoffending among formerly incarcerated young men.[26] Their ties to their children and babies' mothers have served both as a push away from and as a pull toward the underground economy. Neither returned to regularly using the "street corner" model of hustling. Sincere "dibbed and dabbed," selling small amounts of marijuana or cocaine and putting interested buyers and sellers in contact with one another for a small "finder's fee" (usually marijuana for personal use). More seriously, when an opportunity presented itself to help fence stolen guns, he located willing buyers and received a gun for his effort. Nevertheless, he continued to be cognizant of the consequences of his hustles for his new family, minimizing his involvement wherever possible to reduce the risk of arrest.[27] Isaiah earned more consistent income from drug selling, but also diminished his risk by serving as a "silent partner" in an ongoing business. Both young men turned to the underground economy to construct a sense of manhood that they failed to find either in the labor market or, finally, in the family. Their movement back and forth between these two worlds made their success in either domain unlikely.

Gender dynamics in inner-city neighborhoods are profoundly affected by the scarcity of "good" men: those who fulfill their obligations as fathers or support the family financially. This scarcity is compounded by the mass removal of men from poor African American communities through imprisonment.[28] In these impoverished communities, marriage is significantly less common, children are more likely to be born and raised outside of a marital union, and relationships with partners who are themselves engaged in criminal activities are more prevalent than in the U.S. population as a whole.[29] Although romantic relationships and fatherhood have been identified as potential turning points that help move young men away from criminal offending,[30] there is good reason to believe that former offenders who return to inner-city neighborhoods are unlikely to develop enough stability in either domain to facilitate falling back.

CHAPTER 7

"I'm Finally Becoming the Person
I Always Wanted to Be"

MASCULINE IDENTITY, SOCIAL
SUPPORT, AND FALLING BACK

THE YOUNG MEN WHOSE stories have been told thus far occupied marginal roles in relation to the labor market and the family, two important social institutions that are often thought to promote law-abiding behavior. Any sense of masculine identity these men earned by working or by being an involved father and a romantic partner was hard-won and easily lost. In this chapter, I focus on James and Gabe, the only two young men who fell back, becoming stable, law-abiding adults. Both returned to Southwest Philadelphia, a zone of exceptional violence, but they found decent jobs and continued close relationships with significant others. At the same time, their stories are a contrast in how resilience is built and maintained. James carried on an active, conscious struggle to change his trajectory after his stint at Mountain Ridge. Gabe, in contrast, encountered few challenges to falling back. At first glance, Gabe's life looks like a case study in deterrence; after being incarcerated for selling drugs, he was determined never to have his freedom taken away again. Upon closer inspection, however, masculine identity was also important to Gabe's process of "aging out" of delinquency. He viewed Mountain Ridge Academy, especially the emasculating experience of having "another dude" get in his face to give him "feedback," as inconsistent with his self-concept as a man. For both James and Gabe, social ties to meaningful people allowed them to develop law-abiding masculine identities. Just deciding that they wanted to be new people was not enough.

Internal, identity-oriented change relied heavily on external support from others.

JAMES'S STORY

James's catalyst for falling back was his daughter, Maya. After being on the run from the police for six months, James finally decided to turn himself in one month before his eighteenth birthday, just before the deadline when he would have faced the adult court system. Unable to get an on-the-books job or complete his education because of the outstanding arrest warrant, James had been doing day labor on a construction site with his cousin when he decided to "get this [legal problem] out of the way" and return to Philadelphia to be with Maya.

James missed Maya's first and second birthdays while incarcerated at Mountain Ridge. He dreamed of being able to take her to a toy store and buy her anything she pointed to, adding that Dora the Explorer was her current favorite. As his release date neared, James became increasingly frustrated with his counselor's seemingly contradictory expectations. Sitting in one of the tiny, fluorescent back offices in the administration building, James demonstrated a surprising amount of trust at our second meeting. Visibly relieved to be able to speak his mind, he said, "I'm thinking about stopping my clinical work because it doesn't seem to get me anywhere. The more I try, the harder things get. If they point out a problem, I fix it. When I fix it, they say they need to see consistency. If I'm consistent, they point out a new problem. I just don't know what to do."

In order to earn release, James needed to demonstrate his willingness and ability to recognize and amend the "thinking errors" identified by his counselor. Because so many of the program's residents "fake it to make it," each must consistently comply with the facility's code of conduct and pass through therapeutic steps in individual and group counseling sessions. Behavioral compliance with rules and progress in clinical treatment are conceptually intertwined in such a way that program staff view small infractions as evidence of a lack of commitment to going straight. During this interview, James reported that he felt he could no longer talk to his counselor, Richard, after he accused James of stepping out of his dorm lineup and lying about it later. "I tell the truth about so much," James declared, "why would I lie about stepping out of line?" Since then, James felt that he did not want to say anything, since "I'm a liar anyway."

His final few months at Mountain Ridge made James feel helpless and bitter at feeling that his fate was out of his hands. His probation officer, who had promised to schedule a review hearing at the beginning of the year, was fired for drinking on the job. Her supervisor took over James's case, but failed to recommend his release because "she didn't know me from a can of paint." Rumors began to fly at the cafeteria tables, where residents commonly shared information about probation officers and reintegration workers. The word on the street was that the replacement PO was a "hard-ass" and would not be recommending releases for anyone on her caseload.

As spring settled in, the boys on campus collectively began to rebel in small ways, chafing at the staff's strict control over their speech and movement. Their letters suggested frustration at the situation inside Mountain Ridge and little information about important events such as court hearings, often held in absentia. About six weeks before his release in April 2005, James reported in a letter that he and the others were in a campus-wide "slow down" and that most of the small freedoms and privileges they had enjoyed had been suspended until the staff felt their behavior was under better control.

> Jamie,
>
> I received your letter today. To answer your question . . . yes everything is boring on campus. We're still on slow down. Got to play the hand I de[a]lt though. Right? Things'll get better sooner or later. But me, I've been falling back. I haven't been letting these dudes get under my skin.
>
> What's going on with my case, well my next court date is [in April]. My PO said they're thinking about pulling me. The only reason they haven't yet is because they want to make sure I got all I can get out of this place. I'm doing good. I hope by then they are convinced that I am ready to go home. Only time can tell and I got plenty of it.
>
> I'll understand if I don't see you anytime soon. Time is money and money is time and they're not giving you enough of either one. But I'm happy your study is coming along for you.

Let me know how your trip went. When I get home, I'm
never leaving the city again. :) I'll holla at you. . . .

James 2.22.05

Coming Home

James was discharged at the April hearing, and I walked past him in
the waiting room outside J-Court without recognizing him. He called
my name and grabbed my arm, and I greeted him with a hug, com-
menting that I had not recognized him because he was not wearing
the angry scowl I always saw on his face during my visits to Mountain
Ridge. There, in the chaotic and cavernous rooms inside Family Court,
he looked like a normal, happy kid. I noticed, not for the first time, that
he had a remarkable smile and an open, approachable face. He was there
with his Uncle Clifton, a heavy-set man in his mid-thirties, who told
me that James was living with him in Southwest Philly. Clifton appeared
before the juvenile master during his discharge hearing, agreeing to all
the terms of James's release. He reminded me of a social worker, or one of
those traditional "old heads" who were mentors and unofficial caseworkers in their communities.

Clifton's house was in the heart of Southwest Philly, on a small block
just off the major commercial strip of Woodland Avenue. Woodland is
dotted with check-cashing places, takeout restaurants, clothing stores
stocking "urban" labels such as State Property and Rocawear, and African
hair-weaving shops (a likely reflection of the recent influx of African
immigrants to the neighborhood). Turning onto Royale Street, my tires
rolled over broken bottles and other refuse lining the gutters. The houses
were small and shabby, many with cracked concrete stairs leading up to
weather-beaten front doors. Clifton's house stood out because of the
well-used gas grill outside and a rather ornate, white wrought-iron safety
door he had installed to prevent break-ins. James advised me to park
closer to the corner store if I wanted my car to be there when I came
back outside. Even residents of other neighborhoods with rough reputa-
tions, such as Cobbs Creek and Kensington, were wary of this area.

Armed with references from Clifton and me, James set out to get a
job. He returned to Philadelphia owing a $600 debt to a drug dealer in
his neighborhood and was determined to begin paying him back. "I see it

as an investment so I don't have to constantly look over my shoulder," he told me. Three days after his release, he got a job as a fry cook at Popeye's not far from Clifton's house. With the start-up money that Clifton had given him, James bought new clothes, which he wore on the trolley to and from work. "I don't like wearing my work clothes, because everyone on the trolley be lookin' at me," he explained. Working at a low-wage service job commonly invites scorn and public comments that the man must be a "sucka."[1]

During his time off, James tried to spend as much time with Maya as possible, but it did not take long for BMD (baby mama drama) to begin. He and Maya's mother were no longer romantically involved, and she was often jealous when she heard rumors of James talking to other girls. She attempted to assert control by leaving Maya with James long after she was supposed to pick her up or by picking her up suddenly and without explanation. He considered filing custody papers, but was put off by the filing fees and the trips down to the courthouse that were involved.[2]

Because he resided in a neighborhood the city had identified as high risk for violence, James was transferred to a special, intensive probation at a community-based office called YVRP (Youth Violence Reduction Project). A couple of weeks after his return from Mountain Ridge, James asked me to give him a ride to the probation office to meet with his PO. Accompanying him was his best friend, Dell, a tall, dark-skinned, very quiet young man. As James met with his PO for the first time, Dell and I waited in the lobby, where he shared some of his raps with me. I was no expert, but he seemed really talented; he told me he had done a DVD. James came out the door, smiling broadly. Dell looked up at James, saying, "I forgot to tell you that I finished 'Trust' while you were locked up." James nodded with interest as Dell performed it outside the probation office. Not to be outdone, James did some rapping too, but finished quickly as we waited for the elevator, clearly excited to tell us his news.

"My PO said that all the felonies are wiped off my record," he said, practically skipping with glee. "All I have is a misdemeanor and as long as I get off probation without any violations, that will be expunged, too," he said, swinging his arms and doing his signature smile. "Now I can get that job at the airport." "Like security or baggage handling?" I asked. He shrugged and said that he was not sure, but the lady up the street told him about it. He waved his arms back and forth and then to the sides, as if he was one of those tarmac guys who directs planes where to go, smile still firmly planted across his face. I laughed. "All I know is it pays $9.50." He never got a job at the airport. This pattern of half-heartedly making plans based on other people's suggestions but never following through is one I have seen with nearly all the young men I studied. This plan making seemed ritualistic, as if they hoped that the mere act of saying it aloud might enact it.

"You Gotta Leave Your Mark on This Earth"

James's friendship with Dell was the first and most pronounced instance I found of *generativity*, a concern with helping others, usually those who are younger. According to the psychologist Erik Erikson, generativity is a developmental task of adulthood that can be achieved only after the tasks of earlier stages, such as trust, autonomy, initiative, industry, identity, and intimacy, have been met.[3] Criminologist Shadd Maruna adapted Erikson's notion to his study of criminal desistance, noting that helping others or "giving back" is employed explicitly in change regimes such as twelve-step programs because group members believe it is the most effective way to maintain sobriety. Maruna's comparison between current and ex-offenders highlights generativity as a strategy for going straight. Many of his respondents took on the role of "wounded healer" or "professional ex," counseling others in how to succeed. They saw great purpose in saving others, or "even just one," as a way to convince them that their lives were not wasted.[4]

James and I worked together to get Dell into YouthBuild, a paid training program that prepares high school dropouts for jobs in construction. Later, when YouthBuild did not pan out for Dell, James worked to get him a job, giving him money for transportation until his first check came in.

> If you my friend, I wanna see you make it in life, I don't wanna see you deadbeat. Especially if you're gonna be hanging with me, 'cause if you gonna be hanging around me, you're gonna have some impression on my daughter. I mean when you young, you observe stuff like that. If she seen a bunch of drug dealin' and stuff like that going on, that's what she gonna be lookin' for when she get older. She's gonna be lookin' for guys that's sellin' drugs. But if she see a bunch of guys

that's workin', doin' good and they got one female, well, that's what I want in life. That's another reason why I would prefer for all my friends to have some type of job and something to do.

James reached out to help others in innumerable ways: he notified Leo that the pastry shop where he worked briefly was hiring and accompanied him to fill out the application; he prompted his cousin, Manny, to apply for a position at McDonald's as we were eating there together one afternoon; and he volunteered as a coach for a youth basketball league during the summer of 2006. James gave money to Keon, a young man on house arrest whom Clifton had taken in, and gave start-up money to a female friend who had just gotten out of jail. His strategy seemed simple: when those around you are doing well, it is easier to do well yourself. However, these activities also served to support James's narrative as a productive citizen. In addition to viewing himself as a role model as a result of helping others, he hoped they would see him in the same light. With their belief and his own working to reinforce one another, it was easier to fall back and leave the world of hustling behind.

James's generative approach had two other dimensions. The first is his desire to be represented in my book, which he hoped would be used as a manual by others who were trying to fall back. The best evidence of generativity, however, is found in James's relationship with his daughter. In addition to taking pride in his ability to provide for his daughter financially and emotionally, he viewed their relationship as a way to leave a piece of himself behind. He was surprised, almost offended, when I told him that my then husband and I had no plans for children. "You have to leave your mark on this earth. I wouldn't have wanted to be a father this early, but I definitely knew that I wanted to be a father someday," he said. This view echoed that of Sincere, who saw fatherhood as a means of reinventing the self, of "see[ing] a part of me that's never been bad."

"You Find a Struggle Where You Make One"

One of the notable distinctions between James's narrative and those of the other young men who shared their stories with me is his constant talk of self-improvement and his conception of his life as a project of continual, incremental progress. While he described his circumstances and goals, I imagined a treadmill on which he needed to constantly exert

effort to stay in the same place. Relaxing or being complacent meant losing ground. Getting ahead required extra effort.

James conveyed a strong sense of self-efficacy, portraying himself as
having the power to control the events in his life. As Maruna argued,
self-efficacy is a central aspect of the "redemption script" or recovery
story commonly employed by those who are able to go straight. In fact,
he pointed out, this notion of control is often an illusion; ex-offenders
frequently fail to see the structural barriers that prevent their efforts
from bearing fruit. Despite the fact that corrections professionals often
connect "cognitive distortions" to offending behavior, Maruna wisely
noted that a belief that one has control over one's surroundings is actually *more* distorted than the realistic, victim-oriented narratives of persistent offenders.[5]

Several excerpts from conversations, interviews, and journals James
shared after his return from Mountain Ridge attest to his fervent sense of
self-efficacy and his view of himself as a work in progress. When Sincere
was complaining to him about the difficulty of finding a job and getting
along with his baby's mom, he responded, "You find a struggle where you
make one." In his reentry journal in June 2005, he said,

> I still think thinking errors are stupid, but I notice I still use them a
> lot. The most common thinking error I use is uniqueness and perfec-
> tionism. I say that because I try to be better at almost everything I do
> than the next person. Sometimes I can't [accept losing]. Often I use
> uniqueness but I think that's good because it helps me. "I came to[o]
> far and I ain't going backwards for nothing"—that's a line I keep in
> my head to stay focus. I think a lot of people can't relate to me or
> understand what I've been through. Those thoughts motivate me to
> do good because I can't go back. Oh yeah, I'm [conceited] too. What
> can I say? I love the person I became.

Later that month, he reflected, "I gotta work on expressing my feelings
with men. It took me a long time to share anything with [my counselor]
Richard. It's easy to talk to you because you're a woman. I can express
my feelings easier. But I need to work on expressing my feelings with
men, because all my problems are with men. So that's what I learned yesterday. You learn something every day." Toward the end of the summer,

he mused that in the past "I became everything I always said I would never be. I said I would never smoke cigarettes, I would never use drugs, and I would never sell drugs. Now I'm finally becoming the person I always wanted to be." His daughter, Maya, was part of his transformation: "I'm 19 and I'm finally getting it, how important it is to be there for your kids." When James he told Sincere that "you find a struggle where you make one," he meant that obstacles to success should not be used as excuses for lack of progress. When things went badly for James, he saw himself as responsible. After moving out of his mother's house, he said, "I put myself in that situation. There's no one to blame but myself." This view is especially remarkable because he could easily have identified his mother as the primary cause of his setbacks.

James continued to express ambivalence toward the intervention used inside Mountain Ridge Academy, saying that he thought the thinking errors intervention was stupid but noticed that he still made these errors. Many of these young men struggled with conflicting feelings about thinking errors. Inside Mountain Ridge, these were presented as scientific facts that had been proven through research, giving them a false character of objectivity that was difficult to challenge. But this frame for analysis was not always consistent with their personal experiences. Although James admitted that he still thought of himself as unique and as a perfectionist, he viewed these qualities as responsible for his success. In order to make something of himself, he felt, he must strive to view himself as a special person and work to achieve more than those around him.

James *performed* this narrative of self-efficacy widely and persuasively, striving to make his audience buy in to his new image. In Erving Goffman's dramaturgical terms, he created a new definition of the situation and risked losing face if he failed to carry out a successful performance.[6] When an individual makes it clear to others that he is striving for success, he risks public failure and ridicule. Worse still, many of James's peers seemed eager to see him fail. For James, a public show of "doing good" created a level of accountability that would not otherwise exist. When he told Clifton, me, or anyone else in his social network members that he wanted to stop smoking or cursing, he opened the door for us to follow up on his progress. Stating a goal aloud creates an obligation to at least appear to be engaged in change.

James's resilience became particularly visible when his life fell apart. In the fall of 2005, he enrolled in a technical school to earn a certificate in carpentry and construction that required him to travel between his morning classes in Northeast Philly and his job in Southwest Philly. During this time, James calculated that he spent five and a half hours per day on public transportation. "It was like really stressful 'cause I had to wake up at 5:00 in the morning, be out the door by 5:30, on the bus by 5:35 to 5:40. Got to school at 7:00, school started at 7:20, so that gave me exactly 20 minutes to do my homework. Stay at school till 2:30 and then go straight to work at Popeye's. I was always a half hour late for work, and then by the time I got off of work, it was 12. I got home like 1:00, I'd be right back up at five." To me, it seemed inevitable that this arrangement would fall apart, and, of course, it did.

> I wasn't prepared. I was in a no-win situation. You could just look at me, every day I was looking like a zombie and I couldn't stay awake in class, I couldn't stay awake at work. And then when I went home I wasn't really even getting no sleep because I'm arguing with my mom and I'm arguing with my girlfriend. And I was stressing because I wanna see my daughter and my baby mom won't let me see her because I got another girlfriend and she still want me. Like a person only could take like so much in life.

The trigger, however, was not James's demanding schedule but his tenuous relationship with his mother. As part of his treatment at Mountain Ridge, he had been forced to reconcile with his mother, Diane, whom he really did not know. Although Diane did not visit him at the facility, his counselor arranged a series of conference calls to work on repairing their relationship. Shortly before starting trade school, James moved in with her and started helping her pay the bills. Their relationship was fraught with difficulties. After having missed most of her son's childhood, Diane had little idea how to be a mother to a nineteen-year-old. Although she appeared to have kicked her drug habit, she still sold drugs and encouraged James to pick up a packet here and there. He tolerated the pressure for as long as he could. Following a particularly nasty argument in which Diane accused James of stealing her boyfriend's bag of weed (which, it was later discovered, his brother had taken), James left his mother's house with nowhere else to go. His pride kept him from returning to Clifton's house in Southwest Philly, and he lived on the streets for several days. He could not bring himself to go to school because he had not had the opportunity to wash up or change clothes. After three days of absence, the school told him that he was welcome to return the next semester, but he had missed too much material to continue the semester.

When he attempted to re-enroll in the spring, he was no longer on probation. He learned that, without a court referral and the funding stream that accompanied it, the school required financial aid paperwork and a parent's signature. Diane refused to sign, angry with James after their blowup. Eventually James abandoned the idea of returning to school for the short term and attended to more pressing matters. He continued to look back at this period in his life with regret for the lost opportunity at social mobility.

Nevertheless, James took pride in resisting his mother's requests to make quick cash on the streets by selling drugs, viewing his refusal as evidence that he had made some progress. "In all reality it was gonna hurt my daughter more than it hurt her [his mother] 'cause it don't matter if I leave. If I get locked up today or tomorrow, it wouldn't matter to her. Do you think she'll come up there and see me? I didn't get not one visit while I was locked up. It's gonna hurt my daughter more than it's gonna hurt anybody out here, so I don't care what [Diane thinks]. She can hate me, but I feel as though I made the right choice. I got a daughter out here to look out for."

"Everyone Wants a Taste"

Leaving his mother's house and dropping out of school produced a double whammy for James. In the course of a few days, he had failed at his attempts to progress academically and financially and to establish a meaningful relationship with his mother after nineteen years. James realized, however, that his best interests were served by cutting ties to Diane, who appeared to have only her own interests at heart. Abandoning the hope of a mother-son relationship was painful, and he had been taught at Mountain Ridge that family ties are a means to going straight. Here, he directly confronted an instance in which the facility's rhetoric could not have been further from the truth. "She was never part of my life until they forced me to start talking to her when I was at Mountain Ridge. They always think that what they're doing is for the best, but it's not always for the best. I feel more alone now than when I was alone."

Returning to Clifton's house was a visible marker of losing ground. Soon James found a seasonal job as a landscaper in South Jersey and was able to save enough to move out on his own. He shared a basement apartment with a roommate for $200 a month in rent. During this period, he felt somewhat redeemed. When I asked if he was still in touch with Dell, he said no, that he avoided all of the people from his neighborhood. In poor communities, success such as his—even saving enough to live independently—is big news. In the context of a dense network of exchange, those who are doing well are expected to take care of those who are struggling. Spending time with his peers in Southwest Philly meant constantly negotiating requests for "loans," most of which could not realistically be repaid. Success became a lonely endeavor.

Even that small success, however, was short-lived. The landscaping job ended in the fall, and James found himself back at Clifton's looking for work. By winter 2005-2006, James had worked in three different jobs. He left a pastry shop in Center City to return to Popeye's after not getting enough hours there. As he was training for a manager position at Popeye's, he lost his temper with a female employee who challenged his speedy advancement and ended up quitting.

James had a better sense than most of the young men I followed about what was expected of him when job hunting. He was conscious of the difficulties young black men face in encounters with prospective employers and told me that he knew it was necessary to dress and speak properly when dropping off applications and interviewing for positions. For him this meant wearing a collared shirt (typically a short-sleeved polo shirt), jeans or pants that were not too baggy, and clean shoes. He was also conscious of his hair and always eventually invested in a haircut so he could remove his baseball cap indoors. I was impressed by the fact that he kept a pen in his shirt pocket and made a point of letting employers know that he had brought his own if they offered him a pen to complete their paperwork. He managed his speech during interviews so potential employers would not see him as a "thug on the street."

I'm going in front of somebody that doesn't know me from a can of paint, all they know is what I wrote down on a piece of paper. If I go in there talking real crazy, they're gonna look at me like I'm crazy. See, I feel as though I give everybody respect and I want the same respect back. So if I have to change the way I'm speaking for that present moment, I'm gonna change it because of the simple fact I don't want you to look at me as he's just a thug on the street, because I'm not that person. I might look like that, I might dress like that, but I'm not that person. So in order for them to change their opinion about me, I gotta talk differently. Not act differently but talk differently. I just use it more often when I'm in front of people I don't know, whether it's an interview or somebody on the streets I don't know because of the simple fact I don't like to be labeled as a little hoodlum.

Here, James worked to distance himself from the stereotypical view that many employers hold of young black men, but also from his old self as a hustler.

Prescreening employment questionnaires plagued James the most. He repeatedly failed these tests as a direct result of his refusal to lie on them. For instance, the application at Rite Aid asked if he had ever used drugs. James responded truthfully that until two years before he had smoked marijuana regularly and was astounded when they disqualified him for employment because of his honesty. One on hand, he refused to believe that the managers at an inner-city drug store would find *anyone* who did not have a history of drug use; these applications frequently also ask if candidates *know* anyone who uses drugs. On the other hand, if he denied any history of drug use, the managers would surely know he was lying. James insisted that honesty was key to falling back. He equated lying with his past as a hustler. "Lying is what I used to do, along with selling drugs. Now I don't have anything to lie about," he declared. Implicit in this argument is the notion that any job that required him to lie or did not value truthfulness was not the job for him because it was not conducive to his progress in becoming a productive citizen.

James Becomes "a Working Man"

After several months of looking for work and a week stranded during a public transit strike, James got a job as a dishwasher at a Bob Evans restaurant near the airport, about a forty-five-minute bus ride from Clifton's house. Although he felt he had to be hyper-aware of his speech and mannerisms in this mostly white, quasi-suburban environment, James enjoyed working there. He joked around with his supervisor, Winston, and the other members of the kitchen staff. After several months of regular, on-time attendance and showing initiative on the job, he was promoted to a line cook position.

James flourished at Bob Evans. During the year he worked there, he was a fixture, even on his days off. When I asked him where he wanted to go to lunch one afternoon, he asked to go to Bob Evans to show me how much a part of the place he had become. "Are you here again?" joked Winston as he seated us. "Don't you ever go home?" James smiled broadly. During this lunch I realized how central to his identity work had become. Here, finally, he had achieved a measure of success. He had been promoted, was given multiple raises, and outlasted scores of other employees. More important, he had found a group of peers who knew him as a working man and an involved father and who were not familiar with his history as a hustler.

In addition to Winston, the manager, one of the key members of this new audience was his new girlfriend, Ashley. Ashley was attending a nearby college and held down two jobs to put herself through school. James had never dated a "productive citizen" before, a woman who was striving to make something of herself. They provided one another with important support. He encouraged her to attend her classes, even when she was tired from working, and she refused to let him smoke cigarettes around her. As we were having lunch at Bob Evans that day, he phoned her and asked if she would like a takeout meal. We delivered it to her dorm, and I left him there to spend some time with her.

James's relationships with his old networks, however, were still complicated. As long as James was bringing in regular income, his baby's mom was satisfied to let him see Maya. However, she had filed for child support, which angered him because he provided his daughter with even more than the weekly $55 mandated by the court. He had repaired his relationship with Dell following Dell's arrest for involvement in a cocaine ring and had gotten him a job at Bob Evans. As long as Dell was on the right track, James maintained contact. It is significant, however, that he sought to redefine their relationship in a place where others knew James to be a hardworking and dependable person.

James's relationship with Diane remained fraught with drama. They had reconciled at a family member's wedding, and he worked to repair their relationship while dividing his time between Clifton's and his mother's house. One day Diane's boyfriend, Tiny, commented that James was always welcome there, even if his mother "didn't fuck with you like that [did not bother with him or care about him]." Shocked and hurt, James disappeared for several days, hoping she would call around and show some concern. When she did not, he moved out for good. As I helped him remove his belongings from her house, she left numerous messages on my cell phone threatening to call the police to report that we were stealing her things. When James left his cell phone by mistake, she gave it to Tiny.

James's repeated attempts to reconcile with his mother resulted in a loss of progress each time. During his first stay with her, he dropped out of technical school. During another three-week stay in her basement, for which she charged him $100 per week, he lost his job as a result of calling out from work too many days. "One day, she wanted me to stay home because my brother was coming home on house arrest. The next day, she asked me to stay home and wait for the phone guy. The next day, I had to stay and wait for the gas repair guy. The people at the check cashing place just said they didn't need me anymore." While it seemed obvious to me that missing work repeatedly would put his job at risk, I believe he did it in the hopes that his mother would finally accept him. Eventually, despite the pain of giving up on his mother, James eventually concluded that her refusal to see him as a different person, from both what he was before and what she and his siblings were, made it impossible for him to meet his goal of becoming a productive citizen.

Unlike his mother, Clifton had only James's best interests in mind. The older man carefully monitored his behavior for any signs of slipping back into his old ways. Clifton scrutinized his phone calls, the amount of time he spent on the corner, and his friends. Moreover, he ruled his home with a demand for strict adherence to rules, especially that there were to be no guests when Clifton was not home to supervise them. In Clifton's experience, things had a habit of disappearing when friends were left alone in his house. James chafed under this degree of supervision, saying he was no longer comfortable staying with Clifton and was hoping his tax return would cover the deposit on an apartment of his own. In the meantime, he stayed at work late, hoping to reduce contact with his uncle.

James's relationship with Clifton was probably the most central to his identity, as he was the closest thing James had to a father. James had lived with Clifton since he was nine, after the uncle he was living with died of AIDS-related complications. Clifton was above all things a working man. He owned his home and took obvious pride in it. He also possessed a strong sense of generativity, providing shelter to various members of the extended family who had been in trouble with the law. In his role as an old head, he saw himself as responsible for James's moral upbringing, attempting several times to get his nephew to accompany him to church, and for his safety. During bouts of unemployment, Clifton paid James $25 here and there for running errands and cleaning his house. He also provided transportation to and from James's work when he could.

Clifton was more concerned with being respected than being liked. When James broke his rules, Clifton let it be known by bellowing from his bedroom upstairs. Much to James's chagrin, he also asked the neighbors to report what James was up to when he spent time on the corner. In this way, Clifton and James's relationship was similar to one between a parent and an adolescent as the child struggles to assert his autonomy. But James was twenty and viewed himself as an adult. The more he was accepted as legitimate by his girlfriend and the other employees at Bob Evans, the more frustrated he became with Clifton's refusal to acknowledge that he was both a changed person and a man.

Clifton continually questioned James's commitment to falling back after his return from Mountain Ridge. He did this with good reason, as during his time as a hustler James had lied and betrayed his uncle's trust. Clifton shouldered the responsibility of bailing James out when he was arrested and supporting him financially when he was not working regularly. In sum, the personal cost of extending trust and being wrong was high.

James and Clifton had fewer conflicts when James was stably employed, which reduced the amount of free time over which Clifton felt he needed to exert control as well as minimizing their contact around the house. When James brought in a regular paycheck, he paid Clifton's cable bill and was allowed to bring Maya there to care for her. When he was between jobs, however, he spent time hanging on the corner with friends. Any money in his pocket was a source of suspicion. Clifton worried that it was only a matter of time until the negative influences in the neighborhood began to wear down James's resolve to leave hustling behind.

Clifton's suspicions provoked especially strong reactions in James when he viewed himself as working and "doing what he needed to do" to take care of his financial responsibilities. Several months after his return to Philadelphia, while James was holding down two jobs, they battled over some weed Clifton found in James's room. The following is an excerpt from my field notes.

> The day that we had gone to Youth Build, Dell had given him some bags to hold and Clifton had found them in his room. He said that he was in there looking for the iron, but James knew that was a lie because the bags had been hidden. He must have gone in there with the intention of snooping. James continued, saying that it had gotten back to him that Clifton was asking his friends if he was hustling again. "If he wants to know if I'm hustling again, why doesn't he ask me? No one cared when I was hustling, but now that I'm doing what I got to do, he's accusing me of hustling. If I was hustling, he wouldn't know about it, but I've come too far, and I'm not going back. I've got too much to look forward to. But he doesn't trust me, and it makes me want to get out of this house."

Over time, Clifton grew to trust James more and they had fewer conflicts.[7]

James eventually cut his ties to Dell, who became deeply involved in crime and violence after leaving Bob Evans. James maintained contact while Dell was looking for work, but when he was busted for coke they lost touch. Since Dell chose to cut his electronic monitoring bracelet and go on the run, James gave up on him. Dell's refusal to build on James's attempts to help him suggested that he did not appreciate James's role as a "wounded healer."

Despite the fact that the employees and management at his jobs did not remain part of his social network after he left, they were important in supporting his sense of self as a working man. During periods of unemployment James floundered, with no routine or sense of direction. He began to lose faith in himself and seemed almost panicked about slipping backward into his old life. He was hospitalized twice during these periods for chest pains and seizures. During those times he needed the most encouragement from Clifton and other members of his network.

I would be remiss if I did not mention that I became a stable and meaningful supporter for James, as well as many of the other young men I followed. My belief in his ability to achieve his dreams carried a special weight with him because I represented a connection to the mainstream world. Moreover, I put him into contact with other audiences for which he was able to perform and from which he received affirmation.

James, Sincere, and Isaiah served as guest speakers in my classes at the University of Pennsylvania, as well as for various professors in the Criminal Justice Department at Temple University. Because James was the only one who could honestly make a claim to falling back since his return from Mountain Ridge, he received an overwhelming amount of encouragement from the students. Many came up afterward to shake his hand and tell him not to give up, and others offered to connect him to publishers for his raps or resources for scholarships. A family friend gave him a part-time position as a mentor at an after-school program for high school students in one of the most disadvantaged neighborhoods in Philadelphia. These were rare opportunities to feel a sense of accomplishment and to be accepted in the world of highly educated, high-achieving adults. Although James was known for his smile, he never smiled so widely as when he received this sort of affirmation. It was absolutely critical to receive this sort of audience feedback for him to maintain his identity and continue his performance as someone who was making good.

Although James solicited more concrete assistance from me in terms of social capital and financial assistance than did the other young men I followed, I served as an audience member in much the same way for the others. I never discouraged them as they shared their goals and dreams with me, no matter how unrealistic they seemed at the time, and I did not point out the instances in which they failed to live up to their own expectations.

Probably the most profound impact on James's sense of self came from my extension of trust toward him. In his other relationships, where there was a history of lying and betrayal, he needed to earn trust back. However, my policy with all of the young men I studied was to offer trust until it was violated. That meant taking some risks, such as allowing James to go into my purse for money or matches or giving him my car keys so he could go outside and use the car lighter. He demonstrated time and again that he could be trusted, and that trust held great currency with James and the others. When they came together in my presence, I often heard them make competing claims about who had been extended the greatest degree of trust and intimacy.

"Still a Hustla"

James left Bob Evans after they cut his hours so drastically that he was no longer able to pay for transportation to get to work. After a year's tenure there, he felt betrayed and unappreciated by Winston and the other managers. Subsequently, he worked as a chef in two other food chains and briefly as a cashier at a check-cashing store. At the time I was wrapping up my field research in spring 2008, he was looking for work again and going to trade school in a two-year program to learn computer repair.

His story illuminates some of the tangled issues involved in how people move out of criminal careers, particularly when they occupy a stratum of society in which mobility is limited and respectability is hard to come by. For James, succeeding in being a productive citizen was a daily struggle. His determination and remarkable degree of self-efficacy as well as his commitment to "lifting as he climbs" (to use an old black feminist phrase) lend support to Shadd Maruna's theory that desistance is an ongoing maintenance of nonoffending achieved through the development of a self-narrative supporting change.

James told me, "I'm still a hustla, I just changed up my hustle," which fits well with Maruna's characterization of the redemption script as a way to make good. When he says he is still a hustler, he maintains the consistency of his narrative. Instead of "knifing off" his bad past, he "rewrite[s] a shameful past into a necessary prelude to a productive and worthy life."[8] Creating a law-abiding identity and narrative, according to Maruna, means reconstructing the self, not leaving the "old self" behind. James was still a "hustla" because his survival was still a daily struggle, and he was committed to using every legally acceptable resource available to him to make it.

James's narrative also had an important *social* character. His personal identity was not merely constructed, but performed with a particular audience in mind. He worked diligently to develop new social networks when those in his old peer networks refused to believe that he had "changed up his hustle." At the workplace, where coworkers viewed him as a working man and an involved father, he could reaffirm these roles. When his portrayal of himself and others' reflection of their belief in his performance were congruent, his belief in his own performance grew stronger. Sociologist Charles Horton Cooley summed up this phenomenon of the "looking glass self." "As we see our face, figure, and dress in the glass, and are interested in them because they are ours, and pleased or otherwise with them according as they do or do not answer to what we should like them to be; so in imagination we perceive in another's mind some thought of our appearance, manners, aims, deeds, character, friends, and so on, and are variously affected by it."[9]

The significance of audience speaks to the function of social ties, which is emphasized in the age-graded theory of informal social control of criminologists Robert Sampson and John Laub.[10] The authors argued that desistance is achieved through a strengthening of bonds to legitimate others, such as employers and spouses. Informal social control and cognitive conceptions of desistance often are presented as competing. In one, the driving force is external, whereas the other emphasizes internal processes. In James's story, however, the two came together in a way that made it difficult to determine the primacy of one over the other.

James's devotion to his daughter was deeply rooted in his desire to be a good father and to be accepted by others as fulfilling that role. His commitment to steady work stemmed from both financial necessity and a need to surround himself with others who viewed him as a working man. Social ties are more than a "hook for change"; they are critical to the maintenance of a consistent personal narrative, especially after a significant change.[11] Once James successfully constructed a legitimate, respectable self, offending was no longer a potential course of action. It was not among the repertoire of responses that James used to meet his daily obligations, even when trouble arose.

Gabe's Story

Gabe, who was released from Mountain Ridge Academy when he was eighteen years old, had a reentry experience that could not have been more different from James's trajectory. While James's life was filled with constant upheaval and complete uncertainty from one day to the next about employment, custody of Maya, his relationship with his Uncle Clifton, and where he would lay his head that night, Gabe's return to the city was marked by stability in nearly every important domain. He was the only study participant who had grown up in a house with two parents, Beverly and Gabe Senior, who had been married for thirty-four years. Beverly worked at Prudential Financial in the northern suburbs; it took her almost two hours each way to travel there and back each day. "My friends don't understand why I commute all that way, but I couldn't make that much income working in the city," she told me. "After a while, you get used to it." Gabe's father worked at a large city cemetery before falling ill and being unable to work. Gabe told me, "My pop was always there when I was young. . . . He would work around the house, things pops are supposed to do, but when I got older, I didn't remember none of that." Although Gabe Senior always drank too much, he started using drugs after he became ill. "Crack and alcohol. Cigarettes, weed. All that stuff," Gabe reported. Despite his father's substance abuse, his parents' long marriage and his father's continued presence, along with contributions through his disability insurance, created more domestic stability for him than for any of the other young men.

Gabe had been dating his much-older girlfriend, Charmagne, before getting locked up, and they resumed their relationship as soon as he returned home. "She was with me the whole time," he said. When Gabe was released, Charmagne was twenty-seven; she was employed in medical billing and going to college.[12] She had her own apartment in the

inner-ring suburbs, where she lived with her son from a previous relationship. Gabe split his time between her place and his parents' home in
Southwest Philadelphia. His PO, a YVRP officer, was often frustrated
when he was unable to find Gabe at his parents' home. Staying outside
the city limits was a probation violation, but his steady employment and
clean urine screens prevented Gabe from getting more than an occasional
stern warning.

Perhaps the most important difference between Gabe and every
other study participant was that he was able to get a job immediately after
returning to Philadelphia and had stable employment that paid a living
wage for nearly the entire three years I followed him. He made falling
back look easy, especially compared to those who frequently engaged in
desistance talk, discussing the pulls of the underground economy and
constantly renewing their resolve to go straight.

Gabe had sold drugs for several years before being placed at Mountain Ridge. Looking back on his childhood in Southwest Philadelphia,
he said he always wanted "to be outside, ripping and running with my
friends, not listening to my parents." Like Leo, he entered the drug game,
which was pervasive in his neighborhood, because he began to see himself as a grown man and did not want to rely on his family to buy him
whatever he wanted. "I felt as though I was at that stage when I wanted
to provide for myself. A job was not for me, I didn't want to get a job at
McDonald's. I didn't want to work behind a grill, I wanted real money.
And I grew up seeing it. That's how to get this money. It's not the right
way. But I couldn't get no jobs until I was eighteen or had a diploma."

When I asked him if he sold drugs because there were things his
parents couldn't provide him with, he said, "Nah, it was nothing. I
didn't have to sell drugs. I wanted to because I didn't want to ask my
mom for things. Anything I asked my mom for, she would buy me. But
I ain't want to. I felt like I was grown up and what man wants to ask
his mom for things? And I was only fifteen at the time, but I was too
grown for myself."

Gabe's plan was to sell drugs until he turned eighteen, when he
assumed it would be easier to get a good-paying job and fall back. At
that time, too, he would be sent into the adult court system if he were
arrested again. He seemed to view the age of eighteen as a cutoff; after

that, masculinity could no longer viably be achieved through the drug game, especially given its likely consequences. At eighteen, he, his family, and Charmagne all expected that he would take on the masculine responsibility of holding down a job and contributing equally to his domestic partnership.

He had been arrested and held on two occasions, but Mountain Ridge had been his first placement. It took little time inside Mountain Ridge for Gabe to determine what he needed to do to get out. He was "intervened" with by staff only once, when he forgot to tie his shoelaces properly. At that point, he decided that it was up to him to comport with rules so that he never again had another "dude" screaming in his face, emasculating him. Gabe had a strong sense of masculine identity before he was incarcerated at Mountain Ridge, which helped him resist assaults to his masculine self. He never viewed his incarceration as part of how he defined himself, but rather something temporary and superficial that needed to be endured. Moreover, his unusual degree of maturity resulted in his being able to attract a much older romantic partner who stuck with him throughout his time at Mountain Ridge and with whom he resumed a relatively drama-free relationship when he returned home.

Gabe adjusted so quickly to the rules and expectations at Mountain Ridge that his counselor suspected that he was "faking it to make it." He denied this, pointing out that following the rules was actually quite easy:

It became a habit since I've been up here for a little while. I don't try to do everything right 'cause everybody ain't perfect but, I do what I do. Like if I'm walking in transition [between places], oh, let me zip my jacket up so they won't say nothing to me. I'm gonna make sure my shoes tied so I won't have to hear their mouth. So it's like a habit. Make my bed, that's nothing, it's like a habit. The little expectations up here is for kids. If you up here and you can't follow these expectations then you don't wanna go home, and I wanna go home. So it's like people that come up here and act like knuckleheads really don't got nothing to go home to, that's how I see it. But if you wanna go home, you're gonna follow the expectations so you can go home.

Erving Goffman pointed out that one of the characteristics of total institutions is a reliance on the tension between home life and

institutional life.[13] It is therefore interesting to hear Gabe say that many
of the residents at Mountain Ridge did not necessarily experience that
tension because they "don't got nothing to go home to." Later, he drew a
similar boundary between himself and other neighborhood men without
the same opportunities that he had, framing drug selling in terms of having nothing to lose.

Like many of the other young men, he bought into the deterrence-
based principles of the program. He was determined to avoid being separated from his family and having to relinquish his masculine status again.
Shortly before his release, I asked him to imagine a scenario in which he
had been home in Philadelphia for four to six weeks without a steady
job and ran into an old friend who offered to give him "work" for a
one-time drug deal. "The things I would be thinking is that, damn, no, I
can't even go there. Because if I do, you never know what'll happen, like
it's only a matter of time. I mean I leave this store, get locked up all over
again, so it's not a route that I'm weighing. I wouldn't second guess at all.
You know, if I get a couple of dollars, then it's gonna leave it for me to
keep on doing. I'll probably justify it all over again. I'll be saying like man,
I can't even take that route. So I'm good, I'm cool."

Ironically, this thought experiment came true shortly after his
return to Philadelphia. He had almost immediately gotten a job on
a nighttime cleaning crew through a connection his sister had provided. During the weeks when he was waiting for his first paycheck, he
returned to marijuana sales to fill the gap in his income stream. Much
like the other young men I describe as "selling smarter," Gabe did not
return to hand-to-hand sales, but hired "young bulls" to take the risk
involved in being on the corner. He and a friend in his early twenties
"set it up, we had some young bulls that was willin' to stand out there
for us, so we gave young bulls the weed or whatever, they stood out
there, and we put it together like that. We wasn't out [on the corner]
'cause me an' him, we both just came home" from being locked up. He
estimated that he earned $300 from this short-term hustle: "It was just
some money to have in our pockets, 'cause we just came home we ain't
had no money for real. If we wanted to buy some clothes, we could
buy some clothes, if we wanted to get somein' to eat, we could get
somein' to eat. It wasn't money to go out to a fancy restaurant, drink

champagne, eat steak and potatoes, it wasn't that kinda money. But it was money to have that we didn't."

When I asked if he saw incarceration as a possible outcome of this behavior in the same way he did when he was locked up at Mountain Ridge, he said, "No, no. I ain't see incarceration as a possibility 'cause I'm a firm believer that when you think about something, it happens." Luckily, Gabe was never arrested for his brief involvement in drug sales. Once he got his first paycheck, he never returned to hustling. Gabe was able to resist the pulls of the underground economy because he was steadily employed at a well-paying job throughout the years I followed him. His first job paid a base rate of $9.36 per hour, with full-time hours and the opportunity for overtime. When he did specialized jobs like buffing floors, he got between $10.24 and $11.36. In a typical month, he grossed a minimum of $1,500, compared to the $1,080 that Leo made at Chuck E. Cheese in the suburbs and $1,280 he made four months out of the year at the seasonal landscaping job.

Gabe was fired only once, for running up his employers' phone bill with personal calls, and was almost immediately able to get another job and continue working his way up the pay grade to a regular pay of over $11 per hour. This work trajectory is in stark contrast to those of the rest of the young men I followed, who were employed only intermittently and were fired from or quit most of the jobs they held. I attribute part of Gabe's work stability to growing up in a home in which his mother and father worked full-time through his childhood. Beverly's influence appeared especially powerful given his father's ongoing substance abuse problems.

Charmagne was also a role model in her pursuit of higher education and job stability. When she and Gabe had an unplanned pregnancy, she got an abortion, deciding that another child would derail her plans for social mobility. Charmagne's demands on Gabe's time prevented him from spending as much time with his buddies as he had before he was locked up at Mountain Ridge. "My homies be like, damn, dog! When am I gonna see you? It's like you're locked up again. [laughs] I never be around here like that. I be with my girl most of the time."[14]

Almost a year after he returned to Philadelphia, Gabe told me why he wasn't involved in the drug game anymore.

Before, when I was young, I could give a fuck about getting locked up. I was getting this paper [money] and that's all that mattered. I got locked up and come right back out and do it again. But that's until I got placed. I was up there for a year, [but] I didn't have to be up there for a year to realize I wasn't going to come home and do the same thing 'cause I already knew. I was up in the correctional facility for a month or two, I was like, this shit is corny and I ain't coming up here. And that's what I was thinking, so I wasn't really trying to go back there. It's nothing to be scared of, it's just corny. I mean, who wanna live that life?

But do I see a clear connection between selling drugs and getting locked up? Most people don't care about getting locked up, that's what they do. And some people get locked up, they come home, got no other place to go, can't get a job, they already got felonies, they don't want to work at McDonald's. They grown men! What the hell is $5.25 going to do for them? So that's the only way they gotta go, so they're gonna get that money. And it's easy getting it! It's easy getting it, but the consequences are there, it's gonna always be there. It's so easy, I mean so easy getting it. You don't even got to be out there touching the shit, but the consequences are always going to be there.

Gabe's strong sense of adult masculinity prompted him to vow never to get locked up again, to be in a situation in which he was forced to submit to the will of others. Here we see him employing a rational, deterrence-based thought process similar to the one he demonstrated inside Mountain Ridge. It is worth considering how these principles of deterrence as a path to desistance worked differently for Gabe than for the other young men in my study, and how they were temporarily suspended during the short period when he sold weed while waiting for his first paycheck. His story, when systematically compared to those of the other young men I followed, suggests that deterrence has a more lasting impact when individuals have a solid support network, a secure sense of masculinity, and viable alternatives to offending.

SOCIAL TIES AND LAW-ABIDING MASCULINE IDENTITIES

Despite important differences between James and Gabe, their formulas for success share some important features, including the importance of masculine identity and of support from social networks. For James, falling back hinged upon successfully performing the roles of "good father" and "working man." He cut his ties to those who refused to believe that he was a changed person and established new social networks with people who never knew him as a hustler. At first glance, Gabe's life looks like a case study in deterrence; after being incarcerated for selling drugs, he was determined never to have his freedom taken away again. Upon closer inspection, however, masculine identity also was important to Gabe's process of "aging out" of crime. He viewed Mountain Ridge Academy, especially the emasculating experience of having "another dude" get in his face to give him "feedback," as inconsistent with his self-concept as a man. For both James and Gabe, external and internal sources of change worked together as social ties to meaningful people allowed them to develop law-abiding identities. The contrast between Gabe and James, as well as the other young men who did not fare so well, suggests that the deterrent power of incarceration may be limited to those with enough reliable social resources that they can make the rational cost-benefit analysis of involvement in crime that the theory assumes guides all offenders.

CHAPTER 8

"I Got Some Unfinished Business"

FICTIONS OF SUCCESS AT
MOUNTAIN RIDGE ACADEMY'S
GRADUATION CEREMONY

ALMOST A YEAR AFTER I began my field research, I trekked back to Mountain Ridge Academy with five of the former residents for their graduation ceremony. As we traveled down the six-mile road leading to the facility, I witnessed what sociologist Erving Goffman called "a wonderful putting on and taking off of character" as they prepared to move from the back stage of our van onto the front stage of the facility's campus.[1] During this time, they prepared for the roles they planned to play during the graduation ceremony.

Inside Mountain Ridge Academy, like most total institutions, young men were stripped of many markers of individuality and identity. They were given mandatory haircuts, required to shave off any facial hair, and compelled to speak, dress, and act in ways specified in the facility's rule book. Counselors at Mountain Ridge also attempted to strip away visible signs of cultural identity, requiring young men from urban areas to surrender clothing or jewelry that suggested they were too "image conscious," forbidding sagging pants or clothing with urban or black-associated labels, and prohibiting "strutting," urban slang, and listening to or writing rap music. Once these young men returned to Philadelphia, they had been eager to reassemble their urban identity kits, reveling in their freedom to speak, walk, and dress in a fashion that defined them. Returning to the facility as themselves was a meaningful victory and a symbolic reversal of the identity-stripping process.

This chapter recounts the experience of returning to Mountain Ridge and reflects on its meaning for the young men who traveled with me. This visit offered a rare opportunity for these young men to reclaim the experience on their own terms. Wearing their own clothing, using their own language, and playing their own music, they affirmed not only their personal choices but also the fundamental legitimacy of their cultural identity as black men and its compatibility with success. Going back gave them the chance to reshape the staff's collective memories of them and who they could become, as well as transforming their own narratives of the place and their time there.

The graduation ceremony involved an elaborate performance of "doing good" in which these young men, despite substantial evidence of their failure to achieve anything remotely resembling personal success, aligned themselves with mainstream institutions such as school, work, and family. They felt compelled to present fictive views of their success as the staff at Mountain Ridge defined it, which was not compatible with the conditions under which they lived in Philadelphia. By carrying off this performance, they constructed identities as transformed persons for the duration of the graduation ceremony. As reflected in the audience's eyes, they saw their own potential as productive members of society. In doing so, they were able temporarily to undo the identity-stripping process that had occurred inside Mountain Ridge, leaving in its place a coherent personal and cultural identity whereby their status as poor, young, black, and male was no longer inconsistent with success.

However, unlike most status passages, Mountain Ridge's graduation ceremony failed to confer the concrete privileges of a new status. The young men in my study returned to the same daily challenges of living in impoverished, racially segregated neighborhoods with few opportunities for success. No one in their communities viewed them differently after the ritual, nor did they seem to regard themselves in a new light. Moreover, although their claims to doing good were not challenged by the staff, they were quite shaky. None was able to carry through with the plans for school, work, or family that he had made at his release. Only one was fully committed to desisting entirely from offending and substance use. In fact, the graduation ceremony itself seemed to be successful only in energizing and motivating the facility's staff.

RETURNING TO MOUNTAIN RIDGE

In fall 2005, I returned to the facility with five of the young men for Mountain Ridge's annual graduation ceremony. I was surprised at how many were eager to return to the place where they had been held against their will. Sincere, James, Tony, and Leo, who lived in Ozark dorm together while they were locked up, came together as a group with my then husband, Paul, and me. Warren had also expressed an interest in coming if we had room, but unfortunately our rented minivan was cramped enough as it was, stuffed full of the gangly arms and legs of these near-men. Isaiah, whose trip was paid for by the court because he was still on probation, went by Greyhound with his baby's mom, Tamika. I had seen them off that morning, exchanging $25 for his most recent audio journal entry so they had enough money for snacks on the road. Finally, Eddie had expressed an interest in coming up from south-central Pennsylvania, where he was attending a four-year university; I had sent him a money order that would cover bus fare.[2]

We headed across Cambridge Street behind my apartment complex, throwing everyone's bags into the back of the minivan and getting them seated with a minimum of quarreling. I already had announced that Sincere was riding shotgun because, at six feet four inches, he was the tallest. Leo sat next to me in the middle chairs, and James and Tony took the back seats. Leo had brought CDs at my request, and Sincere was appointed the DJ. The others shouted directions to him, particularly James, who considered himself the expert on hip-hop music. Sincere turned the music up and everyone settled in, making quick work of the snacks we had brought. Leo spent a great deal of time on his cell phone, having immediately spotted the charging port in the minivan. "It's a client," he explained when his phone rang, smiling broadly and hinting around about his job as a gigolo. Tony asked if he could use my phone, after which it spent most of the trip in Tony's and James's possession.

As we left the familiar lights of Philadelphia's skyline, I was eager to get some footage of the guys when the energy level was high. As soon as I turned the video camera on, James began rapping. "Spit it!" Sincere yelled, doing a high-pitched, white-girl impression of me using slang. James was happy to oblige, delivering a couple of rhymes from his throne in the back seat, riddled by references to gats (guns) and hustling. He opened with a classic I had heard several times and was obviously familiar to the others and then did a new rap he had just written. The violent, exaggerated masculinity in the verses seemed incongruous, given James's wide smile and what I knew to be his drug-free lifestyle. When he finished, the other guys showed their appreciation.

"Wooee! That's an MNV offense!" Sincere yelled, referring to the facility's rules against writing raps. Writing or listening to rap or hip-hop music at Mountain Ridge was considered a major norm violation, or MNV. Throughout the trip and during their encounters with one another in Philadelphia, they continued to appropriate the language of the facility to signify their shared experience there and to reclaim some of the power that their forced use of that language had taken from them while they were incarcerated.

After everyone settled in, I asked each of them to reflect on the meaning of the trip. Leo said, "You know what I got to say about Mountain Ridge? Ya'll really want to know? Man, *fuck Mountain Ridge!* They ain't teach me nothin'." I responded, "So, Leo, what does it mean to go back?" He replied, "I got some unfinished business . . . there's some people up there I need to see." James took up the theme: "I'm going up there to tell people how I ain't all bad and shit now. I'm there to curse Richard out. . . . I wanna see Chet and I wanna see Sam [all counselors]. But I'm there to tell Richard, to *curse* Richard because he said I was going to fail as soon as I came home. I ain't failed yet . . . I had a coupla slips, but I got right up."

Turning to Sincere, I asked, "Tell me what it means to go back to Mountain Ridge." He responded, "Y'know, show everybody that I ain't no failure in life, that I ain't locked back up. I made it up out of there. It's better days, you know what I'm sayin?" James joked, "Yo, stop lying." Sincere protested, "Yo, I'm definitely goin' to come at a coupla people's necks." Tony interjected, "Yo, can I curse? Fuck Mountain Ridge. That place ain't do shit. The only thing that helped me was the time they gave me in there. That treatment stuff didn't do shit. I still got plans of goin' straight and I ain't even think about those thinking errors or the other stuff they taught me. That stuff been forgotten about. As soon as I got home, I forgot about all that treatment and I'm still going straight."

The conversation I elicited highlights some important similarities and differences among these young men and the way they thought about the facility's role in their lives.[3] Sincere and James, the two with strongest ties to the facility's staff, discussed their desire to prove their counselors wrong, to demonstrate that they "aren't all bad and shit" and "ain't failed yet," that "better times" were ahead for them. Both had been in regular phone contact with their counselors since discharge, but going back in person was proof that their claims to going straight were legitimate. Arriving with Paul and me, a tax attorney and a Ph.D. student, bolstered the credibility of these claims.

Leo, who admitted to being utterly confused by the facility's conflicting demands and rules, was more ambivalent. At first blush, he and Tony appeared to dismiss the experience as unimportant ("fuck Mountain Ridge!"), but both felt they had unfinished business there. Leo, despite his mixed feelings, wanted to see his counselor and teachers again. Tony, who had maintained that he would never return to Mountain Ridge, had decided to join us the day before, apparently because he did not want to miss the excitement of a road trip. Of the four young men, he had the fewest claims to going straight, though he was the only one who explicitly mentioned it.

Six-Mile Road

It was the morning of the ceremony, and we had had very little sleep. The guys, pleased to have their own room, had immediately disassembled the smoke detector and proceeded to stay up most of the night, smoking and watching movies at high volume. Breakfast had involved a great deal of laughter and mutual teasing, which attracted some stares from the locals. Over the last twelve hours, they had taken a curious trip down memory lane, recalling some of their funnier moments at Mountain Ridge. Strangely enough (to me, at least), most of them seemed to involve moments when they or their dorm mates "wiled out" (became violent) and had to be physically restrained by the staff.

The tenor of the group changed palpably when we turned down the long and bumpy dirt road leading to the facility. Perhaps feeling a little trepidation about truly being able to leave at the end of the day, a quiet settled over the guys in the van. James nervously picked out his hair, tucking his pick into a rubber band around his wrist. Tony pretended to sleep. Leo looked around with interest as the residential area melted away into thick forest.

Sincere put in a Snoop Dogg CD and turned it up to maximum volume, the van shaking with every beat. While Leo chattered nervously, the others bobbed their heads to the music, contemplating what the next few hours might bring. The last time they had headed down this dusty six-mile road, everything was different. Their freedom, their clothing, and their music had been taken away. Now they were returning, with a chance to reshape the staff's collective memories of them and more importantly, to transform their own self-images. The rhythm and the lyrics wove a protective cocoon around us, affirming itself and affirming them.

As we turned into the driveway leading up to the facility, we were greeted by one of the counselors who was directing traffic. Tony perked up and Leo leaned forward in his seat, scanning the grounds for familiar faces. "Get the sign! Get the sign!" James directed me with the camera. "Mountain Ridge Academy" he read aloud, with an air of disbelief. He grabbed the camera and took some footage of the grounds. It was a beautiful day, and even James had to admit the place was prettier than he remembered. "It *look* nice," he said. "But looks can be deceiving."

Within seconds, this van full of "thugs" who had previously been talking about "coming at staff's necks" was transformed into an animated group of kids. "We gotta go to work readiness, man. We gotta go to the [smoke] shack," Leo said. "Oh no, we gotta hurry up and get out," James said excitedly. "Oh, look, there's Lisa!" Tony said, always eager to get his chance to flirt with the female staff. "We about to go talk to Lisa," James said, grinning and sticking his pick in the back of his hair. Tony threw open the door to the minivan before we had fully pulled into the parking spot, and the guys spilled out onto the campus, leaving Paul and me behind.

The facility sparkled. It was nearly impossible to observe the open swaths of space, the carefully landscaped grounds, and the tidy dorms resembling log cabins without buying into the notion of "sentimental pastoralism" that guided reformers more than a century ago to build such facilities in remote areas.[4] The air did seem fresher, and the absence of street noise and crowding created a sense that this place might have curative properties. Having been a professional visitor in many facilities such as this one, I was aware of the effort that had gone into creating such an "institutional display" for parents and other invited guests. These displays offer "an 'appropriate' image of the establishment—this image being calculated to allay [visitors'] vague dread about involuntary establishments."[5]

After signing in, we entered the gymnasium and took the folding chairs behind Tamika, who was all smiles. She and Isaiah had been able to drink without IDs at their hotel bar the night before and had enjoyed the time away from their toddler, Darius. The bleachers were pulled out in the back, and the chairs were arranged in sections so that the graduates would be able to pass close enough for photos during the processional. A dais had been erected at the front, with a blue velvet curtain as a backdrop, an American flag, and a podium for speakers. On the right, facing the stage was a small group of chairs that were reserved for administrators and the keynote speaker. On the walls were inspirational posters announcing the link between Mountain Ridge and attributes such as "Excellence" and "Achievement."

A dark-skinned woman sitting behind me asked, "Are you leaving after this?" She fanned herself with the canary-yellow graduation program, which read "A New Beginning." "Yeah, we're going to try to get them out of here before they find any trouble," I said, only half joking. "I wish I could go with you. We're staying overnight again and this place makes me nervous." The young men in my study were not alone in the apprehension and discomfort they felt in this overwhelmingly white, rural town. I laughed. "Believe me, you don't want to be in our minivan. It smells like a boys' locker room," I replied. She nodded knowingly.

The ceremony itself was similar to any other high school graduation. As the graduates filed in wearing their caps and gowns, "Pomp and Circumstance" played over the PA system, and several young men waved to their family members seated in the audience. They took seats at the front of the gymnasium, just in front of us. Sincere and Leo turned around, acknowledging the video camera. Brian Noland, the program director and one of two black adults among the group of administrators, played the role of emcee, leading us through the Pledge of Allegiance and a prayer. One of the young men currently residing at the facility, a tall white kid with short-cropped blond hair and a shy demeanor, played an impressive piece on the piano. Several of the young men I followed had already received a high school diploma at last year's ceremony, while they were still incarcerated. James, however, was excited to be walking across the stage twice today, once as a high school graduate and once as a program graduate.

After Mr. Noland presented several awards to the graduates and the keynote speaker had wrapped up, we were ready for the medallion ceremony, when each of the graduates had an opportunity to address the audience. Tony, James, Sincere, and Leo had practiced their speeches that morning as they got dressed, recording one another with the video camera. "Yo, y'know what I'm gonna say? I'm gonna curse out my counselor!" Tony had promised.

When the speeches began, however, it was clear that the ceremony came laden with performative expectations similar to those that governed behavior inside the facility. The costs of violating these interactional prescriptions, however, were different. Cursing out their counselors and causing mayhem would not result in any formal sanction, but would violate the shared definition of the situation as an opportunity to confer prestige and respect. Moreover, it might threaten their performance as competent, productive adults. As a result, most graduates extended thanks to the facility's staff and pointed to ways in which they had helped them grow. Many of the young men, including James and Leo, hugged their counselors as they accepted their medallions, prompting the audience to say "Awww" in unison. The mutual affection among counselors, teachers, and graduates was clear.

Sam, one of the counselors from Ozark dorm, called Sincere, Tony, and Leo. Sam was a balding, middle-aged white man wearing a sweater and navy Dockers. "You have a whole bunch," Brian said to him. Sam looked at the list. "Good afternoon," he said into the microphone. "Good afternoon, Sam," the audience responded in unison. Sam called Sincere first. With his height, he needed to bend forward in order for Sam to place the medallion around his neck. Sincere helped him slide it over his bushy afro. Then he looked around and pointed to the current members of his dorm sitting in the pull-out bleachers. "Shout out to Ozark," he said, and the audience clapped. "I was here for a long time, I ain't gonna lie." He mumbled something inaudible and then addressed his counselor. "Thank you, Chet!" Smiling, he returned to his seat.

Tony was next. As he climbed the stairs, someone yelled "Smeagol," Tony's nickname at the facility. He looked embarrassed as he accepted the medallion and looked around, realizing he did not know what to say. He shook his head, and there was an uncomfortable pause. Several people in the audience laughed. "Um . . . I just want to say thank you to all the staff. . . . School staff as well. Where Bev?" He searched the audience and pointed when he found her: "Oh, Bev! Dawg!" The audience laughed and clapped. "Just thank you, that's basically it."

Then came Leo. When his name was called, he sprang from his chair and headed across the stage. After Sam put the medal over his head, Leo hugged him and the audience collectively said "Awww." "All I gotta say is, thank all the staff from Ozark, Brian Noland, . . . especially my man Sam right there. And everybody who made doing my time easier. That's all I gotta say."

By this point, a pattern had developed as each new graduate repeated essentially the same grateful speech. Although staff and graduates both incorporated some humor into their discourse, disrupting the established interactional flow would have diminished its meaning for the participants and undermined the graduates' performance of doing good. Tony's hesitation at the microphone revealed internal conflict as he suddenly recognized that the definition of the situation had shifted and that he was expected to praise the program and its staff instead of expressing his rage at having been locked up. If he had chosen to curse out his counselor, he would have immediately identified himself as unworthy of the occasion.

As his sponsor, James chose Bev, a no-nonsense woman with shoulder-length, curly hair wearing a pants suit. "Good afternoon, family. I got quite a few of these things here." When she called his name, James hugged her and smiled shyly as he approached the microphone, clearly filled with a sense of accomplishment. "I'd like to thank school staff, the counselor I hated over there, Chet [pointing to his right]. Thanks a lot."

Mike, a young white counselor wearing a polo shirt, called Isaiah to the stage. Isaiah accepted the medallion and then gestured to the podium so that Mike could say something nice about him. The audience laughed. Awkwardly, Mike said, "I could say that it was all a piece of cake, and I'd be lying to you, but eventually, he got it together and there he goes." Isaiah rubbed his face before speaking, relishing his moment in the spotlight.

"I'd like to thank my wife, Tamika, for being by my side at all times, and my son, Darius. And also I'd like to say thanks to Jamie, you're cool, Paul, you rock. And also Adirondack [dorm]. I'd like to thank Adirondack, Chris, Matt." He looked out into the crowd, smiling. "What's up, Mark? Shout out! Actually, I'm not supposed to be here right now. One of my best friends got murdered last Friday, so I'm supposed to be at his funeral. But I think he would want me to attend this because it's a special day for me and he would want that. It's all good, I'm attending community college, gonna be an RN, it's pretty hard, and living the sober life. Thank you, Mountain Ridge!"

Isaiah's performance neatly combined strands from several of the previous speeches: gratitude, family, success, growth, and sobriety. Few people in the audience, however, were in a position to judge its veracity or point out its inconsistencies. Isaiah had stopped attending classes at community college, and his relationship with Tamika was frequently marred by bouts of violence. By his own admission, he was a heavy drinker. Although he seemed not to have resumed regular marijuana use, his claim to "living the sober life" was so exaggerated that it made me wonder how far the other graduates had stretched to make their claims to doing good.

Laughter and Humor

The medallion ceremony was punctuated by frequent laughter, evoking memories of the significant role that humor played in daily life inside the facility. According to my pre-release interviews, residents appreciated staff members and students known to have a good sense of humor, and laughter broke up the tedium of the day. Humor was also an important element of the ceremony, intensifying solidarity among graduates, staff, and the audience filled with family members. As they called the young men's names, several of the counselors joked about the length of their stay or how many problems they presented at the program. Tom, a tall white counselor in a tie and sport coat, took this tack. "I'm honored to present this to Lamar Johnson." Lamar, a light-skinned black graduate wearing thin wire glasses, stood next to him while he continued. "Lamar was with us for fifteen long months. I think he was with us during the Reagan administration. [audience laughter] He was also part of the three

steps forward three steps back program for awhile 'til we were able to figure some things out for aftercare. I'm very proud to share with you that
Lamar is in Job Corps in Pittsburgh; he's been there for three months. I'd
like to say congratulations for completing the program and wish you the
best." As Lamar accepted his medallion, there was especially loud applause
from the audience.

The next presenter, Bob, a middle-aged white counselor with a
beard, followed suit. "It's a great honor to present this medallion to a
man who also struggled. He always told me he'd have the last word. This
medallion is for William Parker." William, a short white graduate with a
buzz cut, shook his counselor's hand and put on the medallion. "I gotta
say thanks to . . . Bob, for not takin' anything personal during my stay
here. [audience laughter] I'd probably be somewhere else worse, with my
old ways. I've got to say thanks to my mom, my dad, and the rest of my
family for suffering, for paying thousands of dollars for me to get back,
reenter society. I gotta give thanks to the clients over there who told me
what an idiot I was acting like and when to shut my mouth. Thanks."

The next counselor was a young white man wearing glasses. "This
medallion is for a young man who also struggled for quite some time.
Matter of fact, I think he spent more time in the hallway than I did.
[audience laughter] But on a serious note, it took Mark awhile to be
honest with himself and realize the choices he was making weren't going
to get him anywhere. So I'm glad to present this medallion to Mark
Miller [audience applause and some cheers]." Mark, a tall white kid with
broad shoulders and a blond crew cut, said, "Man, it's good to be back
here. Not! [audience laughter] I want to thank all the staff here, you
really affected my life. And I want to thank my mom [points to her] for
standing by me." He grabbed his medallion and looked down at it. "And
I want to thank my dad, who passed away in 2003. He didn't really get
to see me turn my life around, but I know he'd be happy. Thank you."

Reciprocally Sustained Fictions of Doing Good

Almost as important as what was said during the ceremony was what
was conspicuously left unsaid. At no point during or after the ceremony
were any of the graduates' claims challenged by staff members or other
graduates. At no time, including the drive out to the facility, did anyone

bring up the names of their peers who had not made it because they were either dead or incarcerated. No one mentioned Sharif, who had been murdered five weeks after his release and was found by police clutching thirty-eight bundles of crack. No one mentioned Malik, another Ozark dorm mate, who was serving a one-year sentence in a state-run juvenile facility after being arrested on a weapons charge. No one (including myself) pointed out that several of the young men who had traveled with us had "graduated" from the program despite leaving on bad terms, after being pulled out by their probation officer because they were no longer making any progress.[6]

The staff and administration at Mountain Ridge carefully constructed a setting in which the graduates' performance could be successfully carried off. To do otherwise would diminish the meaning of the ritual for all involved. The institutional ceremony, Goffman contended, is an extraordinary occasion in which the moral boundaries between staff and inmate are temporarily suspended and each is given permission to view each other in a favorable, personable light. This was especially evident after the ceremony, when formalities were further relaxed. Staff and former inmates exchanged hugs and asked about one another's families. Graduates reveled in the freedom from rules and restrictions that were no longer enforced. They visited the "smoke shack" to share a cigarette with staff members and took pleasure in the joyful autonomy of shouting, laughing, or running across campus. "These practices express unity, solidarity, and joint commitment to the institution," allowing the institution and its staff to carry on their work after the graduates departed.[7]

Most important, the ceremony reaffirmed the value and effectiveness of the staff's work. The counselors, social workers, and probation officers whom public policy expert Michael Lipsky called street-level bureaucrats routinely perform thoroughly thankless jobs.[8] They are rarely apprised of success stories since, by definition, "success" takes years to demonstrate and is loosely defined. News of reincarceration or the untimely death of a former resident, however, spreads quickly. Staff members' daily routines involve a fair degree of disrespect from residents, a lack of support from supervisors, and low pay. In a facility like Mountain Ridge, there is also a real physical risk associated with confining young people with violent histories. Without institutional ceremonies such as the annual graduation ceremony and holiday party, staff members might never receive the affirmation they feel they need to face another year of working with incarcerated youth.

For these reasons, staff members were invested in the fictions and exaggerations making up the ceremony. Staff members and graduates "serve as one another's audience for self-supporting tales—tales that are somewhat more solid than pure fantasy and somewhat thinner than the facts."[9] This mutuality of fictions played itself out in a set of interlocking tropes, whereby "I am a good person" and "this is a good place" reinforced one another. Ultimately, the ceremony was not for the graduates at all, but a much-needed opportunity for the staff members to celebrate their successes.[10]

Getting the Last Word

It was less immediately clear to me why returning to Mountain Ridge Academy was so important to the young men I followed. Of the ten who were available to go (two were reincarcerated, two were on the run from the police, and one had been murdered), seven contacted me to ask if I could help provide transportation to the graduation ceremony. Few of these had been known as model citizens at Mountain Ridge, and much of their talk about the facility centered on how angry and powerless it made them feel to be locked up there. Exploring the significance of returning to the facility reveals some of the most important and lasting features of their experience on the inside.

As evidenced in their dialogue about their motivation for attending the graduation ceremony, "getting the last word" is a key concern for these young men. This desire is a logical response to counselors' repeated and often public predictions of their failure. Many of these young men reported that their counselors had pronounced that they would likely be back shortly after being released or, worse, would end up in the adult system or dead.

The significance of "getting the last word" also reveals strong relationships built with the counselors and staff at the program, despite vast differences in their backgrounds. Nearly all of the staff members at Mountain Ridge were white, lived in the rural communities surrounding the facility, and held a healthy disdain for anything they perceived as urban. In spite of very little apparent common ground, many of the young men in my study reported developing close, family-like relationships with their counselors, compounding the pain and frustration of being told they were destined to fail on the outside.

The day before the twelve-month anniversary of his release (five months after the graduation ceremony), I asked Sincere, nineteen, to describe any important events that had occurred over the last year.

> The most significant event, this something I been waiting for my whole life, is my son. Other than my son, what can I say? Just me coming home was a good event and me staying out of trouble is the biggest thing. I really feel as though I had to prove myself to the people at Mountain Ridge, even tomorrow I'm going to call them. Like, yeah, I came home a year ago and I'm still home. Like even sometimes I hit them up [phone them] and let them know I'm still home, doin' good and everything.

"Why is it important to let them know that?" I asked.

> Because, like, they doubted me. Mountain Ridge was like home away from home. That's how I looked at it, me being there so long. That was like family at the time. And when they threw the home pass paper in my face and told me to go around and get people to sign it and see who really thinks I deserve a home pass. Even when I did that, people would not sign it, people put "no" on there. And I was like, dag, I was there a year already and nobody sign it. So you know that hurted me. But just to prove to them that they was wrong make me feel good.

Proving the staff at Mountain Ridge wrong was meaningful because these men were well aware of their marginal status as young, black, poor, and male. During our conversations, they demonstrated an impressive degree of racial consciousness. They had been the victims of unprovoked, sometimes violent contact with the police. They were aware that there were few black fathers in their communities and that unemployment among black men is endemic. Young black men are very conscious that they have come to symbolize danger, violence, and crime to passersby on the street.[11] In sum, their very existence as black men is synonymous with failure. Any claims to legitimacy, to doing good, come on both a personal level and a cultural level.

A REDEMPTION RITUAL?

Despite their desire to defy the odds and make good as black men, their grasp on conformity and their ties to legitimate institutions were not as tight as they wished to portray. The young men used the term "doing good" interchangeably with "doing what you have to do" and "falling back" (slang for staying out of trouble). When pressed, most said that doing good meant meeting whatever obligations you have, paying your cell phone bill or child support, or, if you are committed to being an active father, spending time with your children. Interestingly, only James viewed abstaining from drug use as part of doing good, which may reflect a failure of the others to "buy in" to the addictions component of the program. However, not even James, the most committed to falling back, could lay an honest claim to following through on the plans he set up for himself at the time of release.

Although their grip on success was precarious, for these young men, traveling to the graduation ceremony proved that they were not locked up and they were not dead. Doing good in these terms was both measureable and achievable at that point in the reentry process, although like most disadvantaged youth, they retained a longer-term commitment to mainstream success.[12] This low threshold defining success also reflects staff members' own definitions, common among many corrections professionals. Although most hope their young charges will eventually achieve great things, avoiding the "cemetery or penitentiary" appears a modest but worthy goal.[13]

Goffman noted that "an important aspect of every [moral] career is the view the person constructs when he looks backward over his progress."[14] Former inmates may reflect upon the role incarceration played in their lives and construct what Goffman called either a "success story" or a "sad tale." The reconstruction of a person's life story is more than an expression of past events; narrating an autobiography is an active process of identity construction that, in turn, shapes the lines of action that individuals perceive as open and worth pursuing.[15] In short, the way a person sees himself has much to do with how he will behave after release. If, like

James, he can convince himself and others that he is a "working man" or a "good father," he may sustain a self-story that supports falling back.

Speeches made during the medallion ceremony were a public opportunity for young men to claim to be doing good and to align themselves with mainstream institutions such as work, school, and family. The audience's acceptance of these claims, marked by applause and other vocal reactions, provided the validation they needed to pull the performance off. For the duration, the young men were able to reverse the identity-stripping process, leaving in its place a coherent personal identity. However, the benefits of the ceremony were limited to the short time they were engaged in the ritual and linked to the audience for which they performed. Although the staff did not challenge their claims to doing good, the graduates were aware of their own precarious positions in the labor market and in their personal relationships, including those with their own children. While they strove to prove counselors wrong about their limited potential, their struggles after release may have sharpened their own fears that their counselors had been right.

The conditions that made the ceremony successful for the staff, though not for the graduates, included collusion between graduates and staff members in which none of the graduates' claims to doing good were challenged and cases of obvious failure went unmentioned. Definitions of success were modest: doing good simply meant avoiding jail and surviving long enough to attend the ceremony. Their tenuous connections to legitimate institutions such as family, school, and work were glossed over in order for both staff members and graduates to enjoy a shared sense of accomplishment. A second condition was the reproduction of the institutional power structure, whereby the young men, who had prepared to use the ceremony as a platform to express their anger about being told they would fail, ultimately followed the interactional prescriptions to thank their counselors for all they had done. The graduates became enmeshed in a ritualized dynamic in which the needs of the group to believe that Mountain Ridge succeeded in transforming people aligned with their own needs for believing that they themselves had been transformed.

The ceremony appeared to meet two of the standards that Shadd Maruna set for a redemption ritual.[16] First, it was symbolic and emotive. The ceremony was marked by laughter, tears, audience responses such as cheering and "Awww," and displays of gratitude. I personally experienced the emotional energy that sociologist Randall Collins contended is produced by rituals; I felt myself wanting to believe in the power of Mountain Ridge Academy to bring about change in the lives of young people, despite my otherwise critical view of this intervention.[17] Second, the ceremony focused not on risk but on the potential for success. This feature was most visible through what Goffman termed "reciprocally-sustained fictions," whereby claims to success were never challenged and the more obvious instances of failure were ignored.

The symbolic victory of returning to the facility and making a claim to doing good was short-lived, perhaps because it failed to meet the third criterion for a redemption ritual. The ceremony was not held in the graduates' communities, which prevented them from being reinstated as law-abiding members of society. With the exception of Tamika, Paul, and myself, few significant others were able to travel to the facility to witness the graduation ceremony. The performance of transformation and the legitimation by the graduates' former denouncers were circumscribed in time and space; the redemptive effects were confined to the few hours they spent on campus enjoying the benefits of being recognized as productive citizens. Ironically, the distance from home allowed the graduates to make claims that no one (but me) was in a position to contradict. Staging the ceremony on the facility's grounds also limited what graduates could say, silencing their critiques and structuring their acceptance speeches to meet the interactional demands of the ritual. Finally, it should be noted that most of Mountain Ridge's former residents did not return for the graduation ceremony and therefore did not experience even the temporary removal of carceral stigma.

Perhaps equally important, the ceremony was held months after the graduates' release, after the challenges of successful reintegration had already made themselves readily apparent but before their hopes had been entirely foreclosed. The young men returned from the ceremony to the ongoing struggles inherent in living in resource-poor communities: few good-paying jobs, an inability to invest in education because of more immediate financial needs, and the constant lure of hustling as a way to make ends meet. Unlike a traditional rite of passage, such as getting married or graduating high school, the ceremony failed to confer concrete privileges of a change in status. Although the ceremony failed to meet all of the criteria for a redemption ritual, we are left to wonder how powerful such a ritual could be in the absence of real, material changes in former prisoners' life circumstances.

The young men's desire to go back as well as their performance once they arrived reflect their sincere desire for inclusion in mainstream society and a connection with legitimate institutions. It was important to them to have staff members acknowledge their progress and their potential for future success. They enjoyed a sense of inclusion, however temporary. Although so many criminologists emphasize the value-based differences between delinquent and nondelinquent youth,[18] these data suggest that "but for" structural disadvantage, they would be eager members of the mainstream. The graduates' shaky claims to doing good during the ceremony exposed the precariousness of their grip on success.

Conclusion

ON A RECENT VISIT to Albany, New York, where he spoke to my students, Sincere said something so honest and profound that it nearly took my breath away. "Sometimes, I wake up in the middle of the night and feel like I should be doing something more. God meant for me to do something more when He decided to let me live when so many people died [in the church van accident]. I know I was meant to do something special, but I haven't." Although we could interpret this as a classic case of survivor's guilt, I think social forces also are at work. Accompanying this guilt is a fatalism that is both realistic and heartbreaking. Sincere has a grim and deterministic view of his future in which because he hasn't been able to meet his own standards for manhood by age twenty-four, he believes he likely never will.[1]

Giving up unrealistic aspirations can be a normal, healthy part of the transition to adulthood. By now, most of those reading this book have realized that we will probably never become rock or rap stars, professional athletes, or astronauts. We adjust our aspirations and work toward making meaningful and fulfilling lives as "regular people" in our occupations and relationships. We take satisfaction in the things we enjoy, rather than fantasies about becoming celebrities. Similarly, now that Sincere has matured, he no longer believes he is going to be drafted into the NFL or even become a top dog in the drug game. The profoundly sad part is that he doesn't see any possibility of holding down a steady job with a living wage, providing regular financial support to his family, or being able to survive without resorting to the occasional hustle.

Over the last few years, he has tried several times to get and keep a job, working as a security guard at the city's recycling plant, a groundskeeper at a city golf course, and a furniture mover in his brother-in-law's company. Sometimes losing the job was his fault, as when he was fired from the recycling plant for making personal phone calls. Other times, such as at the golf course, he demonstrated an impressive degree of dedication but was subject to seasonal work fluctuations. The moving job was emblematic of the nature of work for so many undereducated African American men: he got the job through a family member, was paid under the table, and was often shorted at the whim of his brother-in-law. Most important, it was fragile; when the truck died, the business died with it, as did Sincere's steady paycheck. Realizing that the best pathway out of the secondary labor market was to get more education, he has considered going back to school to become a chef or a mechanic.[2] He rarely does more than mention these plans, though, having few concrete resources to invest in them. I have seen him become more risk averse as he has tried and failed to find decent work. Instead, he has developed a narrative as a father, which offers the best, though hardly foolproof, way of maintaining his dignity.

The one role Sincere has always known he could perform to its fullest is being an active, loving father. He takes little solace, however, in knowing that he has been there for his sons in a way that his father never was for him or even that he is a father to Mercedes, who is not his biological daughter. His limited financial contributions to the household compromise his sense of himself as a parent. While inner-city men are rarely the main breadwinners for their families, given how few jobs are available, Sincere thinks of this masculine ideal as both desirable and impossible for him to achieve. When he talks about his sons, he sees their time together as short. He knows the statistics—that as a young black male he belongs to an endangered species. He fully expects to be locked up or dead at an early age. Moreover, he may have valid but unspoken concerns about how long his relationship with Marta will last and therefore how involved he might be able to be with his children in the future.[3]

When he looks to the future, he sees only his sons—Sincere Junior, age five and a half, and Martín, eighteen months—and says, "It's now on them to make it for the family." He seeks to teach them to fight, to be self-reliant, and to play football so that they can be drafted by the NFL someday. It may be the ultimate irony that he looks regretfully back at his missed educational opportunities but does not see education as the "way out" for his children. Perhaps, however, he is being realistic only about how far a Philadelphia public school education could get his kids and their own families.

Sincere's story and the other life stories shared in this book illuminate one of the most pressing social problems facing Americans today: the precarious position of young black men from impoverished neighborhoods. Although black youth belong to a socially segregated minority group, the problems that afflict them affect families, communities, labor markets, schools, and other important institutions. Their plight is intimately intertwined with the crisis of mass incarceration that has been created through our fear of and desire to contain the "dangerous classes" residing in urban neighborhoods. We now turn to the central questions of this book, which speak to youth incarceration and transitions to adulthood among this very vulnerable group.

How Did the Young Men Experience and Interpret Incarceration?

In his seminal work *Asylums*, Goffman introduced the notion of a moral career, "the regular sequence of changes that career entails in the person's self and in his framework of imagery for judging himself and others."[4] Goffman was concerned with the power that prisons and other total institutions have to send messages to inmates about their moral character and the sorts of behavioral expectations that await them. However, Goffman did not develop the notion of the moral career beyond the confines of the facility's walls. By contrast, I argue that the experience of being an inmate continues to shape the way former prisoners view themselves upon release.

All total institutions construct moral distinctions and social distance between staff, who represent the rest of law-abiding society, and inmates. But these boundaries take a peculiar form at reform schools such as Mountain Ridge. Here criminality is medicalized, and inmates, known as "clients" or "students," are seen as being in need of treatment. Yet unlike other forms of medicalized deviance, such as mental illness, criminal behavior is seen as the person's own fault. The reform school program is premised on the assumption that inmates are morally culpable for their offenses.[5]

The facility gives the young men it seeks to change a set of messages that contradicts the very possibility of personal transformation. It tells them, you are a criminal—that is, you are bad; you are the same as every other criminal found inside the facility's walls; you are here because you suffer from distortions in the way you perceive and respond to the world; and you will likely always be that way. The manner in which these messages are received by young black men from the inner city is complicated by the fact that the senders are nearly always white and from backgrounds very different from their own. The counselors sending these messages wield power both as members of the dominant racial group and as the institutional authorities who regulate rewards, punishments, and freedom. As a result, their messages are viewed as a form of cultural assault on inmates' place- and race-based identities.

Young people take pride in surviving the meanest streets of Philadelphia and other cities; their geographical and racial identities are closely linked, so negative attributions about the city—which often have racial undertones—are interpreted as directed at the self. This linkage may be heightened when they perceive that white youths from rural areas are permitted to listen to country music and wear clothing associated with the outdoors. They develop a sense of injustice in reaction to being deprived of cultural symbols associated with urban blackness. Ironically, this protest may reaffirm youths' commitment to street culture. Moreover, it contributes to the idea that counselors and other staff members do not understand where youth are coming from, undermining their status as role models who are familiar with the way the world works.

When young men experience this cultural assault, they resist, challenging the right of staff members to stigmatize them and strip them of their sense of self.[6] They reject the messages offered by staff members and focus on ways to maintain the integrity of their identity, engaging in what Goffman termed "secondary adjustments" such as "faking it to make it."[7] They play along during therapeutic sessions, pretending to work on their distorted thinking while stubbornly clinging to the notion that there is nothing wrong with the way they think about or deal with the world. They do this in part because they believe the staff has not shared enough common experiences to give advice that is useful in the real world, but also because the strategies of coping with problems taught inside the facility are likely to be counterproductive in an urban environment. Any more concretely useful lessons taught by the institution, such as job hunting or financial management skills, are also dismissed as useless once they return to Philadelphia.

As they came back to the city, many vowed to prove their counselors wrong by "falling back," or staying out of trouble. Several kept in touch with Mountain Ridge staff, calling periodically to let them know how they were doing. Here, with time and distance, it was easier to see the caring and affectionate nature of their relationships with some staff members at Mountain Ridge. Despite the young men's insistence that they didn't believe in the program's distinctions between criminals and others, one event shed surprising light on the lasting impact of the moral divide between staff and inmates. Approximately two years after his release, Sincere met up with one of his counselors who was visiting Philadelphia for the first time. As soon as he arrived, he asked Sincere to find him a marijuana hookup, and they smoked together before spending a wild evening at a strip club. Sincere was pleased to be on the same side of the moral divide for once. On the other hand, he seemed crushed that the staff engaged in the sorts of activities that were supposed to make one a criminal. He concluded that "all that stuff up there that they told us was bullshit." He and the others had always suspected this sort of hypocrisy was embedded in the program, and here was the proof.

When these young men talk about Mountain Ridge today, they scoff at the idea of "thinking errors" and can name only a few of them. Most, like Sincere, say that they learned they never wanted to be incarcerated and separated from their families again. James is unique in his claim that he has no regrets about his time there because "it made me the person I am today."[8] Still, James rejects the thinking errors approach and says instead that the time away from home allowed him to get his priorities straight. Six years after his release, I was surprised to hear Warren say that he looks back on his time at Mountain Ridge fondly and wishes he could have the structure of the facility, especially the predictable schedule, without the restrictions. Warren's view is shaped by the fact that he has recently lost his mother and is acutely aware of having no adult support.

Despite the rehabilitative aim of many, if not most, juvenile institutions, their residents are often explicitly, repeatedly, and publicly told that they are likely to end up dead or in prison as adults. This common juvenile justice trope is exemplified in Judge Dorn's well-known courtroom diatribe recorded in Edward Humes's *No Matter How Loud I Shout*:

You've seen those homeless people down on Fifth Street, haven't you? That's where you're headed son, if you don't get an education. Don't you understand that if you don't get an education, if you don't go to college or learn you a good trade, all you can expect in this world is a lifetime of degradation and poverty? . . . You're stealing from yourself and no one else. . . . If you keep on the way you're headed, you can only end up in one of two places: the cemetery, or the penitentiary.[9]

Counselors at residential facilities and juvenile court judges may have young people's best interests at heart when they make negative predictions about their futures, but talking to youth about their experiences reveals just how painful and lasting their effects can be, particularly when we consider the very realistic possibility that they will not become successful adults.

These negative messages are consistent with those that young men of color receive in their interactions with representatives of other social institutions, such as schools, family members, employers, the media, white citizens, and the police: little else is expected of them other than continued failure, and they are told they are a drain on the social welfare and criminal justice systems. Racial, class, and criminal stigma are added to existing and cumulative layers of disadvantage. The power and enduring nature of these messages is evidenced in the young men's desire to prove their counselors wrong, and that they "ain't all bad and shit." Ultimately, however, given their lack of legitimate opportunities for success, the fact that they are still alive and not incarcerated may be the only concrete proof that they are "doing good."

Negative predictions about the future become reflected appraisals, sending signals to youth that make self-change difficult to accomplish and thwarting the institutional goals of promoting healthy transitions to adulthood and law-abiding behavior. Without a glimmer of potential seen and reflected by others, it becomes unlikely that formerly incarcerated young men of color will do anything other than fulfill those predictions. Support and encouragement from adults are not in themselves sufficient to enable young people to become respectable, law-abiding citizens, but they may well be necessary.

WHAT ROLE DID INCARCERATION APPEAR TO PLAY IN HELPING THE YOUNG MEN "FALL BACK" AND BECOME HEALTHY ADULTS?

Mountain Ridge offered a few concrete advantages to those who were confined there, including the opportunity to earn a high school diploma and enroll in postsecondary education programs. However, none of the youth were able to capitalize on these advantages after they returned to Philadelphia, since their structural positions remained unchanged. None got a job that required a diploma or were paid more because they had one. And none of the four who pursued higher education and training was able to complete more than a few months before dropping out. Living hand to mouth is incompatible with investing in one's future. This predicament was perhaps most painfully evident in the case of Eddie, who seemed to have a promising future at a four-year university but quickly set up a criminal enterprise in the small college town, landing him in state prison.

These young men were never connected to long-term, stable supports in the community or within their educational institutions that would make success more likely. Juvenile reentry planners, after going through an impressive and lengthy "reinvention" of the system, were forced by budgetary constraints to reduce the period of services to ninety days, regardless of the youth's level of risk. Ironically, after this investment in evidence-based practices, young people received support services for half as long as they had before the policy changes.

The formal reentry plans that young men developed in conjunction with their counselor, probation officer, and reintegration worker unraveled quickly. Within six weeks at least four had returned to drug selling, and a fifth was dead. Sharif, nineteen, was gunned down less than twenty-four hours after being subpoenaed by the police to testify in a murder trial, a testament to the consequences of "snitching." By the time they had reached the six-month mark, six more had resumed offending and a seventh was on the run from the police. Hassan was pressured by police to name the person who had shot him after a friendly neighborhood basketball game and decided it was safer to flee, violating his probation. By the time three years had passed, seven had spent time in jail or prison, and the group of fifteen had generated a combined total of thirty-six arrests.

None completed any additional educational training, including the three who returned to the Philadelphia public schools. Most fathers struggled to stay involved in their children's lives. Only one found steady employment at a job that paid a living wage. Realizing the high likelihood of returning to trouble, the men developed a great interest in how the others I followed were faring since their return. They constantly asked how the other young men were doing, and several reconnected through me—to my chagrin, often to sell weed to one another. Many had the sense that the story I was telling would be grim, and each hoped to be the exception who had made it.

My analysis of how and why things fell apart for most of the young men I followed leads me to believe that even the most therapeutic of reform schools (and most are not as therapeutic as Mountain Ridge) is a problematic site for promoting change among adolescents. In addition to the application of stigma that limits the futures young people are likely to imagine for themselves, they must practice new skills in a setting far from home. In part because sentimental pastoralism still pervades our notions of treatment in juvenile justice and in part because juvenile correctional facilities are subject to "not in my backyard" public pressures, most facilities are located far away from the city and are staffed by counselors and teachers who are white and live in rural communities. Most are hours away from the youths' homes. As a result, treatment such as cognitive behavioral therapy is carried out in an environment that is entirely different from the one in which it must be put into practice.

Although the young men in my study valued having time out to think, the risk-reward calculations they were encouraged to make inside the facility were inapplicable with their world. In the abstract, a return to offending would result in a new stint of incarceration and a loss of all the privileges they hold dear. In their experience, however, risk takes on new meaning; as they see many others engaging in the drug game and not getting caught, they are constantly reminded of their inability to provide for their children, and their refusal to pick up a package may mean that the lights and heat are cut off. When they were younger, rewards may have meant wearing flashy jewelry and "dressing fresh," but now the rewards more likely involve adult concerns such as feeding and housing the family.

Finally, and most important, reform schools fail to acknowledge the structural sources of offending and are not poised to help young men navigate the very real barriers to making a healthy transition to adulthood. All but one of the young men in this study told me that they intended to fall back after release. However, it took only hours after returning home for them to realize that the daily demands of inner-city life remained, leaving them feeling that "nothing's changed but me." Much like recovering addicts who return to the people, places, and things associated with their substance use, young people must enact their reinvented selves outside of the protective setting of the facility. Lessons learned begin to seem less relevant than ever, and old strategies for navigating the urban environment quickly return.

Treating delinquency as a product of "poor choices," reform schools such as Mountain Ridge ignore the real reasons why young people engage in crime and fail to thrive: endemic unemployment, the unhelpful presence of law enforcement agents, residential segregation, and a lack of social supports and connections to the mainstream that make social mobility possible. Because of this fatal flaw, any reduction in offending that comes directly out of the experience of incarceration is likely the result of deterrence rather than treatment and is necessarily limited in value and duration. This deterrent effect is suggested in the strategy of "selling smarter"—techniques for drug dealing that reduce the risk of arrest, usually shifting it downward to others who are willing to do hand-to-hand sales—in which several of the young men I followed engaged after their return.

How Did the Young Men Navigate
the Dual Transition from
Facility to Community and from
Adolescence to Young Adulthood?

Both the transition to adulthood and that back to the community are typically marked by changes in young men's relationships with their families, the labor market, postsecondary education and training, and religious institutions, as well as the criminal justice system. The first ninety days after release from Mountain Ridge or any other reform school involve continued contact with the juvenile justice system via regular meetings with a probation officer and a reintegration worker. Probation officers typically want their clients to pay court fees, secure a job, and maintain clean urine tests through the period of probation. Reintegration workers may offer transportation to and from these meetings, make sure the young people are enrolled in outpatient substance abuse treatment or are attending school, or help connect them to employment opportunities. As is apparent in Eddie's and Tony's cases, reintegration workers often fill their clients' schedules with a variety of activities that are designed as much to keep them busy as to meet clients' actual needs.[10]

Young men returning from correctional facilities frequently are subject to a great degree of scrutiny from their guardians and family members as well. They may have to earn privileges that were granted automatically before their incarceration, be subject to questioning about their whereabouts or how they got the money in their pockets, and be told that they must earn back the trust they lost during their days as drug sellers. For the young men who spent their time at the facility dreaming of the freedom associated with their return to Philadelphia, this treatment can bring a sense of infantilization completely at odds with the notion of moving toward adulthood.

Sincere pointed out several times that because he was institutionalized, he missed out on lessons typically learned from family and peers about becoming a man: "I was locked up from sixteen to eighteen, so I learned how to be a man inside Mountain Ridge." His statement implies what developmental psychologist Laurence Steinberg has long argued: that youthful incarceration results in arrested psychosocial development. Because reform schools offer few opportunities for the development of the self-governance that maturity requires, any attempt to provide concrete skills will ultimately be undermined by the youth's inability to meet the demands of the adult world.[11]

Reform school graduates returning to Philadelphia may feel *less* like men than when they were locked up years before. During the time in which their drug selling was at its height, many were bringing in a substantial cash flow with which they could supplement their family's income. Moreover, hustling and violence offer an alternate source of respect for those unable to earn it through more conventional means.[12] Stripped of their identity as hustlers and not yet having attained the conventional markers of adult manhood, such as a job, a wife, and a house, these young men find themselves dependent upon their family members, their girlfriends and babies' moms, and agents of the system. They eat food they didn't pay for and live in houses whose rents are paid through their partners' or guardians' income or public subsidies. Their memory of being a competent adult who contributes to the family and earns respect on the street corner may eventually compete with their desire to fall back and earn money and dignity through law-abiding routes. Leo, for example, felt like his status as a "grown man" was threatened when he had to rely on his mother and grandmother to support him after he returned from Mountain Ridge. When he was a serious player in the drug game, he had been able to meet all his own material needs and take care of others.

Many of the young men appeared hyper-vigilant about avoiding trouble and a possible return to confinement during the weeks following their release. They avoided resuming regular marijuana use, not only because they were being tested by their probation officers but also because they associated this behavior with their former lives as hustlers. As in Elijah Anderson's story of Rob, who returned from prison to find that very little had changed except for his commitment to going straight, their buddies were often eager to have them return to the game.[13] Staying in the house to avoid trouble seemed a sensible strategy at first. However, as they began to resume the regular rhythms and patterns of life on the outside, they began to make concessions, bargaining that they could hang out in the old places with the old people and still not return to the old behavior.[14] Both Sincere and James told me during these periods that they worried they were "slipping."

When I began this study, I expected to find a tighter relationship between unemployment and reoffending. Other research has shown that employment can serve as a turning point that reduces the likelihood of further offending by reducing the time and opportunity for illegal activities, cutting down contact with antisocial peer groups, or simply reducing the need to earn income through illegal means.[15] In one well-known study of adults released from prison, parole officers identified employment as the single most important factor preventing rearrest and reincarceration.[16]

However, former prisoners are often shunted into the secondary labor market, resulting in a significant loss of earnings that persists through men's careers; returning prisoners earn between 10 percent and 30 percent less than their counterparts with clean records do.[17] This pattern suggests that it is not just employment, but also steady employment at a living wage, that leads to desistance. Only one of the young men I followed, Gabe, had this sort of employment situation, and he succeeded in remaining free from arrest. Work was also an important part of James's attempts to fall back, although his narrative revealed an important identity component. His successful performance of the "working man" role appeared to be the key to reinforcing his commitment to change. A working man is someone who does not need to earn income illegally, who is respectable and never has to worry about looking over his shoulder in fear of the police or angry competitors.

For the young men whose employment was more intermittent, I was unable to detect a pattern in which working was a strong predictor of "falling back." They appeared to move back and forth between employment and unemployment, offending and conforming on an almost day-by-day basis.[18] Working at a low-wage job did not seem to prevent offending, and unemployment did not appear to necessitate it. Many of these young men are able to make ends meet with very little in their pockets. Small hustles, such as bootlegging CDs or accepting cash for sex, might provide enough to "keep them in the green" (allow them to buy weed), get drinks with the boys on the weekends, or buy food at the corner store.

Another significant aspect of their transition home centered on their relationships with romantic partners and, in many cases, children. In stark contrast to the story of arrested development and extended adolescence, fatherhood was the one realm where these young men were moving forward at a faster rate than would be expected for individuals of their age.[19] Perhaps the most astonishing finding of this study is how eagerly these youth anticipated the birth of their children and the strength and sincerity of their desire to be involved parents. This finding runs counter to more pervasive accounts of inner-city men who take little to no responsibility for their children but take pride only in how many children they can father by different women. Many of the young men I followed came home from Mountain Ridge to establish households with their girlfriends and babies' mothers, fully intending to be active and loving parents and partners.

The families these young men form are both a risk factor for and a protective factor from further offending. Young men in these living arrangements, such as Sincere and Isaiah, exhibited long periods of stability in nonoffending punctuated by periodic returns to drug selling, often to address a family financial crisis. I often observed their girlfriends cajoling them to spend less time with their crime-involved friends and to avoid any activity that could result in arrest and reincarceration. At the same time, their babies' mothers also regularly reminded them of their tenuous position in the household because of their inability to make regular contributions to the household finances. The young men I followed were kicked out of the house periodically, often after an argument related to their sexual infidelity, or had custody arrangements changed on a whim. For them, "picking up a package" appeared to be a means of regaining a sense of mastery and manhood in the face of these indignities. Moreover, it provided an income stream that could not be monitored or appropriated by a young man's girlfriend.

Employment, fatherhood, romantic relationships, and housing were all characterized by intermittency or precariousness for the majority of these young men. Offending followed the same intermittent patterns as youth moved back and forth across the relatively fluid boundary between the legal and underground economies. "Part-time hustlers" spent the vast majority of their time engaged in law-abiding behavior, but needed to maintain their connections to the underground economy in order to tap them at a moment's notice. The tenuous nature of young black men's relationships to such fundamental social institutions as work and family explains their tendency to rely on the drug game in order to survive and maintain a sense of manhood that persistently eludes them in more conventional domains.

WHAT FACTORS PROMOTED HEALTHY ADULT DEVELOPMENT AND FALLING BACK FROM CRIMINAL ACTIVITY?

Despite these pulls toward the underground economy, some of the young men I followed were able to leave those connections behind because they had stable social supports in the form of family members and girlfriends. Gabe was probably the best example of the importance of social connections through sturdy personal relationships. The important people in his corner included his parents, who were married throughout his childhood and remained still together. His girlfriend, Charmagne, was several years older and attending college. Both Charmagne and his parents expected him to hold down a job, which he did for nearly the entire time I followed him. Gabe's story, in sharp contrast to the others, is marked by stability in his relationships with his family and his girlfriend, in his work and his housing situation. Because he made a steady, living wage, he had a legitimate stake in the apartment he shared with Charmagne. Despite his occasional cheating, she never threw him out. Their joint income allowed them to live in an inner-ring suburb that had significantly less criminal activity than the neighborhoods where the other young men I knew lived.

James had an important social support in his Uncle Clifton, who gave him a place to live and offered short-term financial support when he was out of work or needed transportation to his job. His daughter, Maya, also played an important role, inspiring his determination to be a good father. He also had some toxic relationships: his mother pressured him to sell drugs, and his baby's mom frequently withheld access to Maya. These made his commitment to falling back more difficult. James suffered several setbacks during the three years after release from Mountain Ridge; he was homeless twice, severed ties with his mother, and abandoned his dream of a career in construction because he was unable to finish technical school. Nevertheless, when there were people in his life—me included—who viewed him as a "working man" and a good father, he could sustain his own belief in these roles and his ability to succeed.

Finally, Sincere's trajectory has demonstrated increased stability over the six years since he was released from Mountain Ridge. Although he has been unemployed during most of this period, he played a daily active role in the household he set up with Marta. Before recently splitting up with Marta, he changed diapers, accompanied Sincere Junior and Mercedes to school, and walked the dog. While their first years were characterized by more dramatic breakups and makeups than I could count, their relationship had settled down considerably over time, and I remain convinced that their separation is a temporary hiccup. As with any family subsisting primarily on state aid, they had financial crises; his first line of defense during these times was his own family. Only when they could not offer assistance did he turn to the streets; when he did, he was far more risk averse than he used to be, engaging in just enough criminal activity to meet the demands of the situation.

Since stable social supports are such an important element of pathways to desistance, it is vital to recognize that reform schools such as Mountain Ridge do nothing to foster them; indeed, they undermine youths' connections with significant others. Their distance from urban communities prevents family members and girlfriends from visiting regularly and strains bonds with parents, girlfriends, and children. For this reason, many states, including New York, California, and Missouri, have recently developed policies and practices designed to keep incarcerated youth closer to home. Small, therapeutic facilities located in or close to residents' communities have had remarkable success at reducing the harmful effects of incarceration.

One approach, known as the Missouri Model, employs small, cottage-type facilities close to youths' homes. The state has received national attention for having the lowest recidivism rate in the country (8.4 percent of youth released in 2006, compared to half of juvenile offenders in neighboring Illinois). As a result, the Missouri Youth Services Institute has received representatives from at least twenty-five states who were interested in replicating the model in their own jurisdictions.[20]

In the next section, I offer additional ideas for addressing serious youth crime in ways that balance public safety demands and the need to support vulnerable young people in their quest to become productive citizens.

WHAT SHOULD WE DO ABOUT SERIOUS YOUTH CRIME?

My first suggestion leads directly from my findings on the experiences of urban youth inside Mountain Ridge Academy, which is but another pebble on a growing mountain of evidence that incarceration harms youth and increases their risk for future criminal behavior. It is simply this: avoid incarcerating young people whenever possible. Nationally, only 37 percent of juveniles who are incarcerated (pre- or postadjudication) are violent offenders. Nearly two in five incarcerated youth were confined for drug offenses, public order offenses, technical violations of probation, or status offenses, such as running away or truancy.[21] At a minimum, we should reserve incarceration for those young people who present a serious public safety risk or those for whom community-based alternatives have already proven ineffective.

In cases where there is no alternative to incarcerate, we must provide facilities where young people are safe. One survey of both detention facilities and training schools found that overcrowding remains pervasive; nearly half (47 percent) of facilities were over capacity. Moreover, overcrowded facilities are more likely to have the highest incidence rates of resident-on-resident and resident-on-staff injuries. The U.S. Department of Justice has initiated legal action against facilities in eleven states where supervision was deemed substandard or abusive. Between 2004 and 2007, 13,000 claims of abuse were made by residents of custodial facilities, including beatings, sexual abuse, and the use of aggressive restraint techniques. At least five young people died while being forcibly restrained during this reporting period. The U.S. Justice Department found 2,821 sexual abuse allegations made by staff inside these institutions in one year alone.[22]

As reliance on private corrections corporations is on the increase, we must demand transparency in and accountability for what happens inside juvenile institutions. Where any sort of programmatic theory exists inside juvenile treatment, it is often outdated or has received no empirical support. The widespread use of "criminal thinking errors" is but one example. Often, the "therapeutic" component is really punitive (as in the case of boot camps) based on the theory that harsh discipline will bring about personal reform. Several high-profile cases of deaths and injuries at such programs should be evidence enough to cause concern. Few of these programs have undergone evaluation, relying instead on (often reactive) monitoring by state and local funding agencies. These efforts tend to emphasize *outputs* and compliance with minimum standards for service provision (e.g., staff-to-client ratios), instead of *outcomes* (e.g., recidivism). Accountability, however, should mean that facilities must demonstrate that they actually reduce young people's risk of reoffending and strengthen resilience after release.

With the vast expansion of research on correctional effectiveness, there is little excuse for continuing to fund youth programs that we know do not work. Systematic evaluations using strong experimental research designs have found that a number of family-based approaches can prevent or reduce youth violence, including multisystemic therapy (MST), family functional therapy (FFT), and the nurse-family partnership.[23] Moreover, we know that a number of principles undergird effective interventions, such as targeting interventions toward risk and needs, increasing positive reinforcement, and engaging ongoing support in natural communities.[24]

We must dismantle what sociologist Victor Rios termed the *youth control complex*, "a system in which schools, police, probation officers, families, community centers, the media, business, and other institutions systematically treat young people's everyday behaviors as criminal activity."[25] One solution is to repeal zero-tolerance school policies, which were instated in the wake of several high-profile school shootings in the 1990s. These mandates remove discretion from school administrators, allowing student behavior to be regulated by school resource officers (SROs). Although school violence is at its lowest level in twenty years, U.S. schools have seen a 38 percent increase in the number of SROs, which has in turn led to an increase in school-based referrals to the juvenile justice system, often for nonserious behavior such as swearing.[26]

In its place, we should develop what Rios called a *youth support complex*, which supports and nurtures high-risk youth. Mentoring programs are one proven means of supporting youth, by connecting them to caring adults in their community. Participants in the Big Brothers Big Sisters of America program, for example, are 46 percent less likely to initiate drug use, almost one-third less likely to hit someone, more likely to have better academic behavior and performance, and more likely to have higher quality relationships with their parents and peers than their counterparts.[27] Mentoring programs have shown such promise for preventing delinquency and for supporting youth returning to their communities from juvenile facilities that the Office for Juvenile Justice and Delinquency Prevention invested $97 million in 2010 alone.[28]

Other supportive strategies involve shoring up mainstream opportunities for at-risk youth. Multiple studies have found that graduation incentive programs, where youth are given financial incentives for good grades or for staying in school, reduce crime and violence. Moreover, they do so at a fraction of the cost of incarceration.[29] For example, students participating in the Quantum Opportunities Program, a financial incentive program aimed at low-income ninth graders, were arrested half as often as their counterparts who did not receive the program. In fact, any successful dropout prevention program will also likely ameliorate crime because of the disproportionately high criminal involvement of high school dropouts. One study in California concluded that a 10 percent increase in high school graduation rates would decrease homicide and assault rates by 20 percent.[30]

The Harlem Children's Zone (HCZ) reappropriates the term "pipeline"—typically used to describe how at-risk youth are funneled into the criminal justice system—by providing "cradle to college" comprehensive services to children and families in high-risk blocks of Harlem, New York. The program includes parenting workshops, prekindergarten preparation, charter schools, college support, assistance programs for tenants who want to convert their city-owned buildings into co-ops, and recreation, arts, and health programs for community members. A National Bureau of Economic Research study found that HCZ's charter school eliminated the black-white school achievement gap in just three years.[31] Moreover, although a longitudinal evaluation of this large-scale social experiment only began in 2008, early results are promising. For example, 100 percent of their high school and after-school students stayed in school for the duration of the program.[32] This massive and multidimensional program emphasizing empowerment of community members is a stark contrast to juvenile institutions, which work only at the individual level and must blame their young charges for their own poor choices because they are not designed to address structural conditions such as poverty.

I contend that the struggles the young men in this book experienced after returning to their communities from Mountain Ridge Academy should not be viewed through a "reentry" lens because their problems existed long before their incarceration. However, I would be remiss if I failed to acknowledge that reentry services do matter, perhaps even more for vulnerable youths than for adults. The transition process is a narrow window of opportunity for the provision of support services that may

not be otherwise available. When carried out in ways that address individual and developmental needs of youth and that focus on continuity
of care between facility and community, carefully planned and executed
aftercare programs have been shown to reduce recidivism among returning youth.[33] It is especially important, according to experts, to account
for the developmental needs of adolescents, regardless of their chrono-
logical age.[34]

A final, more speculative idea about programming for urban youth
in the juvenile justice system involves using their knowledge of the street
code in a positive—rather than stigmatizing—manner. The words and
experiences of the young men in this book suggest strongly that their
mastery of the street code is a great source of pride and an important
component of their masculine identities. In some ways, the code has
served them well because it has allowed them to survive the meanest
streets of Philadelphia. In other ways, however, it is clearly a barrier to
their dreams of becoming productive members of society. In short, acting
"street" works well in urban contexts but not so well in interactions with
gatekeepers to mainstream institutions, such as employers.

What might an intervention program look like if it acknowledged the
usefulness and legitimacy of the street code in some situations, but gave
young people the skills to code switch between street and more mainstream performances? This might involve helping youth identify the contexts in which each is appropriate and shoring up their skills in interacting
with others in professional settings. As an example, I noted in chapter 5
that the young men I followed rarely made eye contact with prospective employers during interviews. In inner-city neighborhoods, continuous
eye contact is considered aggressive and can be interpreted by others as a
physical challenge. From an employer's perspective, failing to maintain eye
contact suggests that a job candidate may be less than trustworthy. Practicing eye contact and handshakes, then, might make young people feel more
confident when they are seeking work in settings where they feel out of
their element. The difference between this code-switching approach I am
suggesting and traditional life skills curricula that are often used inside
juvenile correctional institutions is that the former strategy takes great care
to acknowledge the legitimacy and value of the street code so as not to
destroy or damage the sense of self associated with the street.

Before moving onto a snapshot of the young men's status as I complete this book, I shift from some of the possible policy implications of my findings to a brief consideration of the unique advantages of the long-term ethnographic field research study.

METHODOLOGICAL IMPLICATIONS

What does a research design like the one employed in this book offer that traditional large-sample surveys do not? First, it allows us to examine the construction of meaning. As field researchers, we are trained that meaning is situational and fluid, arising out of shared interactions with others. As suggested in the previous section, sustained eye contact in the context of a job interview conveys trustworthiness, while the same degree of eye contact shared between urban males passing on a sidewalk in the inner city could lead to physical conflict. The meaning that individuals construct helps us understand why they make the choices they do and why they behave in certain ways and not others.

In chapters 2 and 3, I presented the meaning of Mountain Ridge Academy's approach to change, first from the perspective of the program administrators and staff and then from the viewpoint of the young men who were part of the program. These two sets of meaning come into conflict with one another when lessons purportedly taught to help young people make better decisions were received as hostile, stigmatizing, and ill fitting. Another place where meaning is important is when it challenges popularly held notions, such as the idea that inner-city fathers have no desire to take responsibility for their children or be involved in their lives. By contrast, many of the young fathers in my study craved the responsibility of a child, although they were less enamored of the responsibility of being faithful romantic partners with their children's mothers.

A second advantage of the approach I have used here is the insight provided by close relationships with many of the young men I studied. My involvement in their lives—as a godmother, as a job reference, as a member of their support networks—allowed me to see things I would have otherwise missed. For example, if I had never helped Leo get a job, I would not have known the limits to his claims about taking any available legal job. My embeddedness in Sincere's family allowed me to learn Marta's side of the story when they had conflicts. Of course, close relationships have drawbacks, too, when participants begin to care too much what the researcher thinks and censor themselves accordingly. Because these relationships are a challenge to maintain, particularly when they are inherently exploitative and when the researcher must eventually withdraw to some degree to write up her findings. However, the strength of ethnographic partnerships is one way in which field researchers establish the validity of their findings.

Third, by conducting longitudinal ethnographic field research, I was able to develop dynamic and contextual narratives of the lives and trajectories for the young men I followed. These narratives are characterized by a nearly constant instability and flux in housing, employment, offending activity, and romantic and father relationship statuses. If we rely on surveys to map out patterns of desistance, for example, we miss all the cyclical activity between data points. We also typically miss all the "shady" activities in which inner-city actors regularly engage: quasi-legal hustles such as bootlegging CDs, under-the-table employment, and offending that is never detected by the police. Long-term ethnographic field research makes visible the contradictions and inconsistencies that characterize all human behavior, as when our actions are inconsistent with our words or when we behave one way today and contradict ourselves tomorrow. In short, ethnographic data gathered over long periods of time are a more accurate reflection of truth because they are messy. The downside, of course, is that this work involves a conscious trade-off between breadth (or generalizability) and depth (or internal validity).

WHERE ARE THEY NOW?

Since moving to Albany to teach criminal justice, I have lost touch with many of the young men who helped me write this book. It has been extraordinarily difficult to maintain relationships with them from such a distance, and some of these men have undoubtedly been frustrated by my inability to stay in regular contact with them while trying to meet the demands of a tenure-track faculty position. Although I remain in touch with Sincere, Leo, Tony, Eddie, Isaiah, James, and Warren, I have had to rely on criminal records to track the others. Of course, arrest is a poor measure of criminal activity and an even worse indicator of transitions to adulthood. The picture these records offer, however, clearly indicates the prominent role of the criminal justice system in the lives of young black males.

More than six years after his release from Mountain Ridge, Sincere, twenty-five, and I are still closely connected. My new husband and I visit him and the kids whenever we are in Philadelphia. He and Marta had another son, Martín, two and a half years ago. Her sister had another daughter at around the same time, bringing the total number of children Marta and Sincere took responsibility for housing and feeding to five. Although Sincere was not employed for most of the past six years, "being there" over the long haul seemed to have won out in his ongoing battle with Marta. Once they moved to a more spacious home in a less impoverished neighborhood, their relationship seemed stable for a period of almost two years. Sincere occasionally hustled but viewed it as the last viable option when a financial crisis arose.

Recently, the two split up when Lakisha revealed Sincere's secret affair with a college student (a different affair from the previously mentioned one ending in an abortion). He has been living with Teresa and saving money from his work at the golf course to get a place of his own. He is still committed to being an active father and is preparing to fight Marta for joint custody. He still admits to loving her and hopes that they will reconcile.

Leo, twenty-five, still lives with his grandmother Ida in her home in North Philadelphia. When he was released from jail for the murder charge in 2008, he was put on probation for ten years. He has worked on and off for the past six years, but his criminal record makes finding a job very difficult. Last year he spent several happy months doing under-the-table car repair in his uncle's shop, and for the past six months he has worked on the maintenance crew at a YMCA in South Philly. He is still the go-to guy on his block for drugs, although he does hand-to-hand sales less frequently than connecting buyers and sellers. He and Gwen recently got engaged to be married.

Warren, twenty-five, has struggled to find work since his release from Mountain Ridge because his case had been originally filed in the adult court, so unlike the other juvenile offenders I followed, he came out of the justice system with a record to which potential employers had access. His mother, with whom he was exceptionally close, died in early 2009 after being given the wrong dose of blood pressure medicine at the emergency room. Warren has dense criminal networks; he refers to himself as a "hustler," as distinct from a drug dealer, because he will sell whatever others will buy (e.g., tasers). He restricts his drug sales to marijuana because of the relatively lenient sanctions associated with it. He has been arrested four times since his discharge from Mountain Ridge. He wants more than anything to leave Philadelphia, where he sees death and imprisonment as the only possibilities, but has not been successful at marshaling the resources to move.

Akeem, twenty-five, has been out of touch since early in my research, and I have been unable to get back in contact with him. He has been arrested twice since, once in 2008 and again in 2009, both for simple assault. In 2009 he was sentenced to two years of probation.

Tony, twenty-five, was in state prison from January 2008, serving a five- to ten-year sentence for robbery and kidnapping. He was paroled in April 2012.

Malik, twenty-four, has been in state prison since 2008, where he is serving a three- to six-year sentence for carrying a firearm (a virtual necessity for drug sellers).

Luis, twenty-five, has been arrested many times but has spent surprisingly little time in prison. Since he was released from Mountain Ridge in December 2004, he has been arrested six times for a variety of charges including robbery, car theft, and drug selling and did two short jail stints in 2006 and 2009. He is currently in violation of his probation and on the run.

Eddie, twenty-four, has spent most of the time since being released from Mountain Ridge in jails and prisons. After going to prison for the check-kiting scheme in his college town, he returned to Philadelphia and spent most of the summer of 2006 in jail after a conflict with the police that ended in his being charged with assault as well as drug possession. In 2007 he was locked up again for drug selling. Two months after his release in late 2008, he was arrested for retail theft, and in early 2009 he was sentenced to up to twenty-three months in jail. More recently, he was involved in a case of mistaken identity when he was charged with a home invasion that he did not commit. He spent nearly two years in jail, refusing to plead guilty, and just when the hearing appeared imminent, the police picked up a suspect in another crime who confessed to the home invasion. He was released and is considering a lawsuit against the city.

Hassan, twenty-four, was arrested several times after the police pressured him to report who had shot him and he went on the run. He was arrested four times over the years for drug selling, possession, carrying a firearm, and DUI. In 2008, he was sentenced to two to four years in prison for the drug-selling charge.

Isaiah, twenty-five, was never arrested for his "silent partnership" in a drug business. He and Tamika broke up, leaving a criminal history dotted with domestic abuse and violations of protective orders. The last entry on his criminal record suggests that he violated probation and went on the run, although Tamika recently directed me to a local news article detailing an arrest for stealing food from a grocery store and possession of cocaine. Tamika moved her kids to Atlanta, where they could afford to rent a large house in a neighborhood with good schools.

Keandre, twenty-five, has been arrested six times since being released from Mountain Ridge for drug selling, receiving stolen property, and possessing an instrument of crime. In late 2009 he was jailed for up to twenty-three months.

Malik, twenty-four, has been in prison since 2007 and is now serving a three- to six-year sentence for carrying a firearm.

Gabe, twenty-five, is the only one I followed who had no criminal record at all.

James, twenty-five, made it through his first three years at home with no criminal justice contact other than the charge that was generated and then dropped when he was the victim of a stabbing in 2007. In August 2008, he was arrested twice for forgery and drug selling; in 2009 he was arrested for DUI. When I ran my first set of criminal record checks, I was heartbroken to find him there. He has now recommitted himself to "falling back" and is training to be a tattoo artist.

My impressions of the young men I met at Mountain Ridge Academy and have followed since their return to Philadelphia leave me simultaneously sad and hopeful for their futures. As young black men from the most disadvantaged neighborhoods of a racially divided city, they occupy the lowest rungs of the social hierarchy. Worse yet, they know it. They are reminded every time they encounter whites in public space, when they seek work, as they navigate the criminal justice system and the welfare state, and when they fail to live up to their own standards for being good fathers or providers. Yet, despite the psychosocial damage inflicted by this realization and their objective lack of opportunities for making good, they remain remarkably resilient. Although they approach change in varied ways, most have taken concrete steps to improve their lives and to be better parents, providers, and role models than their own parents. When I picture Sincere, Warren, Leo, Eddie, James, and the others, I imagine their easy smiles, humor, creativity, and energy, not their struggle. Sincere's voice rings in my ears: "Hate it or love it, the underdog is on top!"

Notes

Preface

1. This statement was recorded by Howard Becker, one of Park's students, and is reported in John C. McKinney, *Constructive Typology and Social Theory* (New York: Appleton-Century-Crofts, 1966), 71.
2. Elijah Anderson, *Code of the Street: Decency, Violence, and the Moral Life of the Inner City* (New York: Norton, 1999); Paul G. Cressey, *The Taxi-Dance Hall: A Sociological Study in Commercialized Recreation and Urban Life* (Chicago: University of Chicago Press, 1932); Mitchell Duneier, *Sidewalk* (New York: Farrar, Straus and Giroux, 1999); Clifford R. Shaw, *The Jack-Roller: A Delinquent Boy's Own Story* (Chicago: University of Chicago Press, 1966); Harvey W. Zorbaugh, *The Gold Coast and the Slum: A Sociological Study of Chicago's Near North Side* (Chicago: University of Chicago Press, 1929).

Introduction

1. Melissa Sickmund, T. J. Sladky, Wei Kang, and C. Puzzanchera, "Easy Access to the Census of Juveniles in Residential Placement," http://www.ojjdp.gov/ojstatbb/ezacjrp/ (accessed August 8, 2012).
2. American Correctional Association, *2008 Directory of Adult and Juvenile Correctional Departments, Institutions, Agencies, and Probation and Parole Authorities* (Alexandria, VA: American Correctional Association, 2008). See also Justice Policy Institute, "The Costs of Confinement: Why Good Juvenile Justice Policies Make Good Fiscal Sense" (policy brief, Justice Policy Institute, Washington, DC, May 2009), http://www.justicepolicy.org/images/upload/09_05_REP_CostsOfConfinement_JJ_PS.pdf.
3. The normal recreation period had been taken away for three days as a collective punishment for "disrespectful behavior" by one or more of the twenty-three boys in the dorm. The medical examiner ruled his death a homicide, although he had an underlying undiagnosed cardiac arrhythmia. Jennifer Gonnerman, "The Lost Boys of Tryon," *New York Magazine*, January 24 2010, http://nymag.com/news/features/63239.
4. For exceptions, see Laura S. Abrams, "Listening to Juvenile Offenders: Can Residential Treatment Prevent Recidivism?" *Child and Adolescent Social Work Journal* 23, no. 1 (2005): 61–85; Alexandra Cox, "Doing the Programme or Doing Me? The Pains of Youth Imprisonment," *Punishment & Society* 13, no. 5 (2011): 592–610; Michelle Inderbitzin, "Inside a Maximum-Security Juvenile Training School: Institutional Attempts to Redefine the American Dream and 'Normalize' Incarcerated Youth," *Punishment & Society* 9, no. 3 (2007): 235–251; Anne M. Nurse, "The Structure of the Juvenile Prison: The Construction of the Inmate

Father," *Youth & Society* 32, no. 3 (2001): 360–394; and Adam D. Reich, *Hidden Truth: Young Men Navigating Lives In and Out of Juvenile Prison* (Berkeley: University of California Press, 2010).

5. Erving Goffman, *Asylums: Essays on the Social Situation of Mental Patients and Other Inmates* (New York: Anchor Books, 1961).

6. Reform schools are often referred to as residential placements, training schools, juvenile correctional facilities, "juvie," or (incorrectly) detention centers. I prefer the old-fashioned but honest term "reform school." See Jerome Miller, *Last One Over the Wall: The Massachusetts Experiment in Closing Reform Schools* (Columbus: Ohio State University Press, 1991). Many practitioners resist correctional terminology or any reference to youth incarceration because they are convinced that the juvenile justice system offers something fundamentally different than adult corrections. I reject the medicalized language of "residential placements" because it obscures the fundamental truth that no matter how therapeutic the treatment, their "residents" are locked up against their will.

7. Joan Petersilia, *When Prisoners Come Home: Parole and Prisoner Reentry* (New York: Oxford University Press, 2003); Jeremy Travis, *But They All Come Back: Facing the Challenges of Prisoner Reentry* (Washington, DC: Urban Institute Press, 2005).

8. The *Urban Dictionary* defines "fall back" as "chill out, relax, stop trippin'"; s.v. "fall back," *Urban Dictionary*, http://www.urbandictionary.com/define .php?term=Fall+Back. I was struck by the comparative imagery of "falling back" from the drug game, which implies the great expenditure of effort involved in selling drugs, and words used to describe selling drugs, such as "grind" and "hustle," or the noun to describe drugs themselves, "work."

9. Fourteen of the fifteen were African American. The last, Luis, was Puerto Rican and white. Luis was different from the others in many ways, including his belief that addiction was his primary barrier to success after leaving Mountain Ridge Academy. He was reincarcerated fairly quickly after his release. Since I lost contact with him after this stint inside another juvenile facility, I refer to him infrequently. Throughout the book, I discuss my findings in relation to the urban African American experience.

10. I conducted record checks for six years from each participant's date of discharge from Mountain Ridge Academy. This period extended to July 2011 even though most of my field research was completed by 2007. Most of what I focus on in this book covers their first three years after leaving Mountain Ridge.

11. Pennsylvania's Act 88, passed in 2001, mandated that delinquent youth from Philadelphia attend disciplinary schools, GED preparation classrooms, or "twilight" night school instead of returning to public schools. See Marsha Levick, "Law Unfairly Excludes Students from Their Regular School: Why Pennsylvania's Act 88 Is Being Challenged in Court," *The Notebook* 10, no. 2 (2002), http://www.thenotebook.org/winter-2002/02980/ law-unfairly-excludes-students-their-regular-school.

12. I refer to aftercare workers as reintegration workers to reflect the changed language after Philadelphia "reinvented" aftercare.

13. William F. Whyte, *Street Corner Society: The Social Structure of an Italian Slum* (Chicago: University of Chicago Press, 1955); Patricia A. Adler and Peter Adler, *Membership Roles in Field Research* (Thousand Oaks, CA: Sage, 1987);

John Lofland and Lyn Lofland, *Analyzing Social Settings: A Guide to Qualitative Observation and Analysis* (Belmont, CA: Wadsworth, 1995).

14. Isaiah called me "Mommy," which I think may also be "Mami," a reference to his familial ties to the Puerto Rican community.

15. Elijah Anderson, "Urban Ethnography," in *International Encyclopedia of the Social & Behavioral Sciences,* ed. Neil J. Smelser and Paul B. Baltes (New York: Elsevier, 2001), 16004–16008.

16. Timothy Black, *When a Heart Turns Rock Solid: The Lives of Three Puerto Rican Brothers On and Off the Streets* (New York: Pantheon Books, 2009).

17. Victor Rios, *Punished: Policing the Lives of Black and Latino Boys* (New York: New York University Press, 2011).

CHAPTER 1   YOUTH INCARCERATION AND REENTRY IN PHILADELPHIA

1. Elijah Anderson, *The Cosmopolitan Canopy: Race and Civility in Everyday Life* (New York: Norton, 2011).

2. Douglas S. Massey and Nancy A. Denton, *American Apartheid: Segregation and the Making of the Underclass* (Cambridge, MA: Harvard University Press, 1993).

3. Rima Wilkes and John Iceland, "Hypersegregation in the Twenty-First Century," *Demography* 41, no. 1 (2004): 23–36.

4. Daniel Amsterdam, "Immigration to the City of Philadelphia: An Economic and Historical Overview" (Philadelphia Migration Project Working Paper, 2008), http://www.history.upenn.edu/philamigrationproject/paper_02.pdf.

5. Ibid.

6. I accepted Luis into the group of young men I would follow before my advisor suggested that I focus on African Americans because that racial group was disproportionately incarcerated.

7. Adams and her colleagues make this point in an elegant and insightful description of the city:

> The economic changes that have swept the city since World War II have transformed the residential landscape of the city, but hardly with the uniformly beneficial effects generally assumed by the ideologies of progress and planning. The decentralization of economic and residential locations . . . has created, in Philadelphia's case, graphic examples of the paradox of poverty and plenty, virtually side by side. The contemporary picture of housing in the city itself is one of gentrified splendor next to public housing, of abandoned houses and homeless people, and of a black population expanding into many of the city's neighborhoods, yet more segregated now than at any time over the past four decades.

> Carolyn Adams, David Bartelt, David Elesh, Ira Goldstein, and William Yancey, *Philadelphia: Neighborhoods, Division, and Conflict in a Postindustrial City* (Philadelphia: Temple University Press, 1991), 66.

8. Lisa Chamberlain, "Tax Breaks Drive a Philadelphia Boom," *New York Times,* January 8, 2006, http://www.nytimes.com/2006/01/08/realestate/08nati.html (accessed June 2, 2008).

9. These men were terrified of my mild-mannered Doberman pinscher, a phenomenon I understood only after reading Elijah Anderson's *Streetwise: Race, Class and Change in an Urban Community* (Chicago: University of Chicago Press, 1990), which explains that in the inner city walking with a powerful dog is similar to brandishing a weapon.

10. Penny Balkin Bach, *Public Art in Philadelphia* (Philadelphia: Temple University Press, 1992).

11. William Julius Wilson writes about this transformation in *The Truly Disadvantaged: The Inner City, the Underclass, and Public Policy* (Chicago: University of Chicago Press, 1987).

12. Adams et al., *Philadelphia*.

13. Ibid.

14. Wilson, *Truly Disadvantaged*, 1987.

15. Karl E. Johnson, "Police-Black Community Relations in Postwar Philadelphia: Race and Criminalization in Urban Social Spaces, 1945–1960," *Journal of African-American History* 89, no. 2 (2004): 118–134.

16. "Philadelphia: A Legacy of Police Brutality" (transcript of *Democracy Now!* radio broadcast, July 3, 2000), http://www.democracynow.org/2000/7/31/philadelphia_a_legacy_of_police_brutality.

17. George Kelling and Anne Marie Rocheleu, "Boston's Comprehensive Communities Program: A Case Study" (report prepared for the National Institute of Justice, 2004), http://www.ncjrs.gov/pdffiles1/nij/grants/204680.pdf.

18. Naci Mocan, "Crime Control: Lessons from the New York City Experience" (paper, International Seminar on Crime and Violence Prevention in Urban Settings, Bogota, Columbia, May 2003), http://www.suivd.gov.co/SEMINARIO_%20INTERNACIONAL/documento/Mocan.pdf.

19. These statistics have recently been called into question as a function of extreme pressure for police to demonstrate their effectiveness. See William R. Rashbaum, "Retired Officers Raise Questions on Crime Data," *New York Times,* February 6, 2010, http://www.nytimes.com/2010/02/07/nyregion/07crime.html.

20. Amanda Petteruti and Nastassia Walsh, "Jailing Communities: The Impact of Jail Expansion and Effective Public Safety Strategies" (Justice Policy Institute, April 2008), http://www.justicepolicy.org/images/upload/08–04_REP_JailingCommunities_AC.pdf.

21. The Bureau of Justice Statistics makes the FBI's Uniform Crime Reports annual data available via a table-building tool: http://bjs.ojp.usdoj.gov/ucrdata/offenses.cfm.

22. Anderson, *Code of the Street.*

23. Anderson, *Streetwise.*

24. Anderson, *Code of the Street*, 33.

25. Timothy J. Nelson and Kathryn Edin, *Doing the Best I Can: Fatherhood in the Inner City* (Berkeley: University of California Press, 2013); Katherine S. Newman, *No Shame in My Game: The Working Poor in the Inner City* (New York: Russell Sage Foundation, 1999); Carl Husemoller Nightingale, *On the Edge: A History of Poor Black Children and Their American Dreams* (New York: Basic Books, 1993).

26. Warren wanted to update this excerpt before publication, so that the slang would remain current. We revised it together in May 2012.

27. Anderson, *Streetwise.*

CHAPTER 2   PREDICTIONS OF FAILURE AND CULTURAL
            ASSAULTS INSIDE MOUNTAIN RIDGE ACADEMY

1. Samuel Yochelson and Stanton E. Samenow, *The Criminal Personality*, vol. 1 (New York: Aronson, 1976), vol. 2 (New York: Aronson, 1977).

2. Program Development and Evaluation System, Crime and Justice Research Center, Philadelphia. ProDES was the evaluation project I worked on from 1997 to 2002 and that tracked all Philadelphia youth who were adjudicated delinquent and committed to programs. System-wide reports and in-depth descriptions of all the programs tracked by ProDES are available at http://www.temple.edu/prodes/. Program-specific reports are not publicly available.

3. During my time as a program evaluator, I had the opportunity to review the program design as well as those of other Philadelphia-contracted institutions. Moreover, our research team had ongoing communication about facilities with probation officers, judges, and DHS administrators.

4. Program Development and Evaluation System.

5. Miller, *Last One Over the Wall;* Anthony Platt, *The Child Savers: The Invention of Delinquency* (Chicago: University of Chicago Press, 1969); Steven Schlossman, *Love and the American Delinquent: The Theory and Practice of "Progressive" Juvenile Justice, 1825–1920* (Chicago: University of Chicago Press, 1977); Eric C. Schneider, *In the Web of Class: Delinquents and Reformers in Boston, 1810s–1930s* (New York: New York University Press, 1992).

6. Schneider, *In the Web of Class.*

7. ProDES was a finalist for the 1999 Innovations in American Government Award presented by the Ford Foundation and the Kennedy School of Government at Harvard University. See Harvard Kennedy School, Ash Center, "Program Development and Evaluation System," http://www.innovations .harvard.edu/awards.html?id=50391.

8. These are drawn from the Mountain Ridge Academy Employee Training Manual (1994/2003), 333–354.

9. Yochelson and Samenow, *Criminal Personality.*

10. Ibid., 36.

11. Hans Toch, personal communication, June 18, 2010.

12. Hans Toch, "Book Review: The Criminal Personality: Volume II, The Change Process," *Journal of Psychiatry and Law* 6 (1978): 257–263.

13. Delbert S. Elliott, Suzanne S. Ageton, David Huizinga, Brian A. Knowles, and Rachelle J. Canter, *The Prevalence and Incidence of Delinquent Behavior: 1976–1980,* National Youth Survey report no. 26 (Boulder, CO: Behavioral Research Institute, 1983); Terrie E. Moffitt, "Adolescent-Limited and Life-Course Persistent Antisocial Behavior: A Developmental Taxonomy," *Psychological Review* 100, no. 4 (1993): 674–701; Elizabeth S. Scott and Laurence Steinberg, *Rethinking Juvenile Justice* (Cambridge, MA: Harvard University Press, 2008).

14. O. J. Keller, "The Criminal Personality or Lombroso Revisited," *Federal Probation* 37 (1980): 37.

15. Subcultural theory posits delinquency as a lower-class phenomenon that arises as a response to limited opportunities and is transmitted to delinquent peers, usually through gangs. See Albert Cohen, *Delinquent Boys: The Culture of the Gang* (Glencoe, IL: Free Press, 1955); and Walter Miller, "Lower Class Culture as a Generating Milieu of Gang Delinquency," *Journal of Social Issues* 14, no. 3 (1958): 5–20.

16. See Linda M. Burton, Dawn A. Obeidallah, and Kevin Allison, "Ethnographic Insights on Social Context and Adolescent Development among Inner-City African-American Teens," in *Ethnography and Human Development: Context*

and Meaning in Social Inquiry, ed. Richard Jessor, Anne Colby, and Richard A. Shweder (Chicago: University of Chicago Press, 1996), 395–418.

17. Goffman, *Asylums,* 20.
18. In detention, youths must wear jumpsuits similar to those of prison inmates.
19. It is worth noting that the criminalization of urban clothing styles has become more widespread, as when Florida governor Rick Scott signed into law the "baggy pants" bill, requiring school boards to adopt dress codes forbidding clothes that "expose underwear or body parts in an indecent of vulgar manner"; Brandon Larabee, "Governor Approves Voucher Expansions, Baggy Pants Bill," *Palm Beach Post,* June 2, 2011, http://www.palmbeachpost .com/news/state/governor-approves-voucher-expansions-baggy-pants -bill-1515689.html. In another case, a University of New Mexico student athlete was arrested and removed from his flight when he refused to pull up his pants; Justin Berton, "Reasoning for SFO Sagging Pants Arrest Debated," *SFGate.com,* June 17, 2011, http://articles.sfgate.com/2011–06–17/bay-area/ 29668700_1_sagging-pants-fashion-statement-arrest.
20. Mountain Ridge Academy Employee Training Manual, 330.
21. Lee Jussim and Kent D. Harber, "Teacher Expectations and Self-Fulfilling Prophecies: Knowns and Unknowns, Resolved and Unresolved Controversies," *Personality and Social Psychology Review* 9, no. 2 (2005): 131–155.

CHAPTER 3   THE EXPERIENCE OF "REFORM" AT
                MOUNTAIN RIDGE ACADEMY

1. Cox's study of incarcerated youth found similarly that they resist some aspects of the institutional regime, attempting to retain continuity in their identities. When they were unable to do this, they experienced a "split" or "disconnect" between the intent and the results of the treatment programme, which created an alienating experience for the young people as they attempted to demonstrate 'change'" (593). Youth articulated a tension between "doing programme" (i.e., doing well in the program) and "doing me," or retaining a strong sense of self apart from the institution. Cox, "Doing the Programme or Doing Me?"
2. See also Frank F. Furstenberg Jr., "How Families Manage Risk and Opportunity in Dangerous Neighborhoods," in *Sociology and the Public Agenda,* ed. William J. Wilson (Thousand Oaks, CA: Sage, 1993), 231–258; and Carol Stack, *All Our Kin: Strategies for Survival in a Black Community* (New York: Harper and Row, 1974).
3. Richard Majors and Janet Mancini Billson, *Cool Pose: The Dilemmas of Black Manhood in America* (New York: Lexington Books, 1992), 5.
4. Anderson, *Code of the Street;* Philippe Bourgois, *In Search of Respect: Selling Crack in El Barrio* (New York: Cambridge University Press, 1996).
5. Mountain Ridge Academy Employee Training Manual, 135.
6. Program Design and Evaluation System, available at http://www.temple.edu/ prodes/.
7. "Don't know _____ from a can of paint" is slang used by many urban youth. It shows up in hip-hop artists' Salt-n-Pepa's 1997 single "Friends" and was used by music producer Timbaland after he won a sampling lawsuit: "This dude is trying to act like I went to his house and took it from his computer. I don't know him from a can of paint. I'm 15 years deep." Terry Hart, "Timbaland Wins 2nd

Sampling Lawsuit in 3 Months," *Copyhype,* June 15, 2001, http://www.copy
hype.com/2011/06/timbaland-wins-2nd-sampling-lawsuit-in-3-months/.
8. Abrams, "Listening to Juvenile Offenders."
9. Anderson, *Code of the Street.*

CHAPTER 4 REINTEGRATION PLANS MEET THE INNER CITY

1. The "Chinese store" is a term used to describe both Chinese food stores,
which are plentiful in poor urban neighborhoods, and corner bodegas run by
Asians of all nationalities.
2. David M. Altschuler and Rachel Brash, "Adolescent and Teenage Offenders
Confronting the Challenges and Opportunities of Reentry," *Youth Violence and
Juvenile Justice* 2, no. 1 (2004): 72–87.
3. Bureau of Data and Research, *National Comparisons from State Recidivism Studies* (Tallahassee: Florida Department of Juvenile Justice, 1999); Barry Krisberg
and John C. Howell, "The Impact of the Juvenile Justice System and Prospects
for Graduated Sanctions in a Comprehensive Strategy," in *Serious and Violent
Juvenile Offenders,* ed. Rolf Loeber and David P. Farrington (Thousand Oaks,
CA: Sage, 1998), 346–366; Daniel P. Mears and Jeremy Travis, "Youth Development and Reentry," *Youth Violence and Juvenile Justice* 2, no. 1 (2004): 3–20.
4. Some caution should be used in accepting labels of conduct disorders as mental health problems because young people who are adjudicated as delinquent
are often diagnosed with conditions such as oppositional defiant disorder
because of the very fact that they were labeled delinquent.
5. Howard N. Snyder, "An Empirical Portrait of the Youth Reentry Population,"
Youth Violence and Juvenile Justice 2, no. 1 (2004): 39–55.
6. Kathryn Edin, Timothy J. Nelson, and Rechelle Paranal, "Fatherhood and
Incarceration as Potential Turning Points in the Criminal Careers of Unskilled
Men," in *Imprisoning America: The Social Effects of Mass Incarceration,* ed. Mary
Pattillo, David Weiman, and Bruce Western (New York: Russell Sage, 2004),
21–45.
7. Some refer to this as the crab mentality, an analogy that compares the upwardly
mobile to a crab trying to escape from the pot as the other crabs drag him
back into the boiling water.
8. Peggy C. Giordano, Stephen A. Cernkovich, and Jennifer L. Rudolph, "Gender, Crime, and Desistance: Toward a Theory of Cognitive Transformation,"
American Journal of Sociology 107, no. 4 (2002): 990–1064.
9. Shadd Maruna, Thomas P. LeBel, Nick Mitchell, and Michelle Naples, "Pyg-
malion in the Reintegration Process: Desistance from Crime through the
Looking Glass," *Psychology, Crime & Law* 10, no. 3 (2004): 271–281, 272.
10. Raymond is missing from this count because I did not have access to his
criminal records after he moved to South Carolina.

CHAPTER 5 EMPLOYMENT, HUSTLING, AND ADULTHOOD

1. This supermarket chain was later the target of class-action suits for gender and
racial discrimination.
2. In Pager's experimental audits in Milwaukee, only 14 percent of black men
applying for entry-level jobs received a callback, compared to 34 percent of
their white counterparts, despite the fact that their résumés were identical.

When the testers' résumés included a criminal record, these rates decreased to 5 percent for the black testers and 17 percent for the white testers. Tellingly, hiring agents were slightly more likely (17 percent) to hire a white applicant with a criminal record than a black applicant without such a record (14 percent). Devah Pager, "The Mark of a Criminal Record," *American Journal of Sociology* 108, no. 5 (2003): 937–975.

3. U.S. Bureau of Labor Statistics, "Table 3—Employment Status of the Civilian Noninstitutional Population by Age, Sex, and Race," ftp://ftp.bls.gov/pub/special.requests/lf/aa2005/pdf/cpsaat3.pdf.

4. Annie Paul Murphy, *The Cult of Personality: How Personality Tests Are Leading Us to Miseducate Our Children, Mismanage Our Companies, and Misunderstand Ourselves* (New York: Free Press, 2004).

5. Kathryn Edin and Laura Lein, *Making Ends Meet: How Single Mothers Survive Welfare and Low-Wage Work* (New York: Russell Sage, 1997); Bettylou Valentine, *Hustling and Other Hard Work: Life Styles in the Ghetto* (New York: Free Press, 1978); Sudhir A. Venkatesh, *Off the Books: The Underground Economy of the Urban Poor* (Cambridge, MA: Harvard University Press, 2006).

6. Although the term "shady" has been used to mean "disreputable" since the mid-nineteenth century, Drake and Cayton used it less pejoratively to describe the "shadow world" of hustling in the Black Belt of Chicago. St. Clair Drake and Horace R. Cayton, *Black Metropolis: A Study of Negro Life in a Northern City* (Chicago: University of Chicago Press, 1945).

7. Edin and Lein, *Making Ends Meet*; Valentine, *Hustling and Other Hard Work*.

8. The notion that employment and offending lie on a continuum is advanced in Jeffrey Fagan and Richard B. Freeman, "Crime and Work," *Crime and Justice* 25 (1999): 225–289.

9. Sociologist Victor Rios has written about this beautifully in *Punished*.

10. See, for example, Patrick J. Carr, Laura Napolitano, and Jessica Keating, "We Never Call the Cops and Here Is Why: A Qualitative Examination of Legal Cynicism in Three Philadelphia Neighborhoods," *Criminology* 45, no. 2 (2007): 445–480.

11. Anderson, *Code of the Street*.

12. Bourgois, *In Search of Respect*; Anderson, *Code of the Street*.

13. John M. Hagedorn, *People and Folks: Gangs, Crime, and the Underclass in a Rustbelt City* (Chicago: Lake View Press, 1988). See also Mercer Sullivan, *"Getting Paid": Youth Crime and Work in the Inner City* (Ithaca, NY: Cornell University Press, 1989).

14. Thomas Sugrue, *The Origins of the Urban Crisis: Race and Inequality in Postwar Detroit* (Princeton, NJ: Princeton University Press, 1992).

15. Shover and Thompson find that "confinement avoidance"—carrying off crime without being arrested—increases individuals' criminal expectations and reduces their likelihood of desistance. Neal Shover and Carol Y. Thompson, "Age, Differential Expectations, and Crime Desistance," *Criminology* 30, no. 1 (1992): 89–104.

16. Pager, "Mark of a Criminal Record"; Harry J. Holtzer, Steven Raphael, and Michael A. Stoll, "Will Employers Hire Ex-Offenders?" in Pattillo et al., *Imprisoning America*, 205–243; Ronald B. Mincy, ed., *Black Males Left Behind* (Washington, DC: Urban Institute Press, 2006).

17. Jomills H. Braddock II and James M. McPartland, "How Minorities Continue to Be Excluded from Equal Employment Opportunities: Research on Labor Market and Institutional Barriers," *Journal of Social Issues* 43, no. 1 (1987): 5–39;

Julie Kmec, "White Hiring Agents' Organizational Practices and Out-Group Hiring," *Social Science Research* 35, no. 3 (2006): 668–701; Philip Moss and Chris Tilly, *Raised Hurdles for Black Men: Evidence from Interviews with Employers* (New York: Russell Sage, November 1995); Philip Moss and Chris Tilly, "'Soft' Skills and Race: An Investigation of Black Men's Employment Problems," *Work and Occupations* 23, no. 6 (1996): 252–276; Philip Moss and Chris Tilly, *Stories Employers Tell: Race, Skill, and Hiring in America* (New York: Russell Sage, 2001); Johanna Shih, "'. . .Yeah, I Could Hire This One, But I Know It's Gonna Be a Problem': How Race, Nativity, and Gender Affect Employers' Perceptions of the Manageability of Job Seekers," *Ethnic and Racial Studies* 25, no. 1 (2002): 99–119.

18. Ehrenreich gives a hilarious and harrowing account of her experience of undergoing pre-employment testing at stores such as Walmart. Barbara Ehrenreich, *Nickel and Dimed: On (Not) Getting By in America* (New York: Henry Holt, 2002).

19. Christopher E. Kelly and Jamie J. Fader, "Computer-Based Employment Applications: Implications for Offenders and Supervising Officers," *Federal Probation* 76, no. 1 (2012): 24–29.

20. Anderson, *Cosmopolitan Canopy.*

21. Amanda E. Lewis, "Everyday Race-Making: Navigating Racial Boundaries in Schools," *American Behavioral Scientist* 47, no. 3 (2003): 283–305.

22. Duneier, *Sidewalk.*

23. Anderson, *Streetwise.*

24. He did pocket money from customers whose orders he failed to ring up, which he viewed as fundamentally different from stealing from the till.

25. Harry J. Holzer, Keith R. Ihlanfeldt, and David L. Sjoquist, "Work, Search and Travel among White and Black Youth," *Journal of Urban Economics* 35, no. 3 (1994): 320–345.

26. Carl H. Nightingale, *On the Edge: A History of Poor Black Children and Their American Dreams* (New York: Basic Books, 1993), 8. For a haunting account of the psychic consequences of poverty and racism, see also Kenneth Clark, *Dark Ghetto: Dilemmas of Social Power* (New York: Harper & Row, 1965).

27. It should be noted that the opposite is true for those on probation or parole, in which case the only acceptable means of proving employment is through a pay stub. Thus, the paper trail becomes an important source of legitimacy.

28. Christopher E. Kelly, "Crime, Work, and Drift: Accounting for Intermittency in Offending and Employment in the Desistance Process" (paper, American Society of Criminology, Atlanta, GA, 2007).

29. Bruce A. Jacobs, *Dealing Crack: The Social World of Streetcorner Selling* (Boston: Northeastern University Press, 1999). Elaborate methods of separating drugs and money are seen in the excellent HBO series *The Wire.* See also Neal Shover, *Great Pretenders: Pursuits and Careers of Persistent Thieves* (Boulder, CO: Westview, 1996), 123.

30. Elijah Anderson argues that the term "old head" used to mean a positive role model for young people growing up in inner-city neighborhoods. As the black middle class left urban neighborhoods and left poor residents socially isolated, "old head" began to mean someone who socialized younger kids ("young bols") into the rules of the drug game. Anderson, *Streetwise.*

31. According to the *Urban Dictionary,* "jablip," which originated in Philadelphia in the 1980s, refers to an unknown place. *Urban Dictionary,* s.v. "jablip," http://www.urbandictionary.com/define.php?term=east+jablip (accessed August 29, 2011).

32. These benefits definitely included food stamps and, given Ida's advanced age, probably also Social Security benefits. Haywood may have had a life insurance policy as well.

33. Leo's private attorney was able to get the prosecutor to downgrade the attempted murder charge for a charge of criminal conspiracy and drop the remaining charges. Nevertheless, the charge remains on his criminal history.

34. Elliot Liebow, *Tally's Corner: A Study of Negro Streetcorner Men* (Boston: Little, Brown, 1967), 63.

CHAPTER 6   FAMILY, FATHERHOOD, AND FURTHER OFFENDING

1. Edin et al., "Fatherhood and Incarceration as Potential Turning Points"; Paul Florsheim and Le Ngu, "Fatherhood as a Transformative Process: Unexpected Successes among High-Risk Fathers," in *Fragile Families and the Marriage Agenda*, ed. Lori Kowaleski-Jones and Nicholas H. Wolfinger (New York: Springer, 2006), 211–232. Giordano et al. also identify children as one of four "hooks for change" that are an important element in the desistance process for members of their sample. See Giordano et al., "Gender, Crime, and Desistance."

2. Rukmalie Jayakody and Ariel Kalil, "Social Fathering in Low-Income, African American Families with Preschool Children," *Journal of Marriage and the Family* 64, no. 2 (2002): 504–516. Nelson and Edin refer to this as "overclaiming paternity." Timothy J. Nelson and Kathryn Edin, *Doing the Best I Can: Fatherhood in the Inner City* (Berkeley: University of California Press, forthcoming).

3. This economic explanation for men's marginal roles in families has been addressed by many sociologists. My contribution is to show how the labor market–family relationship is associated with further offending or desistance among a group of formerly incarcerated youth. See Elijah Anderson, "Sex Codes and Family Life among Poor Inner-City Youths," in *Young, Unwed Fathers: Changing Roles and Emerging Policies*, ed. Robert I. Lerman and Theodora J. Ooms (Philadelphia: Temple University Press, 1993), 74–98; Nelson and Edin, *Doing the Best I Can*; Mercer L. Sullivan, "Young Fathers and Parenting in Two Inner-City Neighborhoods," in Lerman and Ooms, *Young, Unwed Fathers*, 52–73; and Liebow, *Tally's Corner*.

4. Gerson argues that men are currently in a "no-man's land," where the rules of what being a man means are unclear and often contradictory. Kathleen Gerson, *No Man's Land: Men's Changing Commitments to Family and Work* (New York: Basic Books, 1993). Waller's study of low-income fathers finds that most reported that providing emotional support was more important than providing financial support. Maureen R. Waller, *My Baby's Father: Unmarried Parents and Paternal Responsibility* (Princeton, NJ: Princeton University Press, 2002).

5. This motivation for fatherhood is also noted in Nelson and Edin, *Doing the Best I Can*.

6. This favoritism likely came from her own guilt for being the cause of his HIV-positive status, although I am not sure Sincere recognized this.

7. According to the 2000 census data culled from the University of Pennsylvania's Cartographic Modeling Lab's Neighborhood Information System (accessed January 25, 2007), the tract where Sincere lived after returning from the Mountain Ridge facility was 88 percent Hispanic and 11 percent black. Of the neighborhood's residents, 76 percent lived 200 percent below the federally

established poverty line. By this measure, the census tract is the fourth poorest in the city.

8. Elijah Anderson discusses the social capital that stems from knowledge of the street code in *Code of the Street*.

9. The *Urban Dictionary* defines "ride or die" primarily in terms of romantic partners being willing to do anything for their loved ones, but it can also mean "the people in your life who are there through thick and thin.""Ride," a term coined by West Coast gangstas, also refers to retaliating against a targeted individual for a "humiliating stunt or fallen comrade." *Urban Dictionary*, s.v. "ride or die," http://www.urbandictionary.com/define.php?term=ride+or+die/.

10. Anderson, *Code of the Street*; Ulf Hannerz, *Soulside: Inquiries into Ghetto Culture and Community* (New York: Columbia University Press, 1969); Jay MacLeod, *Ain't No Makin' It: Aspirations and Attainment in a Low-Income Neighborhood* (Boulder, CO: Westview, 1995); Liebow, *Tally's Corner*.

11. Liebow says that "going for brothers" is a type of male friendship in which "the usual claims, obligations, expectations, and loyalties of the friend relationship are publicly declared to be at their maximum." Liebow, *Tally's Corner*, 167.

12. Ibid., 180–181.

13. Years later, Sincere ended up working more regularly for his brother-in-law, doing demolition on a house that would eventually become his mother's family home. He was very proud during this time of his role as a working man, eagerly showing off the work that he had personally done to several rooms in the house. A few months later, he had a blowout with his brother-in-law and lost the opportunity to work with him.

14. Liebow, *Tally's Corner*.

15. Furstenberg's study of inner-city parents notes how memories of their own fathers shape both men and women's expectations of fatherhood; Frank F. Furstenberg, "Fathering in the Inner City: Paternal Participation and Public Policy," in *Fatherhood: Contemporary Theory, Research, and Social Policy*, ed. William Marsiglio (Thousand Oaks, CA: Sage, 1995), 119–147. Nelson and Edin also conclude that "fathering a child is still proof that one can accomplish something of value; it still offers the opportunity to see one's potential expressed in another, less damaged individual." Nelson and Edin, *Doing the Best I Can*.

16. In *My Baby's Father*, Waller notes the importance of fathers' involvement in baby naming. When I asked Sincere what his reaction would have been if he had not had a role in naming the baby, he said, "I would have denied him. He wouldn't have been my son. I wouldn't have gotten a blood test for him or nothin' like that. 'Cause I promised my dad. My dad never been there, never asked me for anything, but he asked me for this one thing. He always told me, 'Keep the name going. It's history behind the name.'"

17. The Fragile Families Study has explored this ambivalence in depth. Respondents at one study site identified four financial goals that are prerequisites for marriage: financial stability (consistently being able to make ends meet), financial responsibility (wise use of existing funds), acquisition of assets (which represents the couple's ability to work together toward long-term financial goals), and the accumulation of enough savings to host a respectable wedding. These findings underscore the deep respect that low-income couples have for the institution of marriage and the cultural norms that sanction nonmarital childbearing. Christina M. Gibson-Davis, Kathryn Edin, and Sarah McLanahan, "High Hopes but Even Higher Expectations: The Retreat from

Marriage among Low-Income Couples," *Journal of Marriage and the Family* 67, no. 5 (2005): 1301–1312. See also Kathryn Edin and Maria Kefalas, *Promises I Can Keep: Why Poor Women Put Motherhood Before Marriage* (Berkeley: University of California Press, 2005); Renata Forste, "Maybe Someday: Marriage and Cohabitation among Low-Income Fathers," in Kowaleski-Jones and Wolfinger, *Fragile Families and the Marriage Agenda,* 189–209; Joanna M. Reed, "Not Crossing the 'Extra Line': How Cohabitors with Children View Their Unions," *Journal of Marriage and the Family* 68, no. 5 (2006): 1117–1131.

18. Anderson, *Code of the Street.*

19. Here he is referring to Miss Cleo, a well-known telephone psychic whose infomercials were ubiquitous in the late 1990s and early 2000s.

20. Edin and Kefalas, *Promises I Can Keep.*

21. Interestingly, Lerman has found that black fathers are more likely than their white and Latino counterparts to have contact with their children, to live close by, and to make child support payments. Robert I. Lerman, "A National Profile of Young Unwed Fathers," in Lerman and Ooms, *Young, Unwed Fathers,* 27–51.

22. Waller, *My Baby's Father.*

23. See Edin and Kefalas, *Promises I Can Keep.*

24. Ibid.; Joanna Reed, "Anatomy of the Breakup: How and Why Do Unmarried Parents Break Up?" in *Unmarried Couples with Children,* ed. Paula England and Kathryn Edin (New York: Russell Sage, 2007), 133–155; Stack, *All Our Kin.*

25. This supports findings in Bourgois, *In Search of Respect.*

26. These findings are in line with much of what has been discovered in the Fragile Families Study, a cohort study of five thousand babies in large U.S. cities, roughly three-quarters of whom were born to unmarried parents. See http://www.fragilefamilies.princeton.edu.

27. Sincere was arrested once for possession of a small quantity of marijuana for personal use, a misdemeanor.

28. Todd Clear, *Imprisoning Communities: How Mass Incarceration Makes Disadvantaged Neighborhoods Worse* (New York: Oxford University Press, 2007).

29. These patterns of family formation among African Americans were documented in two seminal works: W.E.B. Du Bois, *The Philadelphia Negro: A Social Study* (Philadelphia: University of Pennsylvania Press, 1899) and Drake and Cayton, *Black Metropolis.* As a result of the transformation of the economy in the 1970s, black and white rates of marriage and single parenthood have diverged even further. See Wilson, *Truly Disadvantaged.* For further historical background, see Steven Ruggles, "The Origins of African-American Family Structure," *American Sociological Review* 59, no. 1 (1994): 136–151.

30. Laub and Sampson argue that the "love of a good woman" was a distinguishing factor between men who went on to become law-abiding citizens and those who continued to engage in antisocial behavior. Wives may act as powerful agents of informal social control, shaping their husbands' routine activities and removing them from criminal networks. See John H. Laub and Robert J. Sampson, *Shared Beginnings, Divergent Lives: Delinquent Boys to Age 70* (Cambridge, MA: Harvard University Press, 2003). See also Edin et al., "Fatherhood and Incarceration as Potential Turning Points"; Florsheim and Ngu, "Fatherhood as a Transformative Process." Giordano et al. also identify children as one of four "hooks for change" that are an important element in the desistance process. See Giordano et al., "Gender, Crime, and Desistance."

CHAPTER 7   MASCULINE IDENTITY, SOCIAL
            SUPPORT, AND FALLING BACK

1. Newman, *No Shame in My Game*.
2. Tach, Mincy, and Edin note that barriers such as these are responsible for the dramatic decline in nonresidential fathers' involvement after relationships with their children's mothers end. Laura Tach, Ronald Mincy, and Kathryn Edin, "Parenting as a 'Package Deal': Relationships, Fertility, and Nonresident Father Involvement among Unmarried Parents," *Demography* 47, no. 1 (2010): 181–204. See also Nelson and Edin, *Doing the Best I Can*.
3. Erik H. Erikson, *Identity and the Life Cycle* (New York: International Universities Press, 1959).
4. Shadd Maruna, *Making Good: How Ex-Convicts Reform and Rebuild Their Lives* (Washington, DC: American Psychological Association, 2001).
5. Ibid.
6. Erving Goffman, *The Presentation of Self in Everyday Life* (Garden City, NY: Doubleday, 1959).
7. Lofland notes that moving from a deviant to a normal identity requires the performance of "exemplary conformity or even hyperconformity and stellar service to society. . . . Even outstanding conformity is likely always to be greeted by the suspicion and fear in the minds and practices of Others that at any time Actor might revert to type." John Lofland, *Deviance and Identity* (Englewood Cliffs, NJ: Prentice Hall, 1969), 210. Calverley and Farrall also note that once the trust of significant others is earned, it is an added incentive to continue going straight. Adam Calverley and Stephen Farrall, "The Sensual Dynamics of Processes of Personal Reform: Desistance from Crime and the Role of Emotions," in *Emotions, Crime and Justice*, ed. Susanne Karstedt, Ian Loader, and Heather Strang (Oxford: Hart, 2011), 81–99.
8. Maruna, *Making Good*, 87. Maruna here refers to Elder's concept of "knifing off," or severing the past from the future. See Glen H. Elder, "The Life Course and Human Development," in *Handbook of Child Psychology*, vol. 1, ed. Richard M. Lerner (New York: John Wiley, 1998). See also Shadd Maruna and K. Roy, "Amputation or Reconstruction? Notes on the Concept of 'Knifing Off' and Desistance from Crime," *Journal of Contemporary Criminal Justice* 23, no. 1 (2007): 104–224.
9. Charles Horton Cooley, *Human Nature and the Social Order* (1902; repr., New Brunswick, NJ: Transaction Books, 1983), 184. Peggy C. Giordano, Ryan D. Schoeder, and Stephen A. Cernkovich, "Emotions and Crime Over the Life Course: A Neo-Median Perspective on Criminal Continuity and Change," *American Journal of Sociology* 112, no. 6 (2001): 1603–1661.
10. Robert J. Sampson and John H. Laub, *Crime in the Making: Pathways and Turning Points through Life* (Cambridge, MA: Harvard University Press, 1993).
11. Giordano et al., "Gender, Crime, and Desistance."
12. Because I was not able to break through Gabe's expectation that we would have a sexual relationship, I was unable to get to know Charmagne in the same way I became acquainted with most of my participants' steady girlfriends. He kept us separated so she would not find out about his fantasy relationship with me.
13. Goffman, *Asylums*.
14. John H. Laub and Robert J. Sampson, *Shared Beginnings, Divergent Lives: Delinquent Boys to Age 70* (Cambridge, MA: Harvard University Press, 2003).

Chapter 8   Fictions of Success at Mountain Ridge
            Academy's Graduation Ceremony

1. Goffman, *Presentation of Self*, 121.
2. Eddie never made the trip, claiming that he did not receive the money order in time. Although this certainly was possible, I was aware at the time that he was not living up to the staff's expectations for him when they helped him enroll in college. I wondered if his absence was a reflection of his concern that he would not be equipped to carry off the performance of "doing good" convincingly. I later learned that by the time of the ceremony, he had already set up a small drug sales business in the small town where he attended college.
3. Although the young men clearly were performing for each other, the reasons they gave for returning for the graduation ceremony were consistent with what each of them had told me individually.
4. Schneider, *In the Web of Class*.
5. Goffman, *Asylums*, 102.
6. "Maximum benefit" is the preferred terminology that probation officers and facility staff use to describe a case in which a youth has reached a treatment plateau and does not seem to be progressing any further but has not transgressed seriously enough to be placed elsewhere. The notion of maximum benefit is tied to funding since juvenile court judges often invoke a scarcity of funds in their discourse around decision making. Mountain Ridge Academy and other similar reform schools often cost over $250 to $300 per youth per day.
7. Goffman, *Asylums*, 94.
8. Michael Lipsky, *Street-Level Bureaucracy: Dilemmas of the Individual in Public Services* (New York: Russell Sage, 1980).
9. Goffman, *Asylums*, 153.
10. Since the current inmates of the program were also required to attend the ceremony, it is likely that staff and administrators considered graduation an important part of the intervention, providing a ray of hope that success is achievable as well as a series of testimonials about the program's role in graduates' success.
11. Anderson, *Streetwise*; Duneier, *Sidewalk*.
12. Katherine S. Newman, *Chutes and Ladders: Navigating the Low-Wage Labor Market* (New York: Russell Sage, 2006).
13. Edward Humes, *No Matter How Loud I Shout: A Year in the Life of Juvenile Court* (New York: Simon & Schuster, 1996).
14. Goffman, *Asylums*, 145.
15. Maruna, *Making Good*; Dan P. McAdams, *The Stories We Live By: Personal Myths and the Making of the Self* (New York: William Morrow, 1993).
16. Shadd Maruna, "Reentry as a Rite of Passage," *Punishment & Society* 13, no. 1 (2011): 3–28.
17. Randall Collins, *Interaction Ritual Chains* (Princeton, NJ: Princeton University Press, 2004).
18. Cohen, *Delinquent Boys*; Miller, "Lower Class Culture."

Conclusion

1. Brezina et al. also find that inner-city youth are likely to share this sense of fatalism, which they argue comes from frequent exposure to violence. Timothy

Brezina, Erdal Tekin, and Volkan Topalli, "'Might Not Be a Tomorrow': A Multimethods Approach to Anticipated Early Death and Youth Crime," *Criminology* 47, no. 4 (2009): 1091–1129.

2. Most recently, he considered responding to a solicitation he received from the Philadelphia Art Institutes. These for-profit technical schools help students access federal financial aid. I learned from talking to some students at other technical schools that the financial aid counselors often present this money as a scholarship or grant when in reality it involves repayment. For a discussion of trade schools and debt, see Peter S. Goodman, "In Hard Times, Lured into Trade School and Debt," *New York Times*, March 13, 2010, http://www.nytimes.com/2010/03/14/business/14schools.html.

3. Researchers using the Fragile Families and Child Wellbeing Study data have found that, among parents who were unmarried at the time of their child's birth, father involvement declines precipitously, particularly when the relationship ends and the mother becomes romantically involved with another man. Tach et al., "Parenting as a 'Package Deal.'"

4. Goffman, *Asylums*, 128.

5. Peter Conrad and Joseph W. Schneider, *Deviance and Medicalization: From Badness to Sickness* (St. Louis: Mosby, 1980).

6. Lawrence W. Sherman, "Defiance, Deterrence, and Irrelevance: A Theory of the Criminal Sanction," *Journal of Research in Crime and Delinquency* 30, no. 4 (1993): 445–473.

7. Goffman, *Asylums*.

8. See also Cox, "Doing the Programme or Doing Me?"

9. Humes, *No Matter How Loud I Shout*, 38.

10. Jamie J. Fader and Christopher P. Dum, "Doing Time, Filling Time: Bureaucratic Ritualism as a Systemic Barrier to Youth Reentry" (unpublished manuscript).

11. Laurence Steinberg, He Len Chung, and Michelle Little, "Reentry of Young Offenders from the Justice System: A Developmental Perspective," *Youth Violence and Juvenile Justice* 2, no. 1 (2004): 21–38.

12. Anderson, *Code of the Street*; Bourgois, *In Search of Respect*.

13. Elijah Anderson, "Going Straight: The Story of a Young Inner-City Ex-Convict," *Punishment & Society* 3, no. 1 (2001) 135–152.

14. One study of returning youth found that "selective involvement" with old friends prevented them from returning to old habits. Laura S. Abrams, "From Corrections to Community: Youth Offenders' Perceptions of the Challenges of Transition," *Journal of Offender Rehabilitation* 2–3, no. 44 (2006): 31–53.

15. Sampson and Laub, *Crime in the Making*; Christopher Uggen, "Work as a Turning Point in the Life Course of Criminals: A Duration Model of Age, Employment, and Recidivism," *American Sociological Review* 65, no. 4 (2000): 629–646.

16. Petersilia, *When Prisoners Come Home*.

17. Bruce Western, *Punishment and Inequality in America* (New York: Russell Sage, 2006).

18. For the relationship between intermittency in work and intermittency in offending, see Kelly, "Crime, Work, and Drift."

19. Incarcerated youth are substantially more likely to be parents than their nonincarcerated counterparts. Snyder, "Empirical Portrait."

20. Catherine Newhouse, "Beltway Beginnings: D.C. Shifts from Juvenile Corrections Model toward Rehabilitation," *Chicago Reporter*, September/October 2010, http://www.chicagoreporter.com/news/2010/09/beltway-beginnings.

21. Melissa Sickmund, T. J. Sladky, Wei Kang, and Charles Puzzanchera, "Easy Access to the Census of Juveniles in Residential Placement: 1997–2010," http://www.ojjdp.gov/ojstatbb/ezacjrp.

22. Dale G. Parent, "Summary of Conditions of Juvenile Confinement Study," *Prison Journal* 73, no. 2 (1993): 237–245.

23. Center for the Study and Prevention of Violence, University of Colorado, "Blueprints for Violence Prevention" (2012), http://www.colorado.edu/cspv/blueprints/modelprograms.html (accessed March 6, 2012).

24. National Institute of Corrections, "Implementing Evidence-Based Practice in Community Corrections: The Principles of Effective Intervention" (2004), http://static.nicic.gov/Library/019342.pdf; Mark W. Lipsey, David B. Wilson, and Lynn Cothern, "Effective Intervention for Serious Juvenile Offenders," *Juvenile Justice Bulletin* (April 2000), https://www.ncjrs.gov/pdffiles1/ojjdp/181201.pdf.

25. Rios, *Punished*, xiv.

26. Amanda Petteruti, *Education under Arrest: The Case against Police in Schools* (Washington, DC: Justice Policy Institute, November 2011), www.justicepolicy.org/research/3177.

27. Center for the Study and Prevention of Violence, University of Colorado.

28. "Mentoring," Office of Justice Programs Fact Sheet November 2011, http://www.ojp.usdoj.gov/newsroom/factsheets/ojpfs_mentoring.html. See also J. B. Grossman and E. M. Garry, "Mentoring—A Proven Delinquency Prevention Strategy," *Juvenile Justice Bulletin* (April 1997), https://www.ncjrs.gov/pdffiles/164834.pdf.

29. Peter W. Greenwood, Karyn E. Model, C. Peter Rydell, and James Chiesa, *Diverting Children from a Life of Crime: Measuring Costs and Benefits* (Santa Monica, CA: RAND, 1996); Allen Schirm, Elizabeth Stuart, and Allison McKie, *The Quantum Opportunity Program Demonstration: Final Impacts* (Washington, DC: Mathematica Policy Research, 2006).

30. Fight Crime: Invest in Kids California, "School or the Streets: Crime and California's Dropout Crisis" (2007), http://calfightcrime.org/sites/default/files/reports/CA%20dropout.pdf.

31. Will Dobbie and Roland G. Fryer, Jr., "Are High Quality Schools Enough to Close the Achievement Gap? Evidence from a Social Experiment in Harlem" (NBER Working Paper No. 15473, November 2009).

32. Harlem Children's Zone, "Our Results," http://www.hcz.org/our-results (accessed March 7, 2012).

33. David M. Altschuler, Troy L. Armstrong, and Doris L. MacKenzie, *Reintegration, Supervised Release, and Intensive Aftercare* (Washington, DC: Office of Juvenile Justice and Delinquency Prevention, 1999), 1–23; Don A. Josi and Dale K. Sechrest, "A Pragmatic Approach to Parole Aftercare: Evaluation of a Community Reintegration Program for High-Risk Youthful Offenders," *Justice Quarterly* 17, no. 1 (1999): 51–80.

34. Altschuler and Brash, "Adolescent and Teenage Offenders."

Index

AIDS, 38, 90, 130–131, 144, 178, 242n6

Anderson, Elijah: defines "old head," 241n30; defines urban spaces as cosmopolitan canopies, 19; describes code of the street, 33, 76, 235n10, 243n8; describes problems with reentry, 218; mentioned, xii–xiii

black male unemployment, 21–22, 103, 180, 203, 216, 218–219

cognitive behavioral therapy (CBT), 49, 89, 215. *See also* criminal thinking errors

Comprehensive Communities Program (Boston), 30

Cooley, Charles Horton, 182

criminal personality theory: assumes that cognitive distortions set offenders apart from society, 46; assumes that people choose crime, 13; empirical status of, 44; linked to black urban identity at Mountain Ridge, 50, 75; and predictions of failure, 54, 66. *See also* criminal thinking errors; interventions; Mountain Ridge program; Mountain Ridge staff

criminal pride, 46, 59–60, 68, 72

criminal thinking errors: failure of theory of, 47–48, 223; Mountain Ridge program attempts to replace with prosocial thoughts, 3, 46–49,

86; Mountain Ridge staff associate with street code behaviors, 106; and predictions of failure, 48; study participants assess, 58–61, 76, 170–171, 193, 212; theory described, 1; theory presumes that criminality is fixed in childhood, 13, 48, 85. *See also* criminal pride; failure to endure adversity; victim stance

Department of Human Services. *See* Philadelphia Department of Human Services

desistance talk, 90–92

deterrence: masculine identity and, 16–17, 163, 189; prison and, 100; study participants accept aspects of theory of, 85–87, 186, 188; theory of defined, 48, 86; weakens after reentry, 108, 115, 216

Division of Juvenile Justice Services. *See* Philadelphia Department of Human Services; Philadelphia juvenile justice system

doing good: as a public performance, 171, 191, 204–205; study participants define as survival, 17, 204–205, 213; study participants do not meet requirements of, 246n2

domestic violence: against parents of study participants, 129–130; against partners, 100, 148–149, 156–157, 159–160; between siblings, 135

drug addiction: of parents of study
participants, 14, 40, 77, 90, 130–131,
183; in Philadelphia neighborhoods,
35; of study participants, 36, 234n9
drug selling: after reentry, 14, 16, 44,
71, 81, 96, 98–100, 114–116, 123–
125, 154–157, 161, 214–215, 229–
231; and avoiding arrest, 150, 161,
186, 188, 216, 229; before detention
at Mountain Ridge, 14, 36–37, 40,
65, 87, 123, 131–132, 175, 184; by
family members of study participants, 77, 172; and masculine identity, 15, 18, 40, 65, 104, 106, 116,
124–126, 131–132, 155, 157, 184;
and need to provide for family, 215,
217, 220; parenthood as a deterrent to, 170–171, 173; as solution to
financial problems, 98, 126, 131–
132, 220; study participants view
as employment, 142; as supplement
to regular employment, 186–187;
unemployment and, 129. See also
hustling; underground economy
drug trade in Philadelphia, 31–32
drug treatment programs: after reentry,
80, 217; at Mountain Ridge, 49, 71–
72, 76, 204; in prison, 82. See also
Narcotics Anonymous; twelve-step
program

early loss of parents, 36, 38, 90, 129,
132
education: arrest warrants as obstacles
to pursuing, 164; black men less
likely to pursue after high school,
4; lack of benefit to study participants in job market, 214; poverty as
an obstacle to pursuing, 101, 206,
209, 214; study participants' difficulties with after reentry, 80–81,
83–84; study participants do not

see as a way out of poverty for their
children, 209; study participants'
girlfriends pursue, 187; study participants value at Mountain Ridge,
76–77; stunted by incarceration, 84;
white officials' belief in, 212. See
also Empowerment, Education, and
Employment (E3); GED; Job Corps;
job training; labor market
employers: study participants try to
please, 174–175; unwillingness of to
hire study participants, 80, 102–103,
108, 111, 113; use of criminal background checks, 14, 79, 111
employment: in food industry, 79; in
manufacturing, 79; and masculine
identity, 117, 180–183; relationship of to recidivism, 217–218; as a
requirement of probation, 94; seasonal or temporary, 142, 146, 148–
149, 154, 174, 208–209, 243n13; in
service sector, 123, 153, 167, 176,
181, 186–187; types of available to
study participants, 108. See also black
male unemployment; obstacles to
employment; segregation; "working
man" identity
Empowerment, Education, and
Employment (E3), 79–80, 117
eye contact, 33, 37, 50, 157, 226–227

failure to endure adversity, 41, 46, 59
faking it: and graduation ceremony,
191; at Mountain Ridge, 72–74, 76,
164, 211
Family Court. See Philadelphia Family
Court
family functional therapy (FFT), 224
fatherhood: as catalyst for falling
back, 164; constant flux in life
circumstances compromises ability
of study participants to perform,

18, 163, 215, 220, 228–229; and demands for financial contributions to family, 114, 128–129, 141; and ideal of "good man," 162; ideals of in tension with ideals of monogamy, 159–161; and importance of participation in naming children, 243n16; importance of to study participants, 16, 127–129, 141, 149, 159, 203, 209, 219–221, 227, 229, 232, 243n15; and interactions with children, 138, 140, 150, 242n4, 244n21; and masculine identity, 106, 128–129, 149–150; and participation in underground economy, 127–129, 141–142, 150; and predictions of failure, 141; and reinvention of self, 169, 171, 176, 182, 189, 205, 209; study participants' ideals of, 15, 129–131, 137, 149–150, 204

"feedback": fails to help urban residents with life outside Mountain Ridge, 71; as part of Mountain Ridge program, 1, 49; threatens masculine identity, 17, 163, 189; violates norms of street code, 66; willingness to accept necessary for release from Mountain Ridge, 46, 63

Fels Institute of Government, 6

food stamps, 136, 242n32

Fragile Families Study, 243n17, 244n26, 247n3

GED: and applying for jobs, 110; completed at Mountain Ridge, 4, 38–39, 100; completion statistics for incarcerated youth, 84; Pennsylvania law requires incarcerated youth to pursue, 234n11; program at Powelton Aftercare, 6, 36; study participants value, 78

generativity, 168–169, 178

gentrification, 24–26

girlfriends: control access to housing, 15, 129, 144, 152, 157, 159, 220; control household resources, 113–114, 161, 218, 220; demand financial contributions from study participants, 15, 200; described, 137, 152, 176; earn steady incomes, 16, 40, 176; and power struggles with study participants, 16, 113, 145, 156, 159, 167; as source of housing for study participants, 4, 23, 36, 94, 155, 220; as source of life stress for study participants, 172; as source of stability for study participants, 176, 183, 221; study participants see as wives, 34, 127–128, 155, 199. *See also* domestic violence; infidelity; marriage; public assistance; subsidized housing

godmother role, xi, 137, 227

Goffman, Erving: mentioned, 2, 171; theories about prison life, 52, 185, 204, 206, 210–211; theory about institutional ceremonies, 20

graduation ceremony, 17, 191–202, 246n10

Harlem Children's Zone (HCZ), 225

hidden Philadelphia, 13, 19, 27

HIV. *See* AIDS

housing: instability of for study participants, 18, 44, 95, 114, 220, 228; Job Corps program promises, 14; and segregation in Philadelphia, 19–21, 235n8; substandard quality of in black neighborhood of Philadelphia, 20; and upward mobility for study participants, 23. *See also* subsidized housing

hustling: credit card fraud, 124;
defined, 104; and desire for financial independence, 126, 217; family
members watch for signs of, 178–
179; and gang culture, 53; gradual or
sporadic return to after reentry, 15,
125, 141, 161, 186; gun trade, 161;
lack of paper trail, 113–114; and
masculine identity, 220; prostitution, 104–105, 121–123, 125; selling
drugs, 105, 229–230, 234n8; selling
pirated music, 105, 119, 124–125,
228; study participant describes, 35;
study participants regard as a form
of employment, 142; and unemployment, 107–108, 187, 206, 208, 219.
See also underground economy

infidelity, 129, 144, 154, 160, 229. *See
also* fatherhood; girlfriends; romantic
relationships

J-Court, 6–7, 26–27, 151, 166. *See also*
Philadelphia Family Court; Philadelphia juvenile justice system
Job Corps, 14, 41, 78–80, 82, 200
job training: and competing life
demands, 80; dearth of, 117; and
lack of finances, 80; plans for fall
apart, 85, 168, 214–216; in technical schools, 172–173. *See also* Job
Corps; YouthBuild
Justice Policy Institute, 30

labor market: and discrimination, 108,
125–127, 210, 219; and failure of
reentry plans of study participants,
83, 85, 101, 104; and fatherhood,
128, 150; and masculine identity, 161,
163, 205; in Philadelphia, 27–28; and
undereducation, 29, 209. *See also* black
male unemployment; segregation

Laub, John, 182, 244n30
Liebow, Elliott, 126, 134, 243n11

male peer groups: and applying for
jobs, 103, 113, 136; and masculine
identity, 159, 217; Mountain Ridge
staff attempts to undermine, 65,
69–70, 75; predict failure for study
participants, 171; and requests for
loans from wage earners, 174, 182;
and street culture, 10, 133–134. *See
also* masculine identity; street code
marriage: study participants' ambivalence toward entering, 140, 144–148;
study participants value highly, 147
Maruna, Shadd, 168, 170, 181–182, 205
masculine identity: and beliefs about
failure, 208; and breadwinner ideal,
103, 132; defined in opposition
to femininity, 134; development
of interrupted in reform schools,
217–218; and drug selling, 32, 104,
116, 124–126; and employment,
142, 180–183, 243n13; and fatherhood, 128, 149–150; and fidelity of
partners, 144–146; and male peer
groups, 65, 159; as motive for falling back, 188; and pride in survival
skills, 211; and rejection for jobs, 80;
threatened at Mountain Ridge, 16
mass incarceration of black men, 105,
126, 210
mental illness, 4, 39, 84, 99, 210, 239n4
methodology of this book, 5–13, 227–
228, 237n3
Missouri Model, 222
Mountain Ridge Academy: described,
1–3; reputation of, 44; recidivism
rate of, 44, 66. *See also* graduation
ceremony
Mountain Ridge program: creates
double bind for study participants,

62–65, 74; fails to distinguish between drug pushers and drug users, 71; fails to prepare graduates for real life, 14, 17–18, 71, 214–216, 222; and physical restraint, 68–70; strips residents of identity, 13–14, 17, 52–54, 66, 190–191, 205, 211; study participants evaluate positively, 57–60; study participants selectively choose elements of, 60–61, 76; study participants reject utility of, 193; subscribes to criminal personality theory, 3, 13, 43. *See also* criminal personality theory; criminal thinking errors; faking it; street code

Mountain Ridge staff: described, 49–50, 211; disdain of for urban life, 51–52; disrespect families of program residents, 66–67; need of for fictive success of program graduates, 201–202; predict failure for residents, 54–55, 66–67, 202–203, 205, 211–213; stigmatize black urban culture, 48, 50, 42–54; study participants evaluate positively, 56–57; study participants reject legitimacy of, 61–62; verbal baiting, 67, 69–70

MOVE, 29–30

multisystemic therapy (MST), 224

Narcotics Anonymous (NA), 71, 93

negativity bias, 95

obstacles to employment: credit checks, 111; criminal background checks, 14, 79, 108, 111; drug testing, 111; electronic applications, 103, 108–112; lack of driver's license, 135; lack of experience or training, 135–136; lack of jobs, 135, 209; outstanding warrants, 79, 164; personality tests, 104, 111;

prescreening questionnaires, 109, 135, 175; racism of employers, 80, 102, 108, 111, 119–120, 239n2. *See also* black male unemployment; labor market; segregation

old heads: as mentors to young drug sellers, 38, 116, 125; as positive role models, 38, 177–178, 166, 241n30

Park, Robert E., xi–xii, 233n1

performance: of code-switching, 32–33, 226; of "doing good," 191, 198–199; of faking it, 72; of "good father" and "working man" roles, 16, 189, 209, 219; at graduation ceremony, 197–199, 201, 205–207, 246nn2–3; of narratives of self-efficacy, 171; necessity of for successful falling back, 245n7; and need for audience for affirmation, 180, 182; and street code, 33

Philadelphia: drug trade in, 31; employment sectors of, 27–29; escalating gun violence in, 8–9; ethnic neighborhoods of, 20–24; gang life in, 31; increase in crime rate in, 20, 30–31; loss of manufacturing base of, 27–29; patterns of immigration to, 20–21; poor services in black neighborhoods of, 19–20; racial coding of as obstacle to employment, 103; racial divisions in, 19–21

Philadelphia Department of Human Services: mentioned, 26, 67; and Program Development and Evaluation System, 45; removes children from parents, 36, 130, 146–147

Philadelphia Family Court: described, 26–27; discharges study participants, 121, 166; and probation, 92; study participants lose access to children through, 98

Philadelphia juvenile justice system: compared to other systems, 45–46, 52; mentioned, 20, 26. *See also* J-Court; Mountain Ridge Academy; Program Development and Evaluation System (ProDES)

Philadelphia police: crime control strategies of, 30; and drug trade, 20, 33; history of conflict of with black residents, 29–30; racial profiling of, 9, 30, 105–106

Powelton Aftercare, 6

predictions of failure: by family and community members, 141, 213; by Mountain Ridge staff, 54–55, 66–67, 202–203, 205, 211–213

probation: and avoidance of police attention, 105; conditions of, 4, 6, 71, 84, 121, 135, 217, 241n27; delays resumption of hustling, 141, 218; fails to meet needs of study participants, 84, 93, 214; gaps in Philadelphia programs studied, 6–7; and job training, 78–80; meeting conditions of tied to access to housing, 37; police use to try to force information from study participants, 96, 98; and reincarceration, 223; and work, 106, 135, 173, 241n27. *See also* Youth Violence Reduction Project (YVRP)

probation officers: assist with job searches, 38, 151; emphasize employment as condition of probation, 106; evaluate Mountain Ridge program positively, 44; paired with reintegration workers, 20; responsibilities of, 92–93, 217; work with research team to improve reintegration services, 26

Program Development and Evaluation System (ProDES), 45–46, 237n2, 237n7

public assistance: food stamps, 136, 242n32; subsidized housing, 114, 136, 152, 157; Supplemental Security Assistance (SSI), 136, 140; Temporary Assistance to Needy Families (TANF), 136, 140, 154; and women's power in relationships, 161

Quantum Opportunities Program, 225

racially mixed neighborhoods, 24–26

racial profiling, 9, 30, 105–106

recidivism: imprisonment of study participants after reentry, 15, 44, 81–82, 96–100, 214, 230–231; Mountain Ridge and, 66; structural reasons for, 84

reentry, 77–101

Re-entry Transition Initiative—Welcome Return Assessment Process, 7

reform schools, cost of, 2, 224; defined, 234n6; failure of, 214–216; and indeterminate sentencing, 45; injuries and abuse in, 223; number of juveniles in, 2. *See also* Mountain Ridge Academy

reintegration workers: fail study participants, 83, 85, 214; mentioned, 3, 151, 165, 234n12; and methodology of this book, 6–7, 39; and post-reentry employment plans, 14, 41, 79, 92, 106, 117; responsibilities of, 92–93, 217; work with probation officers, 20

Rios, Victor, 18, 224, 240n9

risk aversion: and decisions not to seek employment, 102–103, 126, 135, 209; and deterrence theory, 86, 215–216; and drug selling, 15, 99, 105, 108, 114, 142, 150, 161, 186, 215, 222 romantic relationships: constant flux and, 18, 161–163, 220, 228; and financial support for study partici-pants, 124; importance of to study participants, 127–128; as a source of stability, 185; strained during incarceration of study participants, 3; and struggle for power, 159, 161; and study participants' struggles with demands of monogamy, 161, 227. *See also* domestic violence; girlfriends; infidelity

Samenow, Stanton E., 43, 47–48, 58. *See also* criminal thinking errors
Sampson, Robert, 182, 244n30
segregation: of labor market, 28, 108; of Philadelphia neighbor-hoods, 13, 19–24, 101, 126, 191, 210, 216, 235n8. *See also* black male unemployment
self-efficacy, 170–171, 181
shootings: of family members of study participants, 36; of friends of study participants, 81, 91, 122, 133; of study participants, 59, 96, 214, 231; threats of, 90
social support: dearth of for study participants, 83, 216; importance of for success, 11, 221–222
street code: criminalization of, 238n19; defined, 33; drug trade and, 32–33; and eye contact, 33, 37, 50, 157, 226–227; and identity, 80–81, 88, 106, 226; need of juvenile justice system to incorporate, 226; as obstacle to employment, 102; as obstacle to successful reentry, 98; as a performance, 32–34; and readi-ness for violence, 133; requirements at Mountain Ridge contradict, 48, 50, 42–54, 56, 62–66, 70–71, 74–76,

106; and survival, 27, 42, 56; values of, 63; Warren describes, 34–35. *See also* masculine identity
structural obstacles to success: black male unemployment, 85, 103, 180, 126, 203, 216, 218–291; childhood separation from parents, 31, 60; low-paying jobs, 31, 101; mass incarcera-tion of black men, 85, 105, 126, 210; physical injuries, 60; racial discrimi-nation, 126; violence, 87, 100, 126
subcultural theory, 237n15
subsidized housing, 114, 136, 152, 157
Supplemental Security Income (SSI), 136, 140

Temporary Assistance for Needy Families (TANF), 136, 140, 154
twelve-step program, 49, 71, 76, 168

underground economy: and drug trade, 31, 114–115; and family life, 159, 161, 220; fits structure of urban life, 114; and lack of opportuni-ties in formal economy, 129; and masculine identity, 126, 159, 184, 220; parenthood influences deci-sions of study participants about, 150; participation in supplements legal income, 104–105; psychologi-cal rewards of successful engage-ment in, 106; steady employment as deterrent, 187; study participants participate in after reentry, 108; under-the-table employment, 209, 228–229. *See also* hustling

victim stance, 46, 60

white flight, 20–21, 29
white neighborhoods: discomfort of study participants in, 133, 174–176;

white neighborhoods (*continued*) and search for employment, 103, 112–113

"working man" identity: and absence of steady employment for study participants, 108; Clifton as an example of, 178; importance of to study participants, 16, 176, 180, 182, 189, 205, 219, 221, 243n13; study participants see as impossible goal, 126. *See also* black male

unemployment; labor market; segregation

Yochelson, Samuel, 43, 47–48, 58. *See also* criminal thinking errors

YouthBuild, 168, 179

Youth Study Center (YSC), 26, 44. *See also* reform schools

youth support complex, 18, 224

Youth Violence Reduction Project (YVRP), 167, 184

About the Author

Jamie J. Fader is an assistant professor in the School of Criminal Justice at the University at Albany. She received her Ph.D. in sociology at the University of Pennsylvania in 2008. Her research interests include social inequalities, juvenile justice and delinquency, corrections, urban sociology, and qualitative research methods.

AVAILABLE TITLES IN THE CRITICAL ISSUES IN CRIME AND SOCIETY SERIES:

Tammy L. Anderson, ed., *Neither Villain Nor Victim: Empowerment and Agency among Women Substance Abusers*

Scott A. Bonn, *Mass Deception: Moral Panic and the U.S. War on Iraq*

Mary Bosworth and Jeanne Flavin, eds., *Race, Gender, and Punishment: From Colonialism to the War on Terror*

Loretta Capeheart and Dragan Milovanovic, *Social Justice: Theories, Issues, and Movements*

Walter S. DeKeseredy and Martin D. Schwartz, *Dangerous Exits: Escaping Abusive Relationships in Rural America*

Patricia E. Erickson and Steven K. Erickson, *Crime, Punishment, and Mental Illness: Law and the Behavioral Sciences in Conflict*

Luis A. Fernandez, *Policing Dissent: Social Control and the Anti-Globalization Movement*

Timothy R. Lauger, *Real Gangstas: Legitimacy, Reputation, and Violence in the Intergang Environment*

Michael J. Lynch, *Big Prisons, Big Dreams: Crime and the Failure of America's Penal System*

Raymond J. Michalowski and Ronald C. Kramer, eds., *State-Corporate Crime: Wrongdoing at the Intersection of Business and Government*

Susan L. Miller, *Victims as Offenders: The Paradox of Women's Violence in Relationships*

Torin Monahan, *Surveillance in the Time of Insecurity*

Torin Monahan and Rodolfo D. Torres, eds., *Schools Under Surveillance: Cultures of Control in Public Education*

Leslie Paik, *Discretionary Justice: Looking Inside a Juvenile Drug Court*

Anthony M. Platt, *The Child Savers: The Invention of Delinquency*, 40th Anniversary Edition with an introduction and critical commentaries compiled by Miroslava Chávez-García

Susan F. Sharp, *Hidden Victims: The Effects of the Death Penalty on Families of the Accused*

Jeffrey Ian Ross, ed., *The Globalization of Supermax Prisons*

Dawn L. Rothe and Christopher W. Mullins, eds., *State Crime, Current Perspectives*

Robert H. Tillman and Michael L. Indergaard, *Pump and Dump: The Rancid Rules of the New Economy*

Mariana Valverde, *Law and Order: Images, Meanings, Myths*

Michael Welch, *Crimes of Power & States of Impunity: The U.S. Response to Terror*

Michael Welch, *Scapegoats of September 11th: Hate Crimes and State Crimes in the War on Terror*

Saundra D. Westervelt and Kimberly J. Cook, *Life after Death Row: Exonerees' Search for Community and Identity*